The Philosopher's Alice

The Philosopher's Alice

ALICE'S ADVENTURES IN WONDERLAND & THROUGH THE LOOKING-GLASS

by LEWIS CARROLL with Illustrations by JOHN TENNIEL

INTRODUCTION AND NOTES BY

PETER HEATH

Omne tulit punctum qui miscuit utile dulci.
Lectorem delectando pariterque monendo.

ST. MARTIN'S PRESS   •   NEW YORK

Library of Congress Catalog Card #73-80789
Manufactured in the United States of America
No part of this book may be reproduced without
permission in writing from the publisher.
ISBN 0-312-60518-8
ST. MARTIN'S PRESS
175 Fifth Avenue
New York, N.Y. 10010

Contents

Introduction

A well-known story tells how Queen Victoria, charmed by *Alice in Wonderland,* expressed a desire to receive the author's next book, and was presented, in due course, with a loyally inscribed copy of *An Elementary Treatise on Determinants.* The tale is not true, unfortunately, and was formally contradicted long afterwards by the alleged donor himself.[1] Yet it still dies hard, if only because it coincides all too neatly with the popular picture of Charles Dodgson, alias Lewis Carroll, as an eminent mathematician who wrote nonsense books for children. The sad fact is, however, that this story is no more true than the other. Whatever the world may choose to believe of him, the author of *Alice* was not an eminent mathematician, his books are not nonsense, and of all those who read them, it is children especially who have the smallest chance of understanding what they are about.

Carroll (or rather Dodgson) was indeed a mathematician, who taught the subject—drearily enough, by all accounts—to Christ Church undergraduates for a quarter of a century, and then gave up lecturing for good. An inveterate publisher of trifles, he was forever putting out pamphlets, papers, broadsheets, and books on mathematical topics, but they earned him no reputation beyond that of a crotchety, if sometimes amusing, controversialist, a compiler of puzzles and curiosities, and a busy yet ineffective reformer on elementary points of computation and instructional method. In the higher reaches of the subject he made no mark at all, and has left none since. Compared with such genuine eminences of the time as Cayley, Sylvester, or Henry Smith, to name only fellow-countrymen, Dodgson the mathematician is little better than a valley, and deserves no special interest or esteem.

In the infant science of mathematical logic his place is a notch or two higher. He at least paid more attention to it than anyone else in Victorian Oxford, which is not saying much, and two short papers he published in *Mind* (in 1894 and 1895) toward the end of his life have a tiny corner in logical history, as do the diagrams he invented and made known in *The Game of Logic* (1886) and *Symbolic Logic,* Part I (1896).[2] The general effect of these works, however, is to show that on this subject also, Dodgson's outlook was provincial, even trivial, and somewhat behind that of his predecessors De Morgan and Boole, to say nothing of his contemporaries, Jevons, Venn, and C. S. Peirce. The one enduring legacy he has bequeathed to logicians is a large stock of entertaining examples, which are still regularly drawn upon, or unsuccessfully imitated, by writers of textbooks too modest or unimaginative to manufacture their own.

Dodgson's most interesting and original work in this line, although, strangely enough, it was never fully published, is an investigation of the mathematical theory of voting, which arose out of his discontent with the proceedings of electoral boards and other academic bodies in Oxford. Here he broke ground that has since been cultivated. With the recovery of his work by Duncan Black,[3] he now enjoys, in one small area at least, the recognition due to a pioneer. But it is virtually certain that, without his extramathematical reputation to sustain them, few of his other professional writings would command the slightest attention today.

These facts, though unexciting, are of some importance. Dodgson, the drab exponent of dilemmas and determinants, has been so far overshadowed by the more colorful figure of Carroll, the theater-goer, photographer, gamesman, perennial pursuer of small girls, and creator of the best-known seven-year-old in literature, that it is easy to forget that they are one and the same man. It is equally easy to progress from this to the theory of Dodgson-Carroll as a schizophrenic author, whose two sides are unconnected with—even opposed to—each other. The Carroll persona then comes to be represented as a rebellious escapee from the tedious sobrieties of Dodgson, whereby all that the latter stands for in the way of Victorian orthodoxy is implicitly rejected and denied. Pleasingly romantic as it appears, such a view enforces an almost total misconception of what is best and most individual in Carroll's peculiar art. If *Alice* and his other writings in this vein are interpreted as a protest against the academic conventionality of his outward existence, the 'nonsense' element in them is bound to seem an irrational or anti-rational product of a mind on holiday from the constraints of ordinary logic and ordinary life. If this book has any purpose at all, it is to demonstrate the exact opposite, namely that *Alice's Adventures in Wonderland* and *Through the Looking-Glass* are works of unsleeping rationality, whose frolics are governed throughout, not by a formal theory of any kind, but by close attention to logical principles, and by a sometimes surprising insight into abstract questions of philosophy. The earliest version of Alice's adventures may have been extemporized by Carroll on the famous boat-trip to Godstow; but all its more characteristic details, plus the whole of *Through the Looking-Glass*, were meticulously elaborated in Dodgson's study in Christ Church. Unless Carroll's work is also seen as Dodgson's, it sinks into mere entertainment; half its merits go unrecognized, and the nature and quality of its humor are thoroughly misunderstood. Once the identification is made, it soon becomes apparent not only why *Alice* is so much less boring than other writings for the same alleged age-group, but also why so many intellectual persons, not otherwise nostalgic for the nursery, should cherish and reread it from year to year. Their motive for doing so is the enjoyment of play, certainly; but it is play of a highly intelligent and not at all childish kind.

Carroll's fame as a nonsense-writer is by now so firmly established that it is probably too late to persuade anyone that, apart from a few isolated instances such as the *Jabberwock* poem, he is not strictly a writer of nonsense at all. The term 'nonsense' is admittedly used imprecisely for anything that fails to make sense. But this may happen in more ways than one, and with very different results. Aristotle seems not to have considered the question, but if he had, he would almost certainly have held that the virtue of making sense is a mean between extremes: nonsense on the one hand, and absurdity on the other. The difference between the two is that whereas the former neglects or defies the ordinary conventions of logic, linguistic usage, motive, and behavior, the latter makes all too much of them. In these terms it is easy to see that Carroll stands at the opposite pole from the true nonsense-writer. Although as a literary category the term had not been invented in his day, his proper genre is that of the absurd. Instead of blithely departing from the rules, as the nonsense-writer does, the absurdist persists in adhering to them long after it has ceased to be sensible to do so, and regardless of the extravagances which thereby result. This is what Carroll and his characters habitually do. Their opinions, however ridiculous, are held on principle and backed by formal argument (often, of course, ill-grounded or fallacious), and consist, most typically, in extreme or perverse or ultra-literal-minded versions of idioms normally quite acceptable, or theories otherwise perfectly sane. The humor lies not in any arbitrary defiance of principle, but in seeing a reasonable position pushed or twisted by uncritical acceptance into a wholly unreasonable shape.

To enlarge for a moment on this contrast between nonsense and absurdity, it may be worth renewing the old and by now rather threadbare comparison between Carroll and his near contemporary Edward Lear. The comparison, indeed, is scarcely to be avoided; for when two undomesticated bachelors, both amateur and part-time authors writing (as they think) for the amusement of children, are an instant, permanent, and unparalleled success with a multitude of adults as well, it is not only natural to couple them, but irresistible to suppose that they must both have found an identical key to the same little door. On closer examination, however, the differences soon appear; in spite of their seeming likeness, there is not, after all, so very much in common between Lear, the itinerant landscape painter, and Carroll, the stay-at-home clerical don. The commentators find it surprising, for example, but it can scarcely be an accident, that though quite a few people shared an acquaintance with both of them, they were never brought together, and neither of them anywhere betrays the slightest awareness of the other's existence. Nor has it ever been shown that even such casual resemblances as do occur in their writings are the result either of borrowing, or the use of a common source. The most probable reason for this is that there was nothing to borrow. Their aims are divergent, and the means of achieving them almost entirely distinct.

Lear, for the most part, is a true nonsense-writer, who gets his effects by random aberration from a norm he does not respect. His nonsense, like his life, is essentially of a wayward and bohemian kind, and so far as it is more than merely the defensive expression of a melancholy temperament, is undertaken chiefly for the rebellious pleasure of irresponsible rule-breaking as such. Carroll makes a different point by the more insidious method of simply working to rule. Authority, as he sees it, is not there to be defied, or even seriously resented. The logical proprieties cannot be dispensed with, nor should they be, at least in waking life. Absurdity, the disgrace of reason, arises not from logic itself, but only when carelessness, obtuseness, or pedantry are permitted to usurp its mantle, to the confusion of common sense. It is unmistakably the abuses of logic, not its sovereign authority, that Carroll is concerned to repudiate, and its bungling practitioners whom he is anxious to correct.

The carefully regulated formality of Carroll's method enables him, unlike Lear, to construct an extended design. The quasi-mathematical patterns of cards and chess in the *Alice* books and their themes of size-change and mirror-reversal are only a part of this. Wonderland and the looking-glass world are closed universes, ruled by elaborate conventions of chivalry, with monarchs and nobilities and feudal retainers, courts of justice, duels, and ritual observances that recall the Middle Ages, though most of the trappings, from cucumber frames to railway carriages, come straight from Victorian England. Lear's world, if he can be said to have such a thing, is a great deal wider in extent, but by comparison a loose and anarchic place—a dafter Albania, say, or a wilder West, where nobody (except 'they') is in charge, and where radical individualists and social misfits like the Dong or Uncle Arly are free to roam interminably on the hills, the Jumblies sail the seas, and well-nigh anyone is welcome to roost forever, if they wish to, on the Quangle-Wangle's hat. The Jumblies, too, take a marvelously random collection of baggage on their travels, and are wholly indifferent to where they are going or the safety of their vessel. Carroll's only comparable nomad, the White Knight, is as carefully equipped for emergencies as any Victorian tourist, though the needs foreseen are as unlikely as the precautions are exact.

In Lear, also, there is a persistent search for peace and happiness, to be achieved (as it is, for example, by the Owl and the Pussycat, the Duck and the Kangaroo, the Pelicans, and the Discobolus family) by settling down somewhere and doing nothing from then on. Carroll's two narratives are entirely free from such sentimental quests and yearnings. As Professor Empson has rightly discerned, their mood is essentially pastoral and picaresque. Alice is not looking for anything special in Wonderland, apart from the entry to the garden, and wanders at random or is passed from hand to hand by the inhabitants. In *Through the Looking-Glass* she is propelled by the Red Queen into a pilgrimage not of her own choosing, and sleepwalks through it to her final apotheosis as a Queen. But there is no evidence that she particularly wanted this, or greatly enjoys it when she gets there. Aims and ambitions play little part in the story, therefore. As a child and a dreamer, adventures happen to Alice, but she encounters them passively and cannot be said to seek them out.

Lear, furthermore, has no great cult of childhood, and does not employ the child's point of view. Carroll uses it throughout, partly because he is interested in how children think, but more because

Alice as an embodiment of the *gesunde Menschenverstand*—the naive but not uncritical voice of common sense—enables him to telegraph his own departures from it, and to join the reader in protest at the excesses of *Vernunft* (reason), the overweening logical faculty of Humpty Dumpty and his peers, which persistently outsteps its appointed bounds, and ends, as any Kantian could have predicted, in antinomies, paralogisms, and paradoxes. Carroll is admittedly no Kant, and his books are no rival to the *Critique of Pure Reason*, but his underlying message is concerned, no less than the Critical Philosophy itself, with the bounds of sense and the limitations of reasnn. The form of the message is that of a *sottisier*: a horrendous catalog of philosophical blunders, logical fallacies, conceptual confusions, and linguistic breakdowns, which not only entertain but persistently tease the reader, compelling him to ask himself, 'What has gone wrong here? Why won't this do?' and to find that it is not always perfectly easy to supply the answer. Lear's nonsense seldom makes use of such devices (the mouse-stuffing Bachelors, who sought out the wrong kind of sage, are a rare but notable exception) and in most hands they would soon become wearisome. Carroll's advantage, as a professional logician, is that he has an extensive repertory of tricks up his sleeve, and is very adroit at deploying them, often within the space of a single chapter, as variations on a particular theme.

Alice, although nominally the heroine and undoubtedly the central figure throughout, is in fact the chief butt and victim of most of the author's jokes, and is carefully prevented by her own earnestness from ever seeing them, or realizing the sources of her chronic confusion of mind. In this she resembles such other literary simpletons as Candide or Don Quixote,[4] though she has of course no guide or follower to assist her, and combines in her own person both the stoic realism of Sancho Panza and the resilient optimism of Dr. Pangloss. Her apparent fortitude in traveling, Gulliver-like, alone through an alien society is tempered by the fact that she takes its strangeness almost entirely for granted, and reacts to it mainly with innocent politeness or mild astonishment, rather than revulsion or fear. Since she never actually encounters any serious danger, and is required to assert herself only in bringing the stories to an end, this attitude sees her through. She is not quite the heroine *sans peur et sans reproche* that certain commentators have made her. She talks too much, for one thing, is often snobbish, tactless, or imprudent, and tends to be rude to the lower orders. Nor is the author by any means blind to these faults; on the contrary, he is only too ready to draw attention to them, and here again there can be little doubt that his motives in doing so are didactic and practical, rather than aesthetic. Alice (the real life Alice for whom the adventures were written) was intended to recognize and blush for her failings, and to find in her fictional history not only a lesson in logic, but a sermon on morals as well.

Whether these excellent purposes were ever realized, there is now no need to conjecture; but the chances are that they were not. Alice very probably did what other children do when they are made to read about her, namely to get a fair measure of slightly bewildered fun from the narrative, and to miss the point of everything else. As a work of instruction and profit for the infant reader, *Alice* has never been anything less than a total failure. It is at once too difficult and insufficiently serious in tone for its deeper implications to come across. The same miscalculation, as it happens, has wholly prevented the *Game of Logic* from finding favor in the nursery. It has a board and colored counters, and purports to teach syllogisms to the young, but no sane parent is going to inflict on his family a recreation which, however edifying, he soon finds tedious and barely intelligible even to himself; those who have attempted it have soon repented of their choice. Logic is a dry subject, even to undergraduates. Carroll had a genuine fondness for children, and up to a point, a genuine understanding of how their minds work, but he never had any hope of making little logicians of them, however artfully he might endeavor to sugar the pill, and there is no record that he has succeeded yet.

Alice's unfortunate miscarriage as a child's logic-book should not, however, be taken to imply that this aspect of the work is of no value, and that the world has been right to neglect it in favor of the more popular view of the piece as a mere farrago of amiable nonsense. Not only is it *not* nonsense, in the sense already described; it also contains, by implication, a great deal of excellent sense. The very defects that more or less rule it out as fit reading for children are precisely the qualities to recommend it to mature and intelligent adults. The notion that *Alice* is a grown-up book is certainly nothing new. Many readers find this out for themselves, and the fact has long been familiar to various sections of the academic world, including professional philosophers and logicians. Fiction, of course, is normally of no interest to philosophers—any more than facts are—but *Alice* is a book they can all understand, and many of them find it compulsive reading. Their habit, however, has been to keep this news to themselves, as if slightly ashamed of it, and to notify their addiction only by a growing propensity to quotation (dating from the early 1920s onward) and by the occasional insertion of a discreet article in a learned journal, remote from the vulgar gaze. Their interest in the matter has therefore largely remained unknown to the general public, which continues to enjoy *Alice* in its own fashion, without suspecting its true nature, and with no opportunity for discovering what lies behind its simple-seeming façade.

The results have been somewhat unfortunate. *Alice* has been left in the hands of literary critics and journalists, who until quite recently have been content to applaud its virtues in general terms, and have seldom examined it in depth. With few exceptions, the standard of earlier critical writing about the book and its author is depressingly low. Within this vacuum, both have been liable to fall prey to two classes of specialist interpreter, the allegorists and the psychoanalysts, who deserve some credit for attempting to dig below the surface, but whose efforts, for the most part, have been more successful in adding to the literature of nonsense than in lighting a path to truth. The allegorists, in any case, are a self-canceling group, turning every one to his own way, and may be left to their anagrams and secret histories in the confidence that, until they are able to persuade one another, they deserve no hearing from anyone else. The analysts, after a determined attempt some years ago to take over *Alice* as a guidebook to the Dodgsonian unconscious, seem lately to have wearied of an unrewarding task; which is not to say that, in the hands of an Empson, for example, their approach is unable to add anything to a purely literary appraisal of the book.

The upshot of all this has been that, for want of accessible guidance to its logico-philosophical content, the ordinary adult reader of *Alice* has been left in the dark on matters essential to its understanding; matters which, though sometimes covert or technical, are yet in no way speculative or open to serious dispute. For the commission of logical error is normally a question, not of subjective interpretation, but of ascertainable fact. An invalid argument is invalid in any language and any possible world, and can not only be proved to be such, but may also, on occasion, be recognized intuitively even by those who make no pretension to a knowledge of formal logic. The general reader is thus often able to agree with Alice that "there's a mistake somewhere"; but further than that he cannot always go. If you don't know the principle that has been violated, or the name and nature of the mistake, then you don't know much, as the Duchess would say, and it might be worth knowing more. While the present book does not offer to teach philosophy for nothing, or to spell out every single thing in words of one letter, it can at least claim to be the first full attempt at a serial—if not wholly serious—account of Alice's logico-philosophical misadventures in which she appears, for a change, in her true colors—no longer as the sweet little girl of tradition, but as a mind driven almost to the verge of unhingement by its encounter with the dark forces and mysterious taboos of language and thought.

To advance such a claim to priority is no disparise of the excellent philosophical articles on *Alice* by Professors Alexander, Pitcher, Holmes, and others, which have often been a source of suggestion and are frequently cited in the text. Still less does it disparage two admirable books on the subject whose aid it is a pleasure to acknowledge: Martin Gardner's *Annotated Alice,* and Robert D. Sutherland's *Language and Lewis Carroll.* Gardner's well-known guide to the literary, biographical, and philosophico-scientific background of *Alice* has furnished a model for the format of this book, as well as much helpful and hard-won information, thankfully utilized wherever it has been found appropriate. A similar and still larger overlap of interest occurs in Sutherland's book, the only full-scale scholarly treatise on Carroll's complete output, seen from the point of view of modern linguistics. Since logic, philosophy, and the study of language have nowadays much in common, and since Carroll had a somewhat unnerving knack of anticipating points in all three fields that were wholly neglected by his contemporaries and have only more recently acquired importance, it is not surprising that Sutherland's learned and perceptive treatment should likewise anticipate much that a philosophical critic would also wish to say. On one point especially it is easy to agree with him, namely that Carroll's uncommonly shrewd understanding of the 'logic' of language is essentially an intuitive business, and does not spring from, or terminate in, a general theory or philosophy of language. As Sutherland happily puts it, the scattered insights to be found in Carroll's writings represent the fossil bones of an animal that never actually existed, and the quest for its reconstruction is therefore one enterprise that a commentator may justifiably neglect. Another such animal, hopefully pursued in certain quarters, is Carroll's philosophical system, or more vaguely, his view of life. But of this too, it must be admitted, no plausible sightings have yet been made, and none are reported in the present work. *Alice* (as will soon appear) can explain all the philosophies that ever were invented, and a good many that hadn't been invented when it was written. But that is a very different matter from finding in the book an indigenous philosophy attributable to Carroll himself. The somewhat lugubrious nihilism ascribed to it by Gardner and other critics is in fact an attempt in this direction, but seems far too anachronistic and out of character to have any hope of success. No more improbable existentialist than Carroll could possibly be suggested, and, rather than proclaim him an apostle of ultimate meaninglessness, it seems altogether safer to read into *Alice* no meaning, message, or moral *attitude* at all. An author should have more meaning than a child, perhaps (particularly his own child); but if he happens not to, then that, as the King of Hearts observed, "saves a world of trouble, you know, as we needn't try to find any."

Another thing which saves a world of trouble is that although the text of *Alice* is subject to considerable variation, due to the many small emendations introduced in succeeding editions, there do not appear to be any changes that materially affect the sense. The text used here is that originally issued by St. Martin's Press (1958) and deriving from the first editions of 1865 and 1872. The most covetable modern one-volume edition for the adult reader is now, however, that in the Oxford English Novels series, edited, introduced, and annotated by Roger Lancelyn Green (1971). Mr. Green, the author of a scholarly monograph on Carroll and editor of his *Diaries,* is also responsible for the revised version of Williams and Madan's standard bibliography, *The Lewis Carroll Handbook* (1970). Three other useful volumes are: *Alice's Adventures in Wonderland, a Critical Handbook,* edited by Donald Rackin (1969); *Alice in Wonderland,* edited by Donald J. Gray (1971); and *Aspects of Alice,* edited by Robert Phillips (1971), which between them reprint a large number of journal articles not otherwise easy to obtain. For purposes of reference, and to save encumbering the notes, the writings of these and other commentators are cataloged together in Appendix A. References in the text by name and pagination only (Gardner, p. 29), are to works in this list. Such references indicate that the writer cited has alluded to the passage under discussion, but do not affirm or deny that his views have been adopted. References that also contain a number (Kemeny [24], p. 95), are to Appendix B, which assembles at random the titles of fifty philosophical or logical books and papers in which passages from *Alice* are quoted, mentioned, or otherwise drawn on for professional purposes. Since philosophers have already been cited as among the most habitual quoters of the book, it has seemed worthwhile to provide a little evidence that this is indeed the case.

It remains only to express my obligations, and apologies, to all those authors, living and dead, whose wise saws or modern instances have been laid under contribution in this affair; and to thank the many kind friends who have abetted me with encouragement, information, and advice.

1. Advertisement prefixed to *Symbolic Logic,* 2nd ed. (1896).
2. Reprinted together in *Mathematical Recreations of Lewis Carroll,* Vol. I (New York: Dover, 1958).
3. *The Theory of Committees and Elections* (Cambridge, Eng.: Cambridge University Press, 1958).
4. The latter comparison is elaborated in an article by John Hinz, "Alice Meets the Don," *South Atlantic Quarterly*, LII (1953), 253-66.

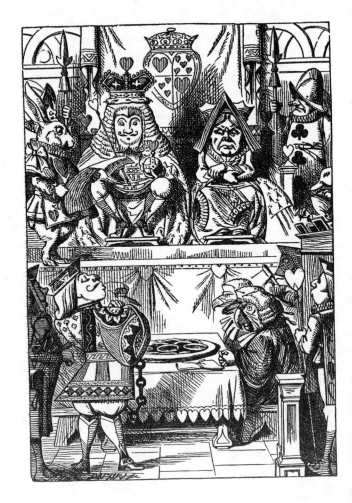

Part I

Alice's Adventures in Wonderland

ALL in the golden afternoon
   Full leisurely we glide;
For both our oars, with little skill,
   By little arms are plied,
While little hands make vain pretence
   Our wanderings to guide.

Ah, cruel Three! In such an hour
   Beneath such dreamy weather,
To beg a tale of breath too weak
   To stir the tiniest feather!
Yet what can one poor voice avail
   Against three tongues together?

Imperious Prima flashes forth
   Her edict 'to begin it' —
In gentler tone Secunda hopes
   'There will be nonsense in it!' —
While Tertia interrupts the tale
   Not *more* than once a minute.

Anon, to sudden silence won,
   In fancy they pursue
The dream-child moving through a land
   Of wonders wild and new,
In friendly chat with bird or beast —
   And half believe it true.

And ever, as the story drained
   The wells of fancy dry,
And faintly strove that weary one
   To put the subject by,
'The rest next time —' 'It *is* next time!'
   The happy voices cry.

Thus grew the tale of Wonderland:
   Thus slowly, one by one,
Its quaint events were hammered out —
   And now the tale is done,
And home we steer, a merry crew.
   Beneath the setting sun.

Alice! a childish story take,
   And with a gentle hand
Lay it where Childhood's dreams are twined
   In Memory's mystic band,
Like pilgrim's wither'd wreath of flowers
   Pluck'd in a far-off land.

CHAPTER I

DOWN THE RABBIT-HOLE

ALICE was beginning to get very tired of sitting by her sister on the bank, and of having nothing to do: once or twice she had peeped into the book her sister was reading, but it had no pictures or conversations in it, 'and what is the use of a book,' thought Alice, 'without pictures or conversation?'[1]

So she was considering in her own mind (as well as she could, for the hot day made her feel very sleepy and stupid) whether the pleasure of making a daisy-chain would be worth the trouble of getting up and picking the

1. The same thought—or one very like it—is in the minds of those many modern philosophers for whom ostensive definition (pictures) and the use of words in everyday speech-situations (conversation) are the twin fountains of verbal meaning. Alice is on the verge of discovering linguistic analysis. If she had only substituted 'word' for 'book' and pushed on from there, a great deal of recent philosophy could have remained unwritten. (Sutherland, p. 227; Shibles, p. 14; High [21], p. 76)

daisies, when suddenly a White Rabbit with pink eyes ran close by her.

There was nothing so *very* remarkable in that; nor did Alice think it so *very* much out of the way to hear the Rabbit say to itself, 'Oh dear! Oh dear! I shall be too late!' (when she thought it over afterwards, it occurred to her that she ought to have wondered at this, but at the time it all seemed quite natural); but when the Rabbit actually *took a watch out of its waistcoat-pocket*, and looked at it, and then hurried on, Alice started to her feet, for it flashed across her mind that she had never before seen a rabbit with either a waistcoat-pocket, or a watch to take out of it, and burning with curiosity, she ran across the field after it, and fortunately was just in time to see it pop down a large rabbit-hole under the hedge.

In another moment down went Alice after it, never once considering how in the world she was to get out again.

The rabbit-hole went straight on like a tunnel for some way, and then dipped suddenly down, so suddenly that Alice had not a moment to think about stopping herself before she found herself falling down a very deep well.

Either the well was very deep, or she fell very slowly, for she had plenty of time as she went down to look about her, and to wonder what was going to happen next.[2] First, she tried to look down and make out what she was coming to, but it was too dark to see anything; then she looked at the sides of the well, and noticed that they were filled with cupboards and book-shelves: here and there she saw maps and pictures hung upon pegs. She took down a jar from one of the shelves as she passed; it was labelled 'ORANGE MARMALADE', but to her great disappointment it was empty:[3] she did not not like to drop the jar for fear of killing

2. 'Suppose again a man to be supported in the air, and to be softly convey'd along by some invisible power. . . .' (David Hume, *Treatise of Human Nature*, Bk. I, Pt. II, Sect. 5). Alice, in free fall, discovers the fact pointed out by Hume and by now familiar to astronauts and aircraft passengers, namely that motion, by itself, gives no impression of distance covered, or therefore of velocity. From the elapsed time she can infer that her descent has been either short and slow or fast and far, but she cannot at present tell which.

3. Sutherland (p. 123) calls this a case of false labeling, which seems unduly severe. If the jar had ever contained marmalade, or was ever destined to do so, its label, though temporarily misleading, could scarcely be called incorrect. Only if Alice had found the jar full of gelignite, say, or raspberry jam, could the charge of false labeling apply.

4. A death joke—the first of many (Empson, p. 268; Gardner, p. 27)

5. Alice brings out these words without knowing their definitions or what they stand for, though she has a fair idea of their use, namely to specify one's position on or in the earth. A moment later she produces the word 'antipathies,' evidently with no idea of its meaning, but with a vague sense that it is being wrongly used. In this case, though ignorant of the use, she knows quite well what she is referring to, and had she picked the right word, instead of a mere approximation to it, would have successfully said what she meant.

As Sutherland observes (pp. 123*ff.*), if she is actually at the earth's center, or crossing its axis, the notion of longitude ceases to apply. On the problem of what happens to a body falling through a hole to the antipodes, and on the interest taken in this question by Plutarch, Nicole Oresme, Francis Bacon, Galileo, and Voltaire, see Gardner, p. 27.

somebody, so managed to put it into one of the cupboards as she fell past it.

'Well!' thought Alice to herself. 'After such a fall as this, I shall think nothing of tumbling down stairs! How brave they'll all think me at home! Why, I wouldn't say anything about it, even if I fell off the top of the house!' (Which was very likely true.) [4]

Down, down, down. Would the fall *never* come to an end? 'I wonder how many miles I've fallen by this time?' she said aloud. 'I must be getting somewhere near the centre of the earth. Let me see: that would be four thousand miles down, I think —' (for, you see, Alice had learnt several things of this sort in her lessons in the schoolroom, and though this was not a *very* good opportunity for showing off her knowledge, as there was no one to listen to her, still it was good practice to say it over) '— yes, that's about the right distance — but then I wonder what Latitude or Longitude I've got to?' (Alice had no idea what Latitude was, or Longitude either, but thought they were nice grand words to say.) [5]

Presently she began again. 'I wonder if I shall fall right *through* the earth! How funny it'll seem to come out among the people that walk with their heads downwards! The Antipathies, I think —' (she was rather glad there *was* no one listening, this time, as it didn't sound at all the right word) '— but I shall have to ask them what the name of the country is, you know. Please, Ma'am, is this New Zealand or Australia?' (and she tried to curtsey as she spoke — fancy *curtseying* as you're falling through the air! Do you think you could manage it?) 'And what an ignorant little girl she'll think me! No, it'll never do to ask: perhaps I shall see it written up somewhere.'

Down, down, down. There was nothing else to do, so Alice soon began talking again. 'Dinah'll miss me very much to-night, I should think!' (Dinah was the cat.) 'I hope they'll remember her saucer of milk at tea-time. Dinah, my dear, I wish you were down here with me! There are no mice in the air, I'm afraid, but you might catch a bat, and that's very like a mouse, you know. But do cats eat bats, I wonder?' And here Alice began to get rather sleepy, and went on saying to herself, in a dreamy sort of way, 'Do cats eat bats? Do cats eat bats?' and sometimes, 'Do bats eat cats?' for, you see, as she couldn't answer either question, it didn't much matter which way she put it.[6] She felt that she was dozing off, and had just begun to dream that she was walking hand in hand with Dinah, and saying to her very earnestly, 'Now, Dinah, tell me the truth: did you ever eat a bat?' when suddenly, thump! thump! down she came upon a heap of dry leaves, and the fall was over.

Alice was not a bit hurt, and she jumped up on to her feet in a moment: she looked up, but it was all dark overhead; before her was another long passage, and the White Rabbit was still in sight, hurrying down it. There was not a moment to be lost: away went Alice like the wind, and was just in time to hear it say, as it turned a corner, 'Oh my ears and whiskers, how late it's getting!' She was close behind it when she turned the corner, but the Rabbit was no longer to be seen: she found herself in a long, low hall, which was lit up by a row of lamps hanging from the roof.

There were doors all round the hall, but they were all locked; and when Alice had been all the way down one side and up the other, trying every door, she walked sadly

6. However, it does matter, as Alice learns on p. 67. Eating is not a symmetrical relation, like being a colleague or cousin or compatriot of somebody, which obliges him to be the same of you. So 'C eats B' is not simply convertible to 'B eats C.' Nor does the inability to answer either question mean that the answers are not worth troubling about. Alexander (p. 562) suspects Alice of flirting here with logical positivism, that is, of rejecting questions that admit of no empirical answer as meaningless. It would, however, be a more old-fashioned positivism (of Comte's type) which dismissed a straightforwardly empirical question simply because there was no practical way of settling it. Alice's behavior shows clearly that she does not, in fact, subscribe to either view; so far from believing the questions to be meaningless or impossible to answer, she immediately tries to get an answer to the first of them by seeking the evidence of a competent witness. Not that such evidence would have been worth much, even if she had obtained it. (Sutherland, p. 191; Shibles, p. 15)

7. Obviously, these are not genuinely alternative explanations, since they come to the same thing. In ordinary language (unlike propositional logic) *or* normally means 'one or the other, but not both.' Here, if one explanation is correct, the other must be so too, that is, both must be true together, if true at all. A particular key may, of course, be too large or too small for a *given* lock, or vice versa. But this presupposes a standard already set, which is hardly the case here. (Sutherland, p. 189; Shibles, p. 15)

down the middle, wondering how she was ever to get out again.

Suddenly she came upon a little three-legged table, all made of solid glass; there was nothing on it except a tiny golden key, and Alice's first thought was that it might belong to one of the doors of the hall; but, alas! either the locks were too large, or the key was too small, but at any rate it would not open any of them.[7] However, the second time round, she came upon a low curtain she had not noticed before, and behind it was a little door about fifteen inches high: she tried the little golden key in the lock, and to her great delight it fitted!

Alice opened the door and found that it led into a small passage, not much larger than a rat-hole: she knelt down and looked along the passage into the loveliest garden you ever saw. How she longed to get out of that dark hall, and wander about among those beds of bright flowers and those

cool fountains, but she could not even get her head through the doorway; 'and even if my head would go through,' thought poor Alice, 'it would be of very little use without my shoulders. Oh, how I wish I could shut up like a telescope! I think I could, if I only knew how to begin.' For, you see, so many out-of-the-way things had happened lately, that Alice had begun to think that very few things indeed were really impossible.[8]

There seemed to be no use in waiting by the little door, so she went back to the table, half hoping she might find another key on it, or at any rate a book of rules for shutting people up like telescopes: this time she found a little bottle on it, ('which certainly was not here before,' said Alice,) and round its neck a paper label, with the words 'DRINK ME' beautifully printed on it in large letters.

It was all very well to say 'Drink me', but the wise little Alice was not going to do *that* in a hurry. 'No, I'll look first,' she said, 'and see whether it's marked *"poison"* or not;' for she had read several nice little histories about children who had got burnt, and eaten up by wild beasts, and many other unpleasant things, all because they *would* not remember the simple rules their friends had taught them: such as, that a red-hot poker will burn you if you hold it too long; and that, if you cut your finger *very* deeply with a knife, it usually bleeds; and she had never forgotten that, if you drink much from a bottle

8. It is sometimes disputed whether one can try (or even wish) to do what one believes to be impossible. Alice later maintains against the White Queen (p. 180) that you cannot believe impossible things (to be possible, that is), and her present attitude is consistent with this, since (on rather weak inductive evidence) she no longer believes, if she ever did, that shutting up *is* impossible; she is thus at least not logically precluded from attempting it.

9. Alice here commits the formal fallacy of 'denying the antecedent.' From the true, if recklessly understated, premise that bottles marked 'poison' are not wholly safe to drink from, it cannot be validly inferred that unmarked bottles are necessarily safe. She gets off comparatively lightly, as it turns out. From a purely logical point of view, the book might have been more instructive if her adventures had ended abruptly at, or soon after, this point. That these are the author's own sentiments, can scarcely be in doubt. His heroine is making an idiot of herself, and fully deserves destruction; only his charity permits her to survive. (Sutherland, pp. 121-22)

10. As the sequel makes clear, Alice has unwittingly consumed a hallucinatory drug. But her previous sensations of falling, and present remarkable powers of sensory discrimination, make it regrettably likely that she is already no stranger to the experience. A generation accustomed to such things has not failed to recognize in Alice a kindred spirit. The Jefferson Airplane (whatever that may be, exactly) has celebrated her excesses in indifferent song, and Fensch (who reprints it, pp. 90*ff*.) has seen fit to interpret the entire narrative in a psychedelic light. Alice, with eight further lapses to her discredit, is undoubtedly the worst offender; but suspicion falls heavily also on the Caterpillar, Frog-Footman and Dormouse, and to a lesser extent on several others as well.

   The widespread use of laudanum as a nineteenth-century household remedy makes it not impossible that Carroll was personally acquainted with its effects. If the fact could be established, Fensch's hypothesis would be no laughing matter, but a serious critical resource. (On the classification of sensations, *cf*. Sutherland, pp. 100, 111.)

11. A puzzle about existence. Like Goethe, Freud, and some others, Alice is unable to conceive of her own total extinction, for she wonders what *she* would be like after she had 'gone out.' She distinguishes, in Cartesian fashion, between her body and herself, but then runs into difficulties through trying to visualize the state of disembodied existence. (Holmes, p. 141)

marked 'poison', it is almost certain to disagree with you, sooner or later.[9]

However, this bottle was *not* marked 'poison', so Alice ventured to taste it, and finding it very nice (it had, in fact, a sort of mixed flavour of cherry-tart, custard, pineapple, roast turkey, toffee, and hot buttered toast,) she very soon finished it off.[10]

* * * *

* * * *

* * * *

'What a curious feeling!' said Alice. 'I must be shutting up like a telescope.'

And so it was indeed: she was now only ten inches high, and her face brightened up at the thought that she was now the right size for going through the little door into that lovely garden. First, however, she waited for a few minutes to see if she was going to shrink any further: she felt a little nervous about this; 'for it might end, you know,' said Alice, 'in my going out altogether, like a candle. I wonder what I should be like then?' And she tried to fancy what the flame of a candle is like after it is blown out, for she could not remember ever having seen such a thing.[11]

After a while, finding that nothing more happened, she decided on going into the garden at once; but, alas for poor Alice! when she got to the door, she found she had forgotten the little golden key, and when she went back to the table for it, she found she could not possibly reach it: she could see it quite plainly through the glass, and she tried her best to climb up one of the table-legs, but it was too slippery; and when she had tired herself out with trying, the poor little thing sat down and cried.

'Come, there's no use in crying like that!' said Alice to herself, rather sharply. 'I advise you to leave off this minute!' She generally gave herself very good advice (though she very seldom followed it), and sometimes she scolded herself so severely as to bring tears into her eyes; and once she remembered trying to box her own ears for having cheated herself in a game of croquet she was playing against herself, for this curious child was very fond of pretending to be two people. 'But it's no use now,' thought poor Alice, 'to pretend to be two people! Why, there's hardly enough of me left to make *one* respectable person!'[12]

Soon her eye fell on a little glass box that was lying under the table: she opened it, and found in it a very small cake, on which the words 'EAT ME' were beautifully marked in currants. 'Well, I'll eat it,' said Alice, 'and if it makes me larger, I can reach the key; and if it makes me smaller, I can creep under the door; so either way I'll get into the garden, and I don't care which happens!'

She ate a little bit, and said anxiously to herself, 'Which way? Which way?' holding her hand on the top of her head to feel which way it was growing, and she was quite surprised to find that she remained the same size:[13] to be sure, this generally happens when one eats cake, but Alice had got so much into the way of expecting nothing but out-of-the-way things to happen, that it seemed quite dull and stupid for life to go on in the common way.[14]

So she set to work, and very soon finished off the cake.

*　　*　　*　　*
　*　　*　　*
*　　*　　*　　*

12. On failing to secure the key, she undergoes a smart attack of schizophrenia, which ends in a reversal of her previous standpoint; for in complaining that there is now almost too little of her to make even one person, she is evidently identifying body and personality, or at least assuming that the amount of the one determines the amount of the other. If so, disembodied existence would be impossible, for it would entail a simultaneous annihilation of personality and, for lack of a complainant, an end to further complaint.

13. As Wittgenstein noted ([48] § 279), this is not a sensible way of finding out. Alice has adopted a measuring rod that is part of the system to be measured, and even if that system is expanding (or contracting), there will be no way of discovering the change from within it. For this reason, suggestions such as that the universe may have doubled in size overnight (measuring rods included), are generally rejected as meaningless. (Pitcher [in Fann], p. 319; Shibles, p. 16)

14. To anticipate and prepare for the unexpected is possible enough, but only as an exception to the general rule. If *everything*, virtually, is to be out-of-the-way, the commonplace becomes the unexpected, and there is then no way for anything to be out of. If (as is sometimes said) we are all of us 'abnormal,' the idea of normality no longer makes any sense.

THE POOL OF TEARS

'CURIOUSER and curiouser!' cried Alice (she was so much surprised, that for the moment she quite forgot how to speak good English); 'now I'm opening out like the largest telescope that ever was! Good-bye, feet!' (for when she looked down at her feet, they seemed to be almost out of sight, they were getting so far off).[1] 'Oh, my poor little feet, I wonder who will put on your shoes and stockings for you now, dears? I'm sure I shan't be able! I shall be a great deal too far off to trouble myself about you: you must manage the best way you can — but I must be kind to them,' thought Alice, 'or perhaps they won't walk the way I want to go! Let

1. Her sudden expansion, this time demonstrated by the visual recession of her nether extremities, leads Alice to distinguish once more between herself and the parts of her own body. 'She,' apparently, is where her head is, and her feet are now regarded as colonial outposts—still hers, but of doubtful loyalty, and requiring bribery to secure a continuing obedience to her will. (On Alice's departure from standard English, *cf.* Sutherland, p. 202.)

me see: I'll give them a new pair of boots every Christmas.'

And she went on planning to herself how she would manage it. 'They must go by the carrier,' she thought; 'and how funny it'll seem, sending presents to one's own feet! And how odd the directions will look!

> *Alice's Right Foot, Esq.*
> *Hearthrug,*
> > *near the Fender,*
> > *(with Alice's love).*

Oh dear, what nonsense I'm talking!'[2]

Just then her head struck against the roof of the hall: in fact she was now more than nine feet high, and she at once took up the little golden key and hurried off to the garden door.

Poor Alice! It was as much as she could do, lying down on one side, to look through into the garden with one eye; but to get through was more hopeless than ever: she sat down and began to cry again.

'You ought to be ashamed of yourself,' said Alice, 'a great girl like you,' (she might well say this), 'to go on crying in this way! Stop this moment, I tell you!' But she went on all the same, shedding gallons of tears, until there was a large pool all round her, about four inches deep and reaching half down the hall.

After a time she heard a little pattering of feet in the distance, and she hastily dried her eyes to see what was coming. It was the White Rabbit returning, splendidly dressed, with a pair of white kid gloves in one hand and a large fan in the other: he came trotting along in a great hurry, muttering to himself as he came, 'Oh! the Duchess,

2. Wittgenstein ([48] § 268) similarly discusses—and discounts—the possibility of such self-addressed gifts (Pitcher [in Fann], p. 319). A man may give himself a treat, he may give his feet a rest, or his stomach may give him a pain, but these do not qualify as 'presents' in the usual sense. Alice is not mistaken in suspecting a conceptual absurdity here. (For more on the subject of gifts, see note 6, p. 32.)

the Duchess! Oh! won't she be savage if I've kept her waiting!' Alice felt so desperate that she was ready to ask help of any one; so, when the Rabbit came near her, she began, in a low, timid voice, 'If you please, sir ——' The Rabbit started violently, dropped the white kid gloves and the fan, and scurried away into the darkness as hard as he could go.

Alice took up the fan and gloves, and as the hall was very

hot, she kept fanning herself all the time she went on talking: 'Dear, dear! How queer everything is to-day! And yesterday things went on just as usual. I wonder if I've been changed in the night? Let me think: was I the same when I got up this morning? I almost think I can remember feeling a little different. But if I'm not the same, the next question is, Who in the world am I? Ah, *that's* the great puzzle!'[3] And she began thinking over all the children she knew that were of the same age as herself, to see if she could have been changed for any of them.

'I'm sure I'm not Ada,' she said, 'for her hair goes in such long ringlets, and mine doesn't go in ringlets at all; and I'm sure I can't be Mabel, for I know all sorts of things, and she, oh! she knows such a very little! Besides, *she's* she, and *I'm* I, and — oh dear, how puzzling it all is! I'll try if I know all the things I used to know. Let me see: four times five is twelve, and four times six is thirteen, and four times seven is — oh dear! I shall never get to twenty at that rate![4] However, the Multiplication Table doesn't signify:[5] let's try Geography. London is the capital of Paris, and Paris is the capital of Rome, and Rome — no, *that's* all wrong, I'm certain! I must have been changed for Mabel! I'll try and say "*How doth the little —*"' and she crossed her hands on her lap as if she were saying lessons, and began to repeat it, but her voice sounded hoarse and strange, and the words did not come the same as they used to do:—

'How doth the little crocodile
Improve his shining tail,
And pour the waters of the Nile
On every golden scale!

3. The first of a series of identity crises such as any existentialist might envy, which beset Alice throughout the book (see notes 1 and 2, p. 47). Her problem, it should be noted, is not that of a hopeless amnesiac like the Baker in *The Hunting of the Snark*, who cannot even remember his own name. Except in the nameless wood (p. 158), Alice has a clear enough memory of herself and her own past. What troubles her, rather, is her inability to *use* that past in remembering correctly the facts and routines she has learned, to the point of doubting whether she is any longer the same person. These doubts—in an admittedly schizoid personality (see note 12, p. 20)—are associated with gross disturbances of the body-image, brought on, as we have seen, by a habit of reckless indulgence in every drug and nostrum that comes within her reach. She is, moreover, far too ready to assume that because she is 'not herself' she must therefore be someone else. Despite the obvious difficulty of believing that she (Alice) can be Ada or Mabel, she eventually accepts the latter conclusion, on the inconsequential ground that she now has an attribute in common with Mabel, namely ignorance. More sensibly, a moment later, she decides to let others determine the question, presumably on physical evidence, while reserving the right to reject this identification if it is not to her own taste. (Sutherland, p. 100; Shibles, pp. 17-18, 20; Holmes, p. 141)

4. As Gardner explains (p. 38), four times twelve 'at that rate' takes her to nineteen, which is as far as she would expect to go.

5. Compare the remark attributed to Wittgenstein: 'All mathematical propositions mean the same thing, namely nothing.' Mathematics, in other words, is a purely formal science, having nothing to say (as geography does) about questions of empirical fact. A knowledge of such elementary formal truths would thus be of little help for purposes of identification, since nearly everybody knows them, whereas people tend to differ a good deal in their knowledge of matters of fact.

---

6. Alice's periodic expansions have provided cosmologists with a source of illustrations for the theory of an expanding universe. Her present shrinkage is cited by Gardner (p. 39) as an equally suitable model for a diminishing one proposed (though not seriously) by Sir Edmund Whittaker in his *Eddington's Principle in the Philosophy of Science* (1951), p. 29.

The Pool of Tears

'*How cheerfully he seems to grin,*
How neatly spread his claws,
And welcomes little fishes in
With gently smiling jaws!'

'I'm sure those are not the right words,' said poor Alice, and her eyes filled with tears again as she went on, 'I must be Mabel after all, and I shall have to go and live in that poky little house, and have next to no toys to play with, and oh! ever so many lessons to learn! No, I've made up my mind about it; if I'm Mabel, I'll stay down here! It'll be no use their putting their heads down and saying "Come up again, dear!" I shall only look up and say "Who am I then? Tell me that first, and then, if I like being that person, I'll come up; if not, I'll stay down here till I'm somebody else" — but, oh dear!' cried Alice, with a sudden burst of tears, 'I do wish they *would* put their heads down! I am so *very* tired of being all alone here!'

As she said this she looked down at her hands, and was surprised to see that she had put on one of the Rabbit's little white kid gloves while she was talking. 'How *can* I have done that?' she thought. 'I must be growing small again.' She got up and went to the table to measure herself by it, and found that, as nearly as she could guess, she was now about two feet high, and was going on shrinking rapidly: she soon found out that the cause of this was the fan she was holding, and she dropped it hastily, just in time to avoid shrinking away altogether.[6]

'That *was* a narrow escape!' said Alice, a good deal frightened at the sudden change, but very glad to find herself still in existence; 'and now for the garden!' and she ran with all speed back to the little door: but, alas! the little door was shut again, and the little golden key was

lying on the glass table as before, 'and things are worse than ever,' thought the poor child, 'for I never was so small as this before, never! And I declare it's too bad, that it is!'

As she said these words her foot slipped, and in another moment, splash! she was up to her chin in salt water. Her first idea was that she had somehow fallen into the sea, 'and in that case I can go back by railway,' she said to herself. (Alice had been to the seaside once in her life, and had come to the general conclusion, that wherever you go to on the English coast you find a number of bathing machines in the sea, some children digging in the sand with wooden spades, then a row of lodging houses, and behind them a railway station.)[7]However, she soon made out that she was in the pool of tears which she had wept when she was nine feet high.

'I wish I hadn't cried so much!' said Alice, as she swam about, trying to find her way out. 'I shall be punished for it now, I suppose, by being drowned in my own tears!

7. Alice's weakness for arguing by partial analogies, and for generalizing rashly on scanty inductive evidence, has already been noticed. The best that can be said for her present theory is that its failings are endemic among amateur sociologists, and very common everywhere else.

———

8. A brave attempt at finding a use at last for the English vocative—a virtually nonexistent case created, as here, by the fancy of Latinizing grammarians during the nineteenth century.

9. Although the Mouse's aversion to cats is later claimed to be an unconditioned reflex of genetic origin, it is here displayed as a conditioned response to a purely verbal stimulus. Much the same thing happens with the Fawn, on p. 160, except that on that occasion the name, once recalled, is assigned to a present object. In this instance, Alice is too tactless to prevent herself from reactivating the same response twice more in quick succession; but she eventually learns (p. 33) to avoid it by euphemism. (Sutherland, pp. 217-18)

That *will* be a queer thing, to be sure! However, everything is queer to-day.'

Just then she heard something splashing about in the pool a little way off, and she swam nearer to make out what it was: at first she thought it must be a walrus or hippopotamus, but then she remembered how small she was now, and she soon made out that it was only a mouse that had slipped in like herself.

'Would it be of any use, now,' thought Alice, 'to speak to this mouse? Everything is so out-of-the-way down here, that I should think very likely it can talk: at any rate, there's no harm in trying.' So she began: 'O Mouse, do you know the way out of this pool? I am very tired of swimming about here, O Mouse!'[8] (Alice thought this must be the right way of speaking to a mouse: she had never done such a thing before, but she remembered having seen in her brother's Latin Grammar, 'A mouse — of a mouse — to a mouse — a mouse — O mouse!' The Mouse looked at her rather inquisitively, and seemed to her to wink with one of its little eyes, but it said nothing.

'Perhaps it doesn't understand English,' thought Alice; 'I daresay it's a French mouse, come over with William the Conqueror.' (For, with all her knowledge of history, Alice had no very clear notion how long ago anything had happened.) So she began again: 'Où est ma chatte?' which was the first sentence in her French lesson-book. The Mouse gave a sudden leap out of the water, and seemed to quiver all over with fright.[9] 'Oh, I beg your pardon!' cried Alice hastily, afraid that she had hurt the poor animal's feelings. 'I quite forgot you didn't like cats.'

'Not like cats!' cried the Mouse, in a shrill, passionate voice. 'Would *you* like cats if you were me?'

'Well, perhaps not,' said Alice in a soothing tone: 'don't be angry about it. And yet I wish I could show you our cat Dinah: I think you'd take a fancy to cats if you could only see her. She is such a dear quiet thing,' Alice went on, half to herself, as she swam lazily about in the pool, 'and she sits purring so nicely by the fire, licking her paws and washing her face — and she is such a nice soft thing to nurse — and she's such a capital one for catching mice —— oh, I beg your pardon!' cried Alice again, for this time the Mouse was bristling all over, and she felt certain it must be really offended. 'We won't talk about her any more if you'd rather not.'

'We, indeed!' cried the Mouse, who was trembling down to the end of his tail. 'As if *I* would talk on such a subject! Our family always *hated* cats: nasty, low, vulgar things! Don't let me hear the name again!'

'I won't indeed!' said Alice, in a great hurry to change

the subject of conversation. 'Are you — are you fond — of — of dogs?' The Mouse did not answer, so Alice went on eagerly: 'There is such a nice little dog near our house I should like to show you! A little bright-eyed terrier, you know, with oh, such long curly brown hair! And it'll fetch things when you throw them, and it'll sit up and beg for its dinner, and all sorts of things — I can't remember half of them — and it belongs to a farmer, you know, and he says it's so useful, it's worth a hundred pounds! He says it kills all the rats and — oh dear!' cried Alice in a sorrowful tone, 'I'm afraid I've offended it again!' For the Mouse was swimming away from her as hard as it could go, and making quite a commotion in the pool as it went.

So she called softly after it, 'Mouse dear! Do come back again, and we won't talk about cats or dogs either, if you don't like them!' When the Mouse heard this, it turned round and swam slowly back to her: its face was quite pale (with passion, Alice thought), and it said in a low trembling voice, 'Let us get to the shore, and then I'll tell you my history, and you'll understand why it is I hate cats and dogs.'

It was high time to go, for the pool was getting quite crowded with the birds and animals that had fallen into it: there were a Duck and a Dodo, a Lory and an Eaglet, and several other curious creatures.[10] Alice led the way, and the whole party swam to the shore.

10. Fifteen creatures, not counting Alice, appear in the second illustration in Chapter III: nine birds, four mammals, and two crustaceans are identifiable, of which the oddest, apart from the extinct Dodo, is a baboon (also in Carroll's own illustration), which has only a walk-on part, being nowhere referred to in the text. Empson (pp. 254-55) conjectures the passage to be an obscure satire on the theory of evolution, with the pool of tears as the primal sea of life, and the caucus-race in Chapter III (in which everybody wins) as a covert attack on natural selection. With Darwinism only six years old, the allusion would certainly be topical enough, but the biographical evidence (marshaled by Gardner, p. 44) identifies the party of creatures with the members of a boating expedition that included Alice's sisters (Lory and Eaglet), an Oxford clergyman (Duck), Carroll himself (Dodo), and various sisters and aunts. This still does not explain the baboon.

CHAPTER III

A CAUCUS-RACE AND A LONG TALE

THEY were indeed a queer-looking party that assembled on the bank — the birds with draggled feathers, the animals with their fur clinging close to them, and all dripping wet, cross, and uncomfortable.

The first question of course was, how to get dry again: they had a consultation about this, and after a few minutes it seemed quite natural to Alice to find herself talking familiarly with them, as if she had known them all her life. Indeed, she had quite a long argument with the Lory, who at last turned sulky, and would only say 'I am older than you, and must know better'; and this Alice would not allow without knowing how old it was, and, as the Lory positively refused to tell its age, there was no more to be said.[1]

At last the Mouse, who seemed to be a person of author-

1. Alice should not have allowed it on any terms. The Lory is guilty of *ignoratio elenchi* (the general name for fallacies of irrelevance) in employing an *argumentum ad verecundiam*, or inappropriate appeal to authority. Greater age does not entail superior wisdom, or the expression 'old fool' would be a contradiction in terms. Instead of questioning the principle, Alice merely quibbles about the facts, and if she could have proved herself the older, would doubtless have committed the same fallacy herself.

ity among them, called out, 'Sit down, all of you, and listen to me! *I'll* soon make you dry enough!' They all sat down at once, in a large ring, with the Mouse in the middle. Alice kept her eyes anxiously fixed on it, for she felt sure she would catch a bad cold if she did not get dry very soon.

'Ahem!' said the Mouse with an important air. 'Are you all ready? This is the driest thing I know.[2] Silence all round, if you please! "William the Conqueror, whose cause was favoured by the Pope, was soon submitted to by the English, who wanted leaders, and had been of late much accustomed to usurpation and conquest. Edwin and Morcar, the earls of Mercia and Northumbria ——"'

'Ugh!' said the Lory, with a shiver.

'I beg your pardon!' said the Mouse, frowning, but very politely. 'Did you speak?'

'Not I!' said the Lory hastily.

'I thought you did,' said the Mouse. '— I proceed. "Edwin and Morcar, the earls of Mercia and Northumbria, declared for him: and even Stigand, the patriotic archbishop of Canterbury, found it advisable ——"'

'Found *what*?' said the Duck.

'Found *it*,' the Mouse replied rather crossly: 'of course you know what "it" means.'

'I know what "it" means well enough, when *I* find a thing,' said the Duck: 'it's generally a frog or a worm. The question is, what did the archbishop find?'[3]

The Mouse did not notice this question, but hurriedly went on, '"— found it advisable to go with Edgar Atheling to meet William and offer him the crown. William's conduct at first was moderate. But the insolence of his Normans —" How are you getting on now, my dear?' it continued, turning to Alice as it spoke.

2. Some philosopher has somewhere said of another (names, alas, forgotten), that his works might be recommended to the Mouse as a substitute for the driest thing he knew. The passage is actually from Haviland Chepmell's *Short Course of History* (1862), pp. 143-44 (Gardner, p. 46, citing R. L. Green, ed., *The Diaries of Lewis Carroll* [1953], Vol. I, p. 2).

3. The Duck is a sort of illogical positivist. The word *it* has meaning for him only by standing for some concrete, verifiable, and usually edible object of experience. Holding such a view requires either the dismissal of many ordinary expressions as unintelligible, or a peopling of the world with anonymous agencies, responsible for raining, snowing, and so forth, and with equally mystifying items of the kind supposed here (for another example, see p. 170). Descartes' famous 'I think, therefore I am' has sometimes been amended by purists to the more noncommittal 'it thinks in me.' But if thereby condemned to accepting a faceless demon that does Descartes' thinking for him, most people would find the remedy worse than the disease, and would sooner have Descartes back again, or, failing that, a better account of the word *it*.

The Mouse, unsurprisingly, ducks the issue. Historians generally do. (Sutherland, pp. 172-73; Shibles, p. 18; Baker [4], p. 707)

4. The sesquipedalian circumlocution of the Dodo's utterance is at once denounced as word-magic. The objection is met by paraphrase, followed by ostensive definition (explaining 'caucus-racing' by doing it). (Sutherland, pp. 159, 223; Kemeny [24], p. 244, on the social sciences)

'As wet as ever,' said Alice in a melancholy tone: 'it doesn't seem to dry me at all.'

'In that case,' said the Dodo solemnly, rising to its feet, 'I move that the meeting adjourn, for the immediate adoption of more energetic remedies ——'

'Speak English!' said the Eaglet. 'I don't know the meaning of half those long words, and, what's more, I don't believe you do either!'[4] And the Eaglet bent down its head to hide a smile: some of the other birds tittered audibly.

'What I was going to say,' said the Dodo in an offended tone, 'was, that the best thing to get us dry would be a Caucus-race.'

'What *is* a Caucus-race?' said Alice; not that she much wanted to know, but the Dodo had paused as if it thought that *somebody* ought to speak, and no one else seemed inclined to say anything.

'Why,' said the Dodo, 'the best way to explain it is to do it.' (And, as you might like to try the thing yourself some winter day, I will tell you how the Dodo managed it.)

First it marked out a race-course, in a sort of circle, ('the exact shape doesn't matter,' it said), and then all the party were placed along the course, here and there. There was no 'One, two, three, and away,' but they began running when they liked, and left off when they liked, so that it was not easy to know when the race was over. However, when they had been running half an hour or so, and were quite dry again, the Dodo suddenly called out, 'The race is over!' and they all crowded round it, panting, and asking, 'But who has won?'

This question the Dodo could not answer without a great

deal of thought, and it sat for a long time with one finger pressed upon its forehead (the position in which you usually see Shakespeare, in the pictures of him), while the rest waited in silence. At last the Dodo said, '*Everybody has won, and all must have prizes.*'[5]

'But who is to give the prizes?' quite a chorus of voices asked.

'Why, *she*, of course,' said the Dodo, pointing to Alice with one finger; and the whole party at once crowded round her, calling out in a confused way, 'Prizes! Prizes!'

Alice had no idea what to do, and in despair she put her hand in her pocket, and pulled out a box of comfits (luckily the salt water had not got into it), and handed them round as prizes. There was exactly one apiece all round.

'But she must have a prize herself, you know,' said the Mouse.

'Of course,' the Dodo replied very gravely. 'What else have you got in your pocket?' he went on, turning to Alice.

'Only a thimble,' said Alice sadly.

'Hand it over here,' said the Dodo.

Then they all crowded round her once more, while the Dodo solemnly presented the thimble, saying 'We beg your acceptance of this elegant thimble;' and, when it had finished this short speech, they all cheered.[6]

Alice thought the whole thing very absurd, but they all looked so grave that she did not dare to laugh; and, as she could not think of anything to say, she simply bowed, and took the thimble, looking as solemn as she could.

The next thing was to eat the comfits: this caused some noise and confusion, as the large birds complained that

5. Pitcher (in Fann, p. 323) considers this a nonsensical decision, since winning logically entails that some contestants do better than others. A general dead heat, as he admits, would constitute a possible exception; so, for that matter, would a walk-over, a one-horse race, or a win by disqualification or default. But although these cases resemble the present one in putting the notion of 'winning' under logical strain, they differ radically from it in that here the competitors have not been told, and never discover, what the necessary conditions for 'winning' are. (Shibles, p. 19)

6. Wittgenstein is said (by N. Malcolm, in *Ludwig Wittgenstein, a Memoir* [1958], p. 31) to have been in the habit of 'presenting' companions on his walks around Cambridge with trees encountered en route, on condition that the recipient left them alone and did nothing with them. The Dodo's presentation to Alice of a piece of her own property is a similarly futile example of a 'gift' that transfers nothing, and so fails to qualify as a genuine reward. According to Karl Marx, the capitalist system perpetrates an analogous fraud on the worker, who is merely given a portion of what already belongs to him by right, and is robbed of the remainder, when the surplus value of his product goes into the pockets of his employer.

they could not taste theirs, and the small ones choked and
had to be patted on the back. However, it was over at last,
and they sat down again in a ring, and begged the Mouse
to tell them something more.

'You promised to tell me your history, you know,'
said Alice, 'and why it is you hate — C and D,' she added
in a whisper, half afraid that it would be offended again.

'Mine is a long and a sad tale!' said the Mouse, turning
to Alice and sighing.

'It *is* a long tail, certainly,' said Alice, looking down
with wonder at the Mouse's tail; 'but why do you call it

sad?'[7] And she kept on puzzling about it while the Mouse was speaking, so that her idea of the tail was something like this:[8]—'Fury said to a
      mouse, That he
      met in the
     house,
   'Let us
    both go to
     law: *I* will
       prosecute
       you. Come,
        I'll take no
        denial; We
       must have a
     trial: For
   really this
  morning I've
  nothing
  to do.'
   Said the
    mouse to the
     cur, 'Such
       a trial,
        dear Sir,
         With
        no jury
       or judge,
      would be
    wasting
   our
    breath.'
      'I'll be
       judge, I'll
       be jury,'
        Said
      cunning
     old Fury:
    'I'll
    try the
    whole
     cause,
      and
     condemn
     you
     to
     death.'

7. The confusion here is due to a fallacy of equivocation, turning not on the use of a single word in different meanings, but on the mistaking of one word for another whose pronunciation is the same (homophonic, as opposed to lexical, ambiguity). (Sutherland, p. 175; Terrell and Baker [46], p. 69)

8. As Alice imagines it, the tale is an example of *technopaegnion*, a riddling versification whose shape resembles an object connected with the poem. Found chiefly in Hellenistic writers and the English metaphysical poets, the form is also said (by Gardner, p. 51) to have been experimented with by the American philosopher-logician (and bad poet) Charles Peirce. The judicial travesty recounted finds an echo in the later trial of *Rex v. Knave of Hearts* (pp. 104-119), and elsewhere in the forensic exploits of the Snark (*The Hunting of the Snark*, Fit 6). Carroll evidently had a low idea of the law. For the law's idea of Carroll, see Glanville Williams, *passim*.

'You are not attending!' said the Mouse to Alice severely. 'What are you thinking of?'

'I beg your pardon,' said Alice very humbly: 'you had got to the fifth bend, I think?'

'I had *not*!' cried the Mouse, angrily.

'A knot!' said Alice, always ready to make herself useful, and looking anxiously about her. 'Oh, do let me help to undo it!'

'I shall do nothing of the sort,' said the Mouse, getting up and walking away. 'You insult me by talking such nonsense!'[9]

'I didn't mean it!' pleaded poor Alice. 'But you're so easily offended, you know!'

The Mouse only growled in reply.

'Please come back and finish your story!' Alice called after it. And the others all joined in chorus, 'Yes, please do!' but the Mouse only shook its head impatiently and walked a little quicker.

'What a pity it wouldn't stay!' sighed the Lory, as soon as it was quite out of sight; and an old Crab took the opportunity of saying to her daughter 'Ah, my dear! Let this be a lesson to you never to lose *your* temper!' 'Hold your tongue, Ma!' said the young Crab, a little snappishly. 'You're enough to try the patience of an oyster!'

'I wish I had our Dinah here, I know I do!' said Alice aloud, addressing nobody in particular. 'She'd soon fetch it back!'

'And who is Dinah, if I might venture to ask the question?' said the Lory.

Alice replied eagerly, for she was always ready to talk about her pet: 'Dinah's our cat. And she's such a capital one for catching mice you can't think! And oh, I wish you

9. Alice's inadvertent pun (homophonic ambiguity again) goes unrecognized, of course—the usual thing in Wonderland—and is treated merely as a stupid *non sequitur*. Upset, no doubt, at being chided for this, she soon blunders into another gaffe about cats, and loses her audience altogether.

could see her after the birds! Why, she'll eat a little bird as soon as look at it!'

This speech caused a remarkable sensation among the party. Some of the birds hurried off at once: one old Magpie began wrapping itself up very carefully, remarking, 'I really must be getting home; the night-air doesn't suit my throat!' and a Canary called out in a trembling voice to its children, 'Come away, my dears! It's high time you were all in bed!'[10] On various pretexts they all moved off, and Alice was soon left alone.

'I wish I hadn't mentioned Dinah!' she said to herself in a melancholy tone. 'Nobody seems to like her, down here, and I'm sure she's the best cat in the world! Oh, my dear Dinah! I wonder if I shall ever see you any more!' And here poor Alice began to cry again, for she felt very lonely and low-spirited. In a little while, however, she again heard a little pattering of footsteps in the distance, and she looked up eagerly, half hoping that the Mouse had changed his mind, and was coming back to finish his story.

10. These references to nighttime are puzzling, since the action of the story continues in broad daylight—so far as there can be any such thing underground—and can hardly be occurring later than mid-afternoon, since the Mad Tea-Party (at 6 P.M.) is still some time ahead.

CHAPTER IV

THE RABBIT SENDS IN A LITTLE BILL[1]

It was the White Rabbit, trotting slowly back again, and looking anxiously about as it went, as if it had lost something; and she heard it muttering to itself, 'The Duchess! The Duchess! Oh my dear paws! Oh my fur and whiskers! She'll get me executed, as sure as ferrets are ferrets![2] Where *can* I have dropped them, I wonder?' Alice guessed in a moment that it was looking for the fan and the pair of white kid gloves, and she very good-naturedly began hunting about for them, but they were nowhere to be seen — everything seemed to have changed since her swim in the pool, and the great hall, with the glass table and the little door, had vanished completely.

Very soon the Rabbit noticed Alice, as she went hunting about, and called out to her in an angry tone, 'Why, Mary Ann, what *are* you doing out here? Run home this moment, and fetch me a pair of gloves and a fan! Quick, now!' And Alice was so much frightened that she ran off at once in the direction it pointed to, without trying to explain the mistake it had made.[3]

'He took me for his housemaid,' she said to herself as she ran. 'How surprised he'll be when he finds out who I am! But I'd better take him his fan and gloves — that is, if I can find them.' As she said this, she came upon a neat little house, on the door of which was a bright brass plate with the name 'W. RABBIT' engraved upon it. She went in without knocking, and hurried upstairs, in great fear

1. The complex equivocation, on a phrase beloved of Victorian tradesmen and moneylenders (*cf.*, for example, Anthony Trollope, *Framley Parsonage*, Ch. XII), may by now be just elusive enough to be worth pointing out.

2. An example of the nonvacuous use of a tautology. Anything as sure as this formally necessary truth is presumably as sure as anything can be. Strictly speaking, however, it is also a necessary truth that predictions of the future do not enjoy this degree of certainty. The Rabbit is a victim of a category mistake in equating a factual probability with a logical truth.

3. A better example of false naming than that on p. 14, though, since the name is bestowed in error and accepted without demur, its falsity is apparent only to the nominee. (Sutherland, p. 126)

The Philosopher's Alice

lest she should meet the real Mary Ann, and be turned out of the house before she had found the fan and gloves.

'How queer it seems,' Alice said to herself, 'to be going messages for a rabbit! I suppose Dinah'll be sending me on messages next!' And she began fancying the sort of thing that would happen: '"Miss Alice! Come here directly, and get ready for your walk!" "Coming in a minute, nurse! But I've got to watch this mouse-hole till Dinah comes back, and see that the mouse doesn't get out." Only I don't think,' Alice went on, 'that they'd let Dinah stop in the house if it began ordering people about like that!'

By this time she had found her way into a tidy little room with a table in the window, and on it (as she had hoped) a fan and two or three pairs of tiny white kid gloves: she took up the fan and a pair of the gloves, and was just going to leave the room, when her eye fell upon a little bottle that stood near the looking-glass. There was no label this time with the words 'DRINK ME', but nevertheless she uncorked it and put it to her lips. 'I know *something* interesting is sure to happen,' she said to herself, 'whenever I eat or drink anything; so I'll just see what this bottle does.[4] I do hope it'll make me grow large again, for really I'm quite tired of being such a tiny little thing!'

It did so indeed, and much sooner than she had expected: before she had drunk half the bottle, she found her head pressing against the ceiling, and had to stoop to save her neck from being broken. She hastily put down the bottle, saying to herself 'That's quite enough — I hope I shan't grow any more — As it is, I can't get out at the door — I do wish I hadn't drunk quite so much!'

Alas! it was too late to wish that! She went on growing, and growing, and very soon had to kneel down on the

4. Alice is arguing from past experience, by the not-very-reliable process which J. S. Mill called the method of agreement. Because previous eatings and drinkings have had interesting consequences, it does not follow that the next one will, and she has no right at all to say that she *knows* this. Her imprudence is all the greater for thinking that she does.

floor: in another minute there was not even room for this, and she tried the effect of lying down with one elbow against the door, and the other arm curled round her head. Still she went on growing, and, as a last resource, she put one arm out of the window, and one foot up the chimney, and said to herself 'Now I can do no more, whatever happens. What *will* become of me?'

Luckily for Alice, the little magic bottle had now had its full effect, and she grew no larger: still it was very uncomfortable, and, as there seemed to be no sort of chance of her ever getting out of the room again, no wonder she felt unhappy.

'It was much pleasanter at home,' thought poor Alice, 'when one wasn't always growing larger and smaller, and being ordered about by mice and rabbits. I almost wish I hadn't gone down that rabbit-hole — and yet — and yet

The Philosopher's Alice

— it's rather curious, you know, this sort of life! I do wonder what *can* have happened to me! When I used to read fairy-tales, I fancied that kind of thing never happened, and now here I am in the middle of one! There ought to be a book written about me, that there ought![5] And when I grow up, I'll write one — but I'm grown up now,' she added in a sorrowful tone; 'at least there's no room to grow up any more *here*.'

'But then,' thought Alice, 'shall I *never* get any older than I am now? That'll be a comfort, one way — never to be an old woman — but then — always to have lessons to learn! Oh, I shouldn't like *that*!'[6]

'Oh, you foolish Alice!' she answered herself. 'How can you learn lessons in here? Why, there's hardly room for *you*, and no room at all for any lesson-books!'

And so she went on, taking first one side and then the other, and making quite a conversation of it altogether; but after a few minutes she heard a voice outside, and stopped to listen.

'Mary Ann! Mary Ann!' said the voice. 'Fetch me my gloves this moment!' Then came a little pattering of feet on the stairs. Alice knew it was the Rabbit coming to look for her, and she trembled till she shook the house, quite forgetting that she was now about a thousand times as large as the Rabbit, and had no reason to be afraid of it.

Presently the Rabbit came up to the door, and tried to open it; but, as the door opened inwards, and Alice's elbow was pressed hard against it, that attempt proved a failure. Alice heard it say to itself, 'Then I'll go round and get in at the window.'

'*That* you won't!' thought Alice, and, after waiting till she fancied she heard the Rabbit just under the window,

5. Since Alice is already a fictional character, this is a distinctly idle proposal for her to make. If she had not already found a chronicler, she would not be around to demand one.

6. Alice confuses mere increase of size with maturation, or growing *up*, and also with aging. Because her body can get no larger, and is thus in one sense full-grown, that does not mean that she is now an adult, and still less that she is somehow exempted from the changes that will supervene on her becoming one.

7. Pat (a 'little animal' otherwise unidentified, though he is shortly to get into an Irish stew) takes the line that an arm is to be defined anatomically by criteria that do not include its relative size. The Rabbit argues, unreasonably, that an outsize specimen of the type cannot be a specimen at all.

she suddenly spread out her hand, and made a snatch in the air. She did not get hold of anything, but she heard a little shriek and a fall, and a crash of broken glass, from which she concluded that it was just possible it had fallen into a cucumber-frame, or something of the sort.

Next came an angry voice — the Rabbit's — 'Pat! Pat! Where are you?' And then a voice she had never heard before, 'Sure then I'm here! Digging for apples, yer honour!'

'Digging for apples, indeed!' said the Rabbit angrily. 'Here! Come and help me out of *this*!' (Sounds of more broken glass.)

'Now tell me, Pat, what's that in the window?'

'Sure, it's an arm, yer honour!' (He pronounced it 'arrum'.)

'An arm, you goose! Who ever saw one that size? Why, it fills the whole window!'

'Sure, it does, yer honour: but it's an arm for all that.'[7]

'Well, it's got no business there, at any rate: go and take it away!'

There was a long silence after this, and Alice could only hear whispers now and then; such as, 'Sure, I don't like it, yer honour, at all, at all!' 'Do as I tell you, you coward!' and at last she spread out her hand again, and made another snatch in the air. This time there were *two* little shrieks, and more sounds of broken glass. 'What a number of cucumber-frames there must be!' thought Alice. 'I wonder what they'll do next! As for pulling me out of the window, I only wish they *could*! I'm sure *I* don't want to stay in here any longer!'

She waited for some time without hearing anything more: at last came a rumbling of little cart-wheels, and the sound of a good many voices all talking together: she made out the words: 'Where's the other ladder? — Why, I hadn't to bring but one; Bill's got the other — Bill! Fetch it here, lad! — Here, put 'em up at this corner — No, tie 'em together first — they don't reach half high enough yet — Oh! they'll do well enough; don't be particular — Here, Bill! catch hold of this rope — Will the roof bear? — Mind that loose slate — Oh, it's coming down! Heads below!' (a loud crash) — 'Now, who did that? — It was Bill, I fancy — Who's to go down the chimney? — Nay, *I* shan't! *You* do it! — *That* I won't, then! — Bill's to go down — Here, Bill! the master says you've to go down the chimney!'

'Oh! So Bill's got to come down the chimney, has he?' said Alice to herself. 'Why, they seem to put everything upon Bill! I wouldn't be in Bill's place for a good deal: this fireplace is narrow, to be sure; but I *think* I can kick a little!'

She drew her foot as far down the chimney as she could, and waited till she heard a little animal (she couldn't guess of what sort it was) scratching and scrambling about in the chimney close above her: then, saying to herself 'This

is Bill,' she gave one sharp kick, and waited to see what would happen next.

The first thing she heard was a general chorus of 'There goes Bill!' then the Rabbit's voice alone — 'Catch him, you by the hedge!' then silence and then another confusion of voices — 'Hold up his head — Brandy now — Don't choke him — How was it, old fellow? What happened to you? Tell us all about it!'

At last came a little feeble, squeaking voice, ('That's Bill,' thought Alice,) 'Well, I hardly know — No more, thank ye; I'm better now — but I'm a deal too flustered to tell you — all I know is, something comes at me like a Jack-in-the-box, and up I goes like a skyrocket!'

'So you did, old fellow!' said the others.

'We must burn the house down!' said the Rabbit's voice. And Alice called out as loud as she could, 'If you do, I'll set Dinah at you!'

There was a dead silence instantly, and Alice thought to herself, 'I wonder what they *will* do next! If they had

8. A disjunctive argument, of the form traditionally known as *tollendo ponens*, which asserts one of a pair of alternative possibilities by denying the other. The premises are dubious, but the argument is formally valid. Having drawn the conclusion that eating a cake will make her smaller, Alice uses it as the major premise for a practical syllogism, of which cake-swallowing is the conclusion.

any sense, they'd take the roof off.' After a minute or two they began moving about again, and Alice heard the Rabbit say 'A barrowful will do, to begin with.'

'A barrowful of *what?*' thought Alice. But she had not long to doubt, for the next moment a shower of little pebbles came rattling in at the window, and some of them hit her in the face. 'I'll put a stop to this,' she said to herself, and shouted out 'You'd better not do that again!' which produced another dead silence.

Alice noticed with some surprise that the pebbles were all turning into little cakes as they lay on the floor, and a bright idea came into her head. 'If I eat one of these cakes,' she thought, 'it's sure to make *some* change in my size; and, as it can't possibly make me larger, it must make me smaller, I suppose.'[8]

So she swallowed one of the cakes, and was delighted to find that she began shrinking directly. As soon as she was small enough to get through the door, she ran out of the house, and found quite a crowd of little animals and birds waiting outside. The poor little Lizard, Bill, was in the middle, being held up by two guinea-pigs, who were giving it something out of a bottle. They all made a rush at Alice the moment she appeared; but she ran off as hard as she could, and soon found herself safe in a thick wood.

'The first thing I've got to do,' said Alice to herself, as she wandered about in the wood, 'is to grow to my right size again; and the second thing is to find my way into that lovely garden. I think that will be the best plan.'

It sounded an excellent plan, no doubt, and very neatly and simply arranged; the only difficulty was, that she had not the smallest idea how to set about it; and, while she was peering about anxiously among the trees, a little sharp

9. Apart from the White Knight's horse, the puppy is about the only creature in either narrative which behaves entirely naturally, that is, as its nature would lead one to expect. Presumably it is too young to do otherwise.

bark just over her head made her look up in a great hurry.

An enormous puppy was looking down at her with large round eyes, and feebly stretching out one paw, trying to touch her.[9] 'Poor little thing!' said Alice, in a coaxing tone, and she tried hard to whistle to it; but she was terribly

10. Alice could equally have said this of the puppy. 'Right size' here means normal relative size. As the Caterpillar is soon to inform her, there is nothing *wrong* with being three inches high so long as everything else is to scale. But it is certainly an inconvenient height for training an erratic young animal a great deal larger than yourself.

frightened all the time at the thought that it might be hungry, in which case it would be very likely to eat her up in spite of all her coaxing.

Hardly knowing what she did, she picked up a little bit of stick, and held it out to the puppy; whereupon the puppy jumped into the air off all its feet at once, with a yelp of delight, and rushed at the stick, and made believe to worry it; then Alice dodged behind a great thistle, to keep herself from being run over; and, the moment she appeared on the other side, the puppy made another rush at the stick, and tumbled head over heels in its hurry to get hold of it; then Alice, thinking it was very like having a game of play with a cart-horse, and expecting every moment to be trampled under its feet, ran round the thistle again; then the puppy began a series of short charges at the stick, running a very little way forwards each time and a long way back, and barking hoarsely all the while, till at last it sat down a good way off, panting, with its tongue hanging out of its mouth, and its great eyes half shut.

This seemed to Alice a good opportunity for making her escape; so she set off at once, and ran till she was quite tired and out of breath, and till the puppy's bark sounded quite faint in the distance.

'And yet what a dear little puppy it was!' said Alice, as she leant against a buttercup to rest herself, and fanned herself with one of the leaves. 'I should have liked teaching it tricks very much, if — if I'd only been the right size to do it! Oh dear! I'd nearly forgotten that I've got to grow up again! Let me see — how *is* it to be managed? I suppose I ought to eat or drink something or other; but the great question is, what?'

The great question certainly was, what? Alice looked all round her at the flowers and the blades of grass, but she could not see anything that looked like the right thing to eat or drink under the circumstances. There was a large mushroom growing near her, about the same height as herself; and, when she had looked under it, and on both sides of it, and behind it, it occurred to her that she might as well look and see what was on the top of it.

She stretched herself up on tiptoe, and peeped over the edge of the mushroom, and her eyes immediately met those of a large blue caterpillar, that was sitting on the top with its arms folded, quietly smoking a long hookah, and taking not the smallest notice of her or of anything else.

The Philosopher's Alice

46

CHAPTER V

ADVICE FROM A CATERPILLAR

THE Caterpillar and Alice looked at each other for some time in silence: at last the Caterpillar took the hookah out of its mouth, and addressed her in a languid, sleepy voice.

1. A straightforward request for identification, to which the proper reply is a statement of name or a definite self-description. Alice misinterprets it as a metaphysical enquiry about personal identity, and proceeds to bother the questioner with her own problems. In the face of such prevarication, the Caterpillar's patience soon becomes exhausted, and its temper understandably short.

2. Still preoccupied with her identity problem, Alice again misplaces the emphasis of the question (fallacy of accent), so that a conventionally worded demand to know what she is talking about is literally construed as an injunction to self-analysis. Since she has not even explained yet that the changes in question are changes of size, the Caterpillar, in turn, is quite justified in taking *her* idiom literally, and contradicting it. (Alexander, p. 557; Shibles, p. 21)

3. (Harrison [20], p. 151)

4. Alice presumably concedes this in the belief that she is dealing with a sentient creature physically unlike herself. She can scarcely be said to have broached the more general problem of 'other minds'—the difficulty of knowing about *any* being other than oneself that it is animate. So far as she does glimpse it, she appears to favor Berkeley's opinion, that the existence and nature of mind in others is to be inferred by analogy from their outward resemblance in appearance and behavior to oneself. Since the physical analogy is imperfect here, she concludes that there are probably differences on the mental side as well. (Shibles, p. 21)

'Who are *you*?' said the Caterpillar.[1]

This was not an encouraging opening for a conversation. Alice replied, rather shyly, 'I — I hardly know, sir, just at present — at least I know who I *was* when I got up this morning, but I think I must have been changed several times since then.'

'What do you mean by that?' said the Caterpillar sternly. 'Explain yourself!'

'I can't explain *myself*, I'm afraid, sir,' said Alice, 'because I'm not myself, you see.'[2]

'I don't see,' said the Caterpillar.

'I'm afraid I can't put it more clearly,' Alice replied very politely, 'for I can't understand it myself to begin with; and being so many different sizes in a day is very confusing.'[3]

'It isn't,' said the Caterpillar.

'Well, perhaps you haven't found it so yet,' said Alice; 'but when you have to turn into a chrysalis — you will some day, you know — and then after that into a butterfly, I should think you'll feel it a little queer, won't you?'

'Not a bit,' said the Caterpillar.

'Well, perhaps your feelings may be different,' said Alice; 'all I know is, it would feel very queer to *me*.'[4]

'You!' said the Caterpillar contemptuously. 'Who are *you*?'

Which brought them back again to the beginning of the conversation. Alice felt a little irritated at the Caterpillar's making such *very* short remarks, and she drew herself up and said, very gravely, 'I think you ought to tell me who *you* are, first.'[5]

'Why?' said the Caterpillar.

Here was another puzzling question; and as Alice could

not think of any good reason, and as the Caterpillar seemed to be in a *very* unpleasant state of mind, she turned away.

'Come back!' the Caterpillar called after her. 'I've something important to say!'

This sounded promising, certainly: Alice turned and came back again.

'Keep your temper,' said the Caterpillar.

'Is that all?' said Alice, swallowing down her anger as well as she could.

'No,' said the Caterpillar.

Alice thought she might as well wait, as she had nothing else to do, and perhaps after all it might tell her something worth hearing. For some minutes it puffed away without speaking, but at last it unfolded its arms, took the hookah out of its mouth again, and said, 'So you think you're changed, do you?'

'I'm afraid I am, sir,' said Alice; 'I can't remember things as I used — and I don't keep the same size for ten minutes together!'

'Can't remember *what* things?' said the Caterpillar.

'Well, I've tried to say "*How doth the little busy bee*", but it all came different!' Alice replied in a very melancholy voice.

'Repeat "*You are old, Father William*",' said the Caterpillar.[6]

Alice folded her hands, and began: —

5. Another *ignoratio elenchi*. Alice attempts, unsuccessfully, to shift the burden of proof.

6. The Caterpillar takes a sensibly Lockean view about personal identity, namely that it is primarily based on continuity and consistency of memories. A person knows who he is in remembering his own past, that is, in reviving mutually consistent memories of personal experience, and in demonstrating abilities he recalls having previously acquired. Alice is therefore asked to recite a poem she is supposed to have learned by heart. She fails miserably, of course; but the test is *prima facie* a reasonable one. Its main disadvantage is that if it is *not* passed, there is no clear indication of what ought to be said next. For all the Caterpillar can tell, Alice might have learned the poem all wrong in the first place, and be reproducing what she has learned with perfect accuracy. If so, her mind is in good order; it is only her education that is at fault.

'You are old, Father William,' the young man said,
  'And your hair has become very white;
And yet you incessantly stand on your head —
  Do you think at your age, it is right?'

'In my youth,' Father William replied to his son,
  'I feared it might injure the brain;
But, now that I'm perfectly sure I have none,
  Why, I do it again and again.'

'You are old,' said the youth, 'as I mentioned before,
  And have grown most uncommonly fat;
Yet you turned a back-somersault in at the door —
  Pray, what is the reason of that?'

'In my youth,' said the sage, as he shook his grey locks,
  'I kept all my limbs very supple
By the use of this ointment — one shilling the box —
  Allow me to sell you a couple?'

'You are old,' said the youth, 'and your jaws are too weak
   For anything tougher than suet;
Yet you finished the goose, with the bones and the beak —
   Pray how did you manage to do it?'

'In my youth,' said his father, 'I took to the law,
   And argued each case with my wife;
And the muscular strength, which it gave to my jaw,
   Has lasted the rest of my life.'

'You are old,' said the youth, 'one would hardly suppose
   That your eye was as steady as ever;
Yet you balanced an eel on the end of your nose —
   What made you so awfully clever?'

'I have answered three questions, and that is enough,'
   Said his father; 'don't give yourself airs!
Do you think I can listen all day to such stuff?
   Be off or I'll kick you downstairs!'[7]

7. Father William's explanations for his conduct are first, that his practice is harmless; second and third, that there are causal grounds for his abilities; and fourth, that there comes a point in any enquiry when the search for explanations has to stop. (Austin [1], p. 27)

---

8. Cited by Pitcher (in Fann, p. 323) as an illustration of Wittgenstein's dicta that one cannot always sensibly make the move from 'some' to 'all' ([48] § 344), and that a game consisting entirely of false moves makes no sense (§ 345). Like Shibles (p. 22), Pitcher considers the Caterpillar's verdict 'too harsh to be intelligible,' since if every word of a poem is recited wrongly, it is not being recited, and is not that poem at all. Still, in relation to what she was asked to do, namely, recite '*Father William*,' Alice's effort can legitimately be called a failure. A few of the words are right; but even if they were not, it would still be clear that it is *this* poem, and not some other one, that she is trying to recite. She is not like an examination candidate who misreads or misconstrues the question and gives a totally inappropriate answer. A parody, in short, is *not* just an independent poem, having no relation to its original; neither is it simply a garbled version of the original; it is something between the two.

9. Both parties are prejudiced, and neither is prepared to recognize that the value judgments involved here are relative.

'That is not said right,' said the Caterpillar.

'Not *quite* right, I'm afraid,' said Alice, timidly; 'some of the words have got altered.'

'It is wrong from beginning to end,' said the Caterpillar decidedly, and there was silence for some minutes.[8]

The Caterpillar was the first to speak.

'What size do you want to be?' it asked.

'Oh, I'm not particular as to size,' Alice hastily replied; 'only one doesn't like changing so often, you know.'

'I *don't* know,' said the Caterpillar.

Alice said nothing: she had never been so much contradicted in all her life before, and she felt that she was losing her temper.

'Are you content now?' said the Caterpillar.

'Well, I should like to be a *little* larger, sir, if you wouldn't mind,' said Alice: 'three inches is such a wretched height to be.'

'It is a very good height indeed!' said the Caterpillar angrily, rearing itself upright as it spoke (it was exactly three inches high).[9]

'But I'm not used to it!' pleaded poor Alice in a piteous tone. And she thought to herself, 'I wish the creatures wouldn't be so easily offended!'

'You'll get used to it in time,' said the Caterpillar; and it put the hookah into its mouth and began smoking again.

This time Alice waited patiently until it chose to speak again. In a minute or two the Caterpillar took the hookah out of its mouth and yawned once or twice, and shook itself. Then it got down off the mushroom, and crawled away into the grass, merely remarking as it went, 'One side will make you grow taller, and the other side will make you grow shorter.'

'One side of *what*? The other side of *what*?' thought Alice to herself.

'Of the mushroom,' said the Caterpillar, just as if she had asked it aloud; and in another moment it was out of sight.

Alice remained looking thoughtfully at the mushroom for a minute, trying to make out which were the two sides of it; and as it was perfectly round, she found this a very difficult question.[10] However, at last she stretched her arms round it as far as they would go, and broke off a bit of the edge with each hand.

'And now which is which?' she said to herself, and nibbled a little of the right-hand bit to try the effect: the next moment she felt a violent blow underneath her chin; it had struck her foot![11]

She was a good deal frightened by this very sudden change, but she felt that there was no time to be lost, as she was shrinking rapidly; so she set to work at once to eat some of the other bit. Her chin was pressed so closely against her foot, that there was hardly room to open her mouth; but she did it at last, and managed to swallow a morsel of the left-hand bit.

*　　*　　*　　*　　*
*　　*　　*　　*
*　　*　　*　　*　　*

'Come, my head's free at last!' said Alice in a tone of delight, which changed into alarm in another moment, when she found that her shoulders were nowhere to be found: all she could see, when she looked down, was an immense length of neck, which seemed to rise like a stalk out of a sea of green leaves that lay far below her.

'What *can* all that green stuff be?' said Alice. 'And

10. The uniformity of the circumference offers no opportunity for distinguishing any part of it as a 'side' in relation to any other. Alice's procedure arbitrarily selects two diametrically opposite arcs, and this proves in the event to be good enough.

Hallucinogenic mushrooms are known and used in many parts of the world. Fensch (p. 70) identifies this one as *Teonanacatl*, from Central and South America, whose active agent is psilocybin; but the pharmacological evidence for this is slender, to say the least. (Sutherland, p. 109; Shibles, p. 22)

11. A case of nonuniform bodily contraction, or disappearance, rather than shrinkage proper. Like many another fantasist, the author has modestly failed to consider the effect of these biologically induced fluctuations on his heroine's clothing, which she must inevitably have fallen out of or reduced to tatters long before now.

12. As before, the elongation of her body leads Alice to detach and personify her extremities, even though they are still under voluntary control.

where *have* my shoulders got to? And oh, my poor hands, how is it I can't see you?'[12] She was moving them about as she spoke, but no result seemed to follow, except a little shaking among the distant green leaves.

As there seemed to be no chance of getting her hands up to her head, she tried to get her head down to them, and was delighted to find that her neck would bend about easily in any direction, like a serpent. She had just succeeded in curving it down into a graceful zigzag, and was going to dive in among the leaves, which she found to be nothing but the tops of the trees under which she had been wandering, when a sharp hiss made her draw back in a hurry: a large pigeon had flown into her face, and was beating her violently with its wings.

'Serpent!' screamed the Pigeon.

'I'm *not* a serpent!' said Alice indignantly. 'Let me alone!'

'Serpent, I say again!' repeated the Pigeon, but in a more subdued tone, and added with a kind of sob, 'I've tried every way, and nothing seems to suit them!'

'I haven't the least idea what you're talking about,' said Alice.

'I've tried the roots of trees, and I've tried banks, and I've tried hedges,' the Pigeon went on, without attending to her; 'but those serpents! There's no pleasing them!'

Alice was more and more puzzled, but she thought there was no use in saying anything more till the Pigeon had finished.

'As if it wasn't trouble enough hatching the eggs,' said the Pigeon; 'but I must be on the look-out for serpents night and day! Why, I haven't had a wink of sleep these three weeks!'

'I'm very sorry you've been annoyed,' said Alice, who was beginning to see its meaning.

'And just as I'd taken the highest tree in the wood,' continued the Pigeon, raising its voice to a shriek, 'and just as I was thinking I should be free of them at last, they must needs come wriggling down from the sky! Ugh, Serpent!'

'But I'm *not* a serpent, I tell you!' said Alice. 'I'm a —— I'm a ——'

'Well! *What* are you?' said the Pigeon. 'I can see you're trying to invent something!'

'I — I'm a little girl,' said Alice, rather doubtfully, as she remembered the number of changes she had gone through, that day.

'A likely story indeed!' said the Pigeon in a tone of the deepest contempt. 'I've seen a good many little girls in my time, but never *one* with such a neck as that! No, no! You're a serpent; and there's no use denying it. I suppose you'll be telling me next that you never tasted an egg!'

'I *have* tasted eggs, certainly,' said Alice, who was a very truthful child; 'but little girls eat eggs quite as much as serpents do, you know.'

'I don't believe it,' said the Pigeon; 'but if they do, why, then, they're a kind of serpent, that's all I can say.'[13]

This was such a new idea to Alice, that she was quite silent for a minute or two, which gave the Pigeon the opportunity of adding, 'You're looking for eggs, I know *that* well enough; and what does it matter to me whether you're a little girl or a serpent?'

'It matters a good deal to *me*,' said Alice hastily; 'but I'm not looking for eggs, as it happens; and if I was, I shouldn't want *yours*: I don't like them raw.'

13. An argument worthy of a proverbially brainless species, often cited in logic books as an example of the fallacy of undistributed middle, or (depending on how it is stated) of 'affirming the consequent.' Because little girls and serpents are both egg-eaters, it does not follow that, as classes, they have any members in common. Alternatively, from 'If anything is a serpent, it eats eggs,' and 'Little girls eat eggs', it does not follow that 'Little girls are serpents.' Some writers, however (e.g., Alexander, pp. 559-60; Bradbury [7], pp. 57, 65-67, 75; Carney and Scheer [11], pp. 88-89), have defended the argument as an instance (albeit an incompetent one) of the respectable scientific practice of redefining a concept so as to incorporate new and relevant data. Since the pigeon is averse to egg-eaters of all descriptions, the differences between them matter little compared with the one important and unattractive feature they have in common. Compare the popular use of the term *toadstool* to cover poisonous fungi in general.

Sutherland (p. 105) sees misclassification in this passage; Jourdain (p. 61) accuses the pigeon of accepting the 'identity of discernibles,' a vice attributed to nineteenth-century mathematicians; Pitcher (in Fann, pp. 325-26) detects a satire on essentialism. Alice is eliminated as a little girl for want of one essential characteristic, a short neck, and identified as a serpent for possessing only one, namely egg-eating. Her neck length, however, seems no less important as a mark of serpentinity; it was this, after all, that drew the accusation on her in the first place.

14. But how can she tell what this is, except in relation to surrounding objects? To these she has evidently paid no attention, since her 'usual height,' once attained, is immediately found to be too large, and in need of further reduction. Unless she has a measuring rod about her, there is no seeing how she can possibly tell a priori that the Duchess' house is four feet, or her own stature nine inches high. Of course, if the house is manifestly diminutive by comparison with its own surroundings, she has a clue. But in the illustration at the beginning of Chapter VI, Tenniel, if anything, makes the trees too small for the house, so the difficulty is still there.

'Well, be off, then!' said the Pigeon in a sulky tone, as it settled down again into its nest. Alice crouched down among the trees as well as she could, for her neck kept getting entangled among the branches, and every now and then she had to stop and untwist it. After a while she remembered that she still held the pieces of mushroom in her hands, and she set to work very carefully, nibbling first at one and then at the other, and growing sometimes taller and sometimes shorter, until she had succeeded in bringing herself down to her usual height.[14]

It was so long since she had been anything near the right size, that it felt quite strange at first; but she got used to it in a few minutes, and began talking to herself, as usual. 'Come, there's half my plan done now! How puzzling all these changes are! I'm never sure what I'm going to be, from one minute to another! However, I've got back to my right size; the next thing is, to get into that beautiful garden — how *is* that to be done, I wonder?' As she said this, she came suddenly upon an open place, with a little house in it about four feet high. 'Whoever lives there,' thought Alice, 'it'll never do to come upon them *this* size: why, I should frighten them out of their wits!' So she began nibbling at the right-hand bit again, and did not venture to go near the house till she had brought herself down to nine inches high.

CHAPTER VI

PIG AND PEPPER

FOR a minute or two she stood looking at the house, and wondering what to do next, when suddenly a footman in livery came running out of the wood — (she considered him to be a footman because he was in livery: otherwise,

judging by his face only, she would have called him a fish) — and rapped loudly at the door with his knuckles. It was opened by another footman in livery, with a round face, and large eyes like a frog; and both footmen, Alice noticed, had powdered hair that curled all over their heads. She felt very curious to know what it was all about, and crept a little way out of the wood to listen.

The Fish-Footman began by producing from under his arm a great letter, nearly as large as himself, and this he handed over to the other, saying, in a solemn tone, 'For the Duchess. An invitation from the Queen to play croquet.' The Frog-Footman repeated, in the same solemn tone, only changing the order of the words a little, 'From the Queen. An invitation for the Duchess to play croquet.'

Then they both bowed low, and their curls got entangled together.

Alice laughed so much at this, that she had to run back into the wood for fear of their hearing her; and, when she next peeped out, the Fish-Footman was gone, and the other was sitting on the ground near the door, staring stupidly up into the sky.

Alice went timidly up to the door, and knocked.

'There's no sort of use in knocking,' said the Footman, 'and that for two reasons. First, because I'm on the same side of the door as you are; secondly, because they're making such a noise inside, no one could possibly hear you.' And certainly there was a most extraordinary noise going on within — a constant howling and sneezing, and every now and then a great crash, as if a dish or kettle had been broken to pieces.

'Please, then,' said Alice, 'how am I to get in?'

'There might be some sense in your knocking,' the

1. The attempt to classify by natural signs produces conflicting results. New class-names (Fish-Footman, Frog-Footman) have therefore to be introduced to cover both sets of attributes. (Sutherland, pp. 78, 106)

---

2. The Footman is not so idiotic as Alice later supposes. He is sharp enough, at any rate, to recognize the fallacy known as *plures interrogationes*, or 'many questions,' in which the answers to one or more questions are implicitly assumed in asking another (as in 'When did you stop beating your wife?'). Alice evidently believes, with Aristotle, that there is no deliberating about ends, and addresses herself solely to the means of achieving them. (Shibles, p. 22)

3. Argumentative as she is, Alice does not care to be argued *with*. She speaks here for all plain folk who from the time of Socrates onwards have fallen among philosophers. (Kemeny [24], p. 65)

4. Consulted directly about ends, the Footman has no advice to offer. Alice, as he well knows, will do what she wants, whatever he has to say, and the sequel bears him out.

Footman went on without attending to her, 'if we had the door between us. For instance, if you were *inside*, you might knock, and I could let you out, you know.' He was looking up into the sky all the time he was speaking, and this Alice thought decidedly uncivil. 'But perhaps he can't help it,' she said to herself; 'his eyes are so *very* nearly at the top of his head. But at any rate he might answer questions. — How am I to get in?' she repeated, aloud.

'I shall sit here,' the Footman remarked, 'till tomorrow ——'

At this moment the door of the house opened, and a large plate came skimming out, straight at the Footman's head: it just grazed his nose, and broke to pieces against one of the trees behind him.

'— or next day, maybe,' the Footman continued in the same tone, exactly as if nothing had happened.

'How am I to get in?' asked Alice again, in a louder tone.

'*Are* you to get in at all?' said the Footman. 'That's the first question, you know.'[2]

It was, no doubt: only Alice did not like to be told so. 'It's really dreadful,' she muttered to herself, 'the way all the creatures argue. It's enough to drive one crazy!'[3]

The Footman seemed to think this a good opportunity for repeating his remark, with variations. 'I shall sit here,' he said, 'on and off, for days and days.'

'But what am *I* to do?' said Alice.

'Anything you like,' said the Footman, and began whistling.[4]

'Oh, there's no use in talking to him,' said Alice desperately: 'he's perfectly idiotic!' And she opened the door and went in.

The door led right into a large kitchen, which was full of smoke from one end to the other: the Duchess was sitting on a three-legged stool in the middle, nursing a baby; the cook was leaning over the fire, stirring a large cauldron which seemed to be full of soup.

'There's certainly too much pepper in that soup!' Alice said to herself, as well as she could for sneezing.

There was certainly too much of it in the air. Even the Duchess sneezed occasionally; and the baby was sneezing and howling alternately without a moment's pause. The only things in the kitchen that did not sneeze, were the cook, and a large cat which was sitting on the hearth and grinning from ear to ear.

'Please would you tell me,' said Alice a little timidly, for she was not quite sure whether it was good manners for her to speak first, 'why your cat grins like that?'

'It's a Cheshire cat,' said the Duchess, 'and that's why.[5] Pig!'

She said the last word with such sudden violence that Alice quite jumped; but she saw in another moment that it was addressed to the baby, and not to her, so she took courage, and went on again:—

'I didn't know that Cheshire cats always grinned; in fact, I didn't know that cats *could* grin.'

'They all can,' said the Duchess; 'and most of 'em do.'[6]

'I don't know of any that do,' Alice said very politely, feeling quite pleased to have got into a conversation.

'You don't know much,' said the Duchess; 'and that's a fact.'

Alice did not at all like the tone of this remark, and thought it would be as well to introduce some other subject of conversation. While she was trying to fix on one, the cook took the cauldron of soup off the fire, and at once set to work throwing everything within her reach at the Duchess and the baby — the fire-irons came first; then followed a shower of saucepans, plates, and dishes. The Duchess took no notice of them even when they hit her; and the baby was howling so much already, that it was quite impossible to say whether the blows hurt it or not.

'Oh, *please* mind what you're doing!' cried Alice, jumping up and down in an agony of terror. 'Oh, there goes his *precious* nose;' as an unusually large saucepan flew close by it, and very nearly carried it off.

'If everybody minded their own business,' the Duchess

5. (Kemeny [24], p. 156, on scientific explanation)

6. The Duchess has shifted her ground. If most cats grin any- way, this, and not its Cheshire origin, provides the cover- ing law that explains why her cat grins.

7. Alice seems to suppose that if the day were shorter more labor would be needed to get through a day's work. But this does not follow. The world is already adapted to a 'day' (i.e., daylight period) of varying length, and some Eastern countries have even varied the length of the hour accordingly. But there is no reason why this should make more, or less, work.

said in a hoarse growl, 'the world would go round a deal faster than it does.'

'Which would *not* be an advantage,' said Alice, who felt very glad to get an opportunity of showing off a little of her knowledge. 'Just think what work it would make with the day and night!⁷You see, the earth takes twenty-four hours to turn round on its axis ——'

'Talking of axes,' said the Duchess, 'chop off her head!'

Alice glanced rather anxiously at the cook, to see if she meant to take the hint; but the cook was busily engaged in stirring the soup, and did not seem to be listening, so she ventured to go on again; 'Twenty-four hours, I *think*; or is it twelve? I ——'

'Oh, don't bother *me*,' said the Duchess; 'I never could abide figures!' And with that she began nursing her child again, singing a sort of lullaby to it as she did so, and giving it a violent shake at the end of every line:

> '*Speak roughly to your little boy,*
> *And beat him when he sneezes:*
> *He only does it to annoy,*
> *Because he knows it teases.*'

CHORUS.
(In which the cook and the baby joined):—
'*Wow! wow! wow!*'

While the Duchess sang the second verse of the song, she kept tossing the baby violently up and down, and the poor little thing howled so, that Alice could hardly hear the words:—

Pig and Pepper

'I speak severely to my boy,
I beat him when he sneezes;
For he can thoroughly enjoy
The pepper when he pleases!'

CHORUS.
'Wow! wow! wow!'

'Here! you may nurse it a bit, if you like!' the Duchess said to Alice, flinging the baby at her as she spoke. 'I must go and get ready to play croquet with the Queen,' and she hurried out of the room. The cook threw a frying-pan after her as she went out, but it just missed her.

Alice caught the baby with some difficulty, as it was a queer-shaped little creature, and held out its arms and legs in all directions, 'just like a star-fish', thought Alice. The poor little thing was snorting like a steam-engine when she caught it, and kept doubling itself up and straightening itself out again, so that altogether, for the first minute or two, it was as much as she could do to hold it.

As soon as she had made out the proper way of nursing it, (which was to twist it up into a sort of knot, and then keep tight hold of its right ear and left foot, so as to prevent its undoing itself,) she carried it out into the open air. 'If I don't take this child away with me,' thought Alice, 'they're sure to kill it in a day or two: wouldn't it be murder to leave it behind?'[8] She said the last words out loud, and the little thing grunted in reply (it had left off sneezing by this time). 'Don't grunt,' said Alice; 'that's not at all a proper way of expressing yourself.'

The baby grunted again, and Alice looked very anxiously into its face to see what was the matter with it.

8. It would not. In the absence of *mens rea*, Alice cannot commit murder, nor has she any legal duty in the matter, unless it be that of notifying the proper authorities. In abducting the baby without parental consent she is herself open to a charge of kidnapping, however worthy her intentions may be.

9. The changing attributes of the so-called baby make its correct description a matter of uncertainty, to be settled eventually by reclassifying it under a more appropriate concept. (Sutherland, pp. 108 *ff.*)

There could be no doubt that it had a *very* turn-up nose, much more like a snout than a real nose; also its eyes were getting extremely small for a baby: altogether Alice did not like the look of the thing at all.[9] 'But perhaps it was only sobbing,' she thought, and looked into its eyes again, to see if there were any tears.

No, there were no tears. 'If you're going to turn into a pig, my dear,' said Alice, seriously, 'I'll have nothing more to do with you. Mind now!' The poor little thing sobbed again (or grunted, it was impossible to say which), and they went on for some while in silence.

Alice was just beginning to think to herself, 'Now, what am I to do with this creature when I get it home?' when it grunted again, so violently, that she looked down into its face in some alarm. This time there could be *no* mistake about it: it was neither more nor less than a pig, and she felt that it would be quite absurd for her to carry it any further.

So she set the little creature down, and felt quite relieved to see it trot away quietly into the wood. 'If it had grown up,' she said to herself, 'it would have made a dreadfully ugly child: but it makes rather a handsome pig,

I think.'[10] And she began thinking over other children she knew, who might do very well as pigs, and was just saying to herself, 'if one only knew the right way to change them ——' when she was a little startled by seeing the Cheshire Cat sitting on a bough of a tree a few yards off.

The Cat only grinned when it saw Alice. It looked good-natured, she thought: still it had *very* long claws and a great many teeth, so she felt that it ought to be treated with respect.

'Cheshire Puss,' she began, rather timidly, as she did not at all know whether it would like the name: however, it only grinned a little wider. 'Come, it's pleased so far,' thought Alice, and she went on. 'Would you tell me, please, which way I ought to go from here?'

'That depends a good deal on where you want to get to,' said the Cat.[11]

'I don't much care where ——' said Alice.

'Then it doesn't matter which way you go,' said the Cat.

'—— so long as I get *somewhere*,' Alice added as an explanation.

'Oh, you're sure to do that,' said the Cat, 'if you only walk long enough.'

Alice felt that this could not be denied, so she tried another question. 'What sort of people live about here?'

'In *that* direction,' the Cat said, waving its right paw round, 'lives a Hatter: and in *that* direction,' waving the other paw, 'lives a March Hare. Visit either you like: they're both mad.'

'But I don't want to go among mad people,' Alice remarked.

'Oh, you can't help that,' said the Cat: 'we're all mad here. I'm mad. You're mad.'[12]

10. Beauty and ugliness, in the present context, are relative concepts, predicated of things not absolutely, but as members of an appropriate reference-class. There is a similar distinction to be made in moral contexts, between 'good of its kind' and 'good without qualification.' An instance of this will occur below (p. 68).

11. The question is void for lack of specification. The Cat, like the Footman, is not to be drawn into providing Alice with an objective, and having discovered the utter vagueness of her own purposes, can only point out the necessary truth that *any* action on her part will suffice to satisfy them. Without an end, it is useless to debate over the means of achieving it. (Shibles, pp. 22-23; Gardner, p. 89, citing Kemeny [24], p. 230, who applies these remarks to the distinction between science, which tells what *can* be done, and value, which seeks to determine what *ought* to be done)

12. If the Cat really *is* mad, as it says, then the truth of its statement is open to suspicion. Moreover, the proof offered for its madness is so deplorable as to furnish no reason for believing its conclusion. So maybe the Cat is not mad. But then only an exceptionally weak-minded creature could have used such an argument; so very likely it *is* mad after all. In which case its statements are again no longer to be relied on. The circular reasoning involved here resembles that in the ancient paradox of the *pseudomenos*, or liar. If I truthfully say 'I lie,' I tell an untruth, and so do *not* lie, and therefore tell the truth, which is that I lie, and so on. Bothered, if not actually maddened, by this problem for twenty-four centuries, logicians have lately been reexcavating the foundations of mathematics, in the hope of burying it once and for all.

Shibles (p. 23) argues that where all are mad, it makes no sense to say that anyone is. But his case founders on the admitted sanity of dogs. Gardner (p. 90) quotes at length from Plato, *Theaetetus*, 158, on the resemblance of dreaming and madness. Neilson Graham, in a radio broadcast (on the BBC, November 13, 1971), has contended that the Cat is right. Wonderland is a madhouse, and if its nonsense were not funny, would be very disturbing indeed.

13. Two species may well have two or more contrary attributes; but it does not follow that they are therefore opposed in any *other* respect. The attempt at reasoning by negative analogy here is unsound, not to say ridiculous, because too few properties are involved, and they have, in any case, too little bearing on each other. Compare Augustus De Morgan's verdict on James Smith the circle-squarer: 'He is not mad. Madmen reason rightly upon wrong premises; Mr. Smith reasons wrongly upon no premises at all' (*A Budget of Paradoxes*, 2nd ed. [1915], Vol. II, p. 107). (Holmes, p. 134; Carney and Scheer [11], p. 151)

14. Pitcher (in Fann, p. 324), citing Wittgenstein ([48] § 379), takes exception to the Humpty-Dumptyish view here implied, that the nature of a thing is entirely independent of what it is called. Sutherland (p. 127) supports the Cat. 'Call it what you like' need not, in fact, mean here that *any* word would do; the Cat may be conceding merely that alternative designations are admissible in novel, specialized, or borderline cases.

'How do you know I'm mad?' said Alice.

'You must be,' said the Cat, 'or you wouldn't have come here.'

Alice didn't think that proved it at all: however, she went on. 'And how do you know that you're mad?'

'To begin with,' said the Cat, 'a dog's not mad. You grant that?'

'I suppose so,' said Alice.

'Well, then,' the Cat went on, 'you see a dog growls when it's angry, and wags its tail when it's pleased. Now *I* growl when I'm pleased, and wag my tail when I'm angry. Therefore I'm mad.'[13]

'*I* call it purring, not growling,' said Alice.

'Call it what you like,' said the Cat.[14] 'Do you play croquet with the Queen to-day?'

'I should like it very much,' said Alice, 'but I haven't been invited yet.'

'You'll see me there,' said the Cat, and vanished.

Alice was not much surprised at this, she was getting so used to queer things happening. While she was looking at the place where it had been, it suddenly appeared again.

'By-the-bye, what became of the baby?' said the Cat. 'I'd nearly forgotten to ask.'

'It turned into a pig,' Alice quietly said, just as if it had come back in a natural way.

'I thought it would,' said the Cat, and vanished again.

Alice waited a little, half expecting to see it again, but it did not appear, and after a minute or two she walked on in the direction in which the March Hare was said to live. 'I've seen hatters before,' she said to herself; 'the March Hare will be much the most interesting, and perhaps, as this is May, it won't be raving mad — at least not so mad as it was in March.'[15] As she said this, she looked up, and there was the Cat again, sitting on a branch of a tree.

'Did you say pig, or fig?' said the Cat.[16]

'I said pig,' replied Alice; 'and I wish you wouldn't keep appearing and vanishing so suddenly: you make one quite giddy.'[17]

'All right,' said the Cat; and this time it vanished quite slowly, beginning with the end of the tail, and ending with the grin, which remained some time after the rest of it had gone.[18]

'Well! I've often seen a cat without a grin,' thought

15. Alice, like the Cat, tends to assume that the March Hare is a special kind of hare, rather than just an ordinary one at a special time of year. She thus misconstrues a contingent temporal feature as an essential property, though she is clearly quite familiar with the facts. (Shibles, p. 23)

16. Sutherland (pp. 87*ff*.) notes this as an illustration of signification by morphemic identity. Very similar sounds, that is, may have meanings that are very different.

17. Wittgenstein ([48] § 80) discusses a similarly ill-behaved chair (*cf.* Pitcher [in Fann], p. 330). Intermittent objects raise problems about identity. There can be more than one opinion as to whether a rainbow that fades and then reappears, or a shower that stops and then starts again, is the *same* rainbow, or the same shower. Ordinary objects are believed by common sense to persist even when not under observation, but as Hume showed (*Treatise of Human Nature*, Bk. I, Pt. IV, Sect. 2), this is anything but a necessary truth, and is without justification, even as a belief.

18. An outrageous defiance of the long-established tradition that an attribute must inhere in a substance. The later appearance of the Cat's head without its body (p. 82) does not flout this principle, since a part may exist separately from a whole. But a grin is not a part of anything, being merely, as Alice recognizes, a contingent aspect or feature of cats. The loss of such a feature does not mean, so Aristotle and St. Thomas would say, that it can turn up elsewhere, float about on its own, or remain *in situ* (as here) in the absence of its normal possessor. Smells and

sounds can do this, however, and so can star images, and have thus been regarded by some as substances in their own right. Not so grins, which as mere facial contortions would seem to be no less functionally dependent on faces than the square root of -1 is functionally dependent on -1, and about equally likely to be seen alone in public. Tenniel's illustration is inevitably inaccurate in continuing to show physical features; his author had set him a logically impossible task. (Shibles, pp. 23-24; Holmes, p. 141; Gardner, p. 91, with allusion to Russell on pure mathematics; Findlay [15], p. 45; Russell [41], p. 135; Ryle [42], p. 184, [43], p. 412; Smart [44], p. 4; Terrell and Baker [46], p. 79, diagnosing a fallacy of reification)

Alice; 'but a grin without a cat! It's the most curious thing I ever saw in all my life!'

She had not gone much farther before she came in sight of the house of the March Hare: she thought it must be the right house, because the chimneys were shaped like ears and the roof was thatched with fur. It was so large a house, that she did not like to go nearer till she had nibbled some more of the left-hand bit of mushroom, and raised herself to about two feet high: even then she walked up towards it rather timidly, saying to herself, 'Suppose it should be raving mad after all! I almost wish I'd gone to see the Hatter instead!'

CHAPTER VII

A MAD TEA-PARTY

THERE was a table set out under a tree in front of the house, and the March Hare and the Hatter were having tea at it: a Dormouse was sitting between them, fast asleep, and the other two were resting their elbows on it, and talking over its head.[1] 'Very uncomfortable for the Dormouse,' thought Alice; 'only, as it's asleep, I suppose it doesn't mind.'

The table was a large one, but the three were all crowded together at one corner of it. 'No room! No room!' they cried out when they saw Alice coming. 'There's *plenty* of room!' said Alice indignantly, and she sat down in a large arm-chair at one end of the table.

'Have some wine,' the March Hare said in an encouraging tone.

Alice looked all round the table, but there was nothing on it but tea. 'I don't see any wine,' she remarked.

'There isn't any,' said the March Hare.

'Then it wasn't very civil of you to offer it,' said Alice angrily.[2]

'It wasn't very civil of you to sit down without being invited,' said the March Hare.

'I didn't know it was *your* table,' said Alice; 'it's laid for a great many more than three.'

'Your hair wants cutting,' said the Hatter. He had been looking at Alice for some time with great curiosity, and this was his first speech.

1. The physical resemblance of the Hatter, March Hare, and Dormouse to the Cambridge philosophical trio of Bertrand Russell, G. E. Moore and J. M. E. McTaggart is so striking as to amount almost to a coincidence. First noted in print, apparently, by Norbert Wiener, it seems to have been current before this in the local description of the three as the 'Mad Tea-Party of Trinity.' (Gardner, p. 94)

2. Logically and morally improper as this fraudulent offer may be, Alice has little right to be indignant at it. She is much too young to be drinking wine anyway. Fensch (p. 86) supposes her to share the drug addict's normal disdain for alcohol, but the orgiastic climax of *Through the Looking-Glass*, with its drinking songs, healths, flying decanters, and general pandemonium, does little to confirm this view.

3. Shibles (p. 26) compares this to the unanswerable questions allegedly asked by philosophers. But the real objection to it is that it has too *many* answers, namely all the innumerable negative properties that ravens share with writing-desks. If these do not count, then neither does the property of unanswerability, which the Hatter's riddle is supposed to share with the questions of the philosophers.

4. Having rashly accepted the March Hare's version as a correct account of her meaning, Alice is driven to admit that this was not what she originally said. Cornered, she panics, and instead of arguing that the two statements mean the same (thereby confronting the March Hare with the paradox of analysis), she mistakenly asserts this of two *other* statements, which seem plainly to differ in meaning. The fallacy of conversion involved is duly exposed by way of counterexamples. The Dormouse's example is rejected (*ad glirem*) on the ground that in his case sleeping and breathing are extensionally equivalent. (The argument *ad glirem* is admittedly unknown to the logic books. But what else is one to call an *argumentum ad hominem* addressed to a dormouse?)

In recommending Alice to say what she means, the Hare allies himself with the conceptualists, for whom meaning something is one thing, and saying it another. The Hatter, who insists that meaning what you say is distinct from this, implies that it is words that mean, and thereby sides with nominalism (Jourdain, p. 24). Alice, who amalgamates the two, has a supporter in Wittgenstein, who objected to internal meanings ([49], pp. 34 *ff.*, 145) though it is not likely that he would have approved of her defense of this point of view (*cf.* Pitcher [in Fann],

'You shouldn't make personal remarks,' Alice said with some severity; 'it's very rude.'

The Hatter opened his eyes very wide on hearing this; but all he *said* was 'Why is a raven like a writing-desk?'[3]

'Come, we shall have some fun now!' thought Alice. 'I'm glad they've begun asking riddles. — I believe I can guess that,' she added aloud.

'Do you mean that you think you can find out the answer to it?' said the March Hare.

'Exactly so,' said Alice.

'Then you should say what you mean,' the March Hare went on.

'I do,' Alice hastily replied; 'at least — at least I mean what I say — that's the same thing, you know.'[4]

'Not the same thing a bit!' said the Hatter. 'You might

just as well say that "I see what I eat" is the same thing as "I eat what I see"!'

'You might just as well say,' added the March Hare, 'that "I like what I get" is the same thing as "I get what I like"!'

'You might just as well say,' added the Dormouse, who seemed to be talking in his sleep, 'that "I breathe when I sleep" is the same thing as "I sleep when I breathe"!'

'It *is* the same thing with you,' said the Hatter, and here the conversation dropped, and the party sat silent for a minute, while Alice thought over all she could remember about ravens and writing-desks, which wasn't much.*

The Hatter was the first to break the silence. 'What day of the month is it?' he said, turning to Alice: he had taken his watch out of his pocket, and was looking at it uneasily, shaking it every now and then, and holding it to his ear.

Alice considered a little, and then said, 'The fourth.'

'Two days wrong!' sighed the Hatter. 'I told you butter wouldn't suit the works!' he added, looking angrily at the March Hare.

'It was the *best* butter,' the March Hare meekly replied.[5]

'Yes, but some crumbs must have got in as well,' the Hatter grumbled: 'you shouldn't have put it in with the bread-knife.'

The March Hare took the watch and looked at it gloomily: then he dipped it into his cup of tea, and looked

* *Author's Note:* Enquiries have been so often addressed to me, as to whether any answer to the Hatter's Riddle can be imagined, that I may as well put on record here what seems to me to be a fairly appropriate answer, viz. 'Because it can produce a few notes, though they are *very* flat; and it is never put with the wrong end in front!' This, however, is merely an after-thought: the Riddle, as originally invented, had no answer at all.

p. 329, and Shibles, pp. 24-25). (Holmes, pp. 134-35; Carney and Scheer [11], p. 155; Manicas and Kruger [27], p. 275)

5. Best as butter goes, no doubt, but not absolutely, or, it would seem, as a mechanical lubricant. 'Good,' like its superlative, is often a relative term, meaning 'good of its kind,' or for its standard purpose, whatever that may happen to be. Failing such a reference, the judgment of goodness is indeterminate, and cannot be applied or debated without risk of confusion. (Shibles, p. 27)

6. Analytic philosophers (notably G. E. Moore) have often suffered from the same feeling when confronted with the opinions of their colleagues. As Wittgenstein was fond of pointing out ([48] § 348; [49] p. 56), a sentence may sound like English, be 'apparently quite in order,' and yet be a logical mess (Pitcher, [in Fann], p. 318). (Sutherland, p. 207; Shibles, pp. 26-27)

7. St. Augustine voiced a fairly universal complaint in saying that he knew what time was until anyone asked him to explain it. We are all acquainted with time. The Hatter is alone in treating it as an acquaintance, though one with whom he is unfortunately on bad terms. Alice is being seduced into the fallacy of reification—a common ailment of philosophers—whereby it is assumed of any word functioning grammatically as a name that there must be a concrete thing of which it is the name. (Pitcher [in Fann], p. 333, comparing Wittgenstein [49], pp. 6, 107ff.; Broad [8], pp. 53, 114; Terrell and Baker [46], p. 78)

at it again: but he could think of nothing better to say than his first remark, 'It was the *best* butter, you know.'

Alice had been looking over his shoulder with some curiosity. 'What a funny watch!' she remarked. 'It tells the day of the month, and doesn't tell what o'clock it is!'

'Why should it?' muttered the Hatter. 'Does *your* watch tell you what year it is?'

'Of course not,' Alice replied very readily: 'but that's because it stays the same year for such a long time together.'

'Which is just the case with *mine*,' said the Hatter.

Alice felt dreadfully puzzled. The Hatter's remark seemed to have no meaning in it, and yet it was certainly English.[6] 'I don't quite understand,' she said, as politely as she could.

'The Dormouse is asleep again,' said the Hatter, and he poured a little hot tea upon its nose.

The Dormouse shook its head impatiently, and said, without opening its eyes, 'Of course, of course; just what I was going to remark myself.'

'Have you guessed the riddle yet?' the Hatter said, turning to Alice again.

'No, I give it up,' Alice replied: 'what's the answer?'

'I haven't the slightest idea,' said the Hatter.

'Nor I,' said the March Hare.

Alice sighed wearily. 'I think you might do something better with the time,' she said, 'than waste it asking riddles with no answers.'

'If you knew Time as well as I do,' said the Hatter, 'you wouldn't talk about wasting *it*. It's *him*.'[7]

'I don't know what you mean,' said Alice.

'Of course you don't!' the Hatter said, tossing his head

contemptuously. 'I dare say you never even spoke to Time!'

'Perhaps not,' Alice cautiously replied: 'but I know I have to beat time when I learn music.'

'Ah! that accounts for it,' said the Hatter. 'He won't stand beating. Now, if you only kept on good terms with him, he'd do almost anything you liked with the clock. For instance, suppose it were nine o'clock in the morning, just time to begin lessons: you'd only have to whisper a hint to Time, and round goes the clock in a twinkling! Half-past one, time for dinner!'[8]

('I only wish it was,' the March Hare said to itself in a whisper.)

'That would be grand, certainly,' said Alice thoughtfully: 'but then — I shouldn't be hungry for it, you know.'

'Not at first, perhaps,' said the Hatter: 'but you could keep it to half-past one as long as you liked.'

'Is that the way *you* manage?' Alice asked.[9]

The Hatter shook his head mournfully. 'Not I!' he replied. 'We quarrelled last March — just before *he* went mad, you know —' (pointing with his teaspoon at the March Hare,) '— it was at the great concert given by the Queen of Hearts, and I had to sing

> *"Twinkle, twinkle, little bat!*
> *How I wonder what you're at!"*

You know the song, perhaps?'

'I've heard something like it,' said Alice.

'It goes on, you know,' the Hatter continued, 'in this way:—

8. If four and a half hours pass in one twinkling, how long does the twinkling take? To measure the rate of passage of time requires a time of second order, of which the same question may be asked. The Hatter is embarked on a vicious infinite regress. Alice, though she fails to notice this, does make a useful distinction, for once, between biological time and clock time. (Shibles, pp. 27-29)

9. The rest of the chapter, from here onward, has been analysed at length by Weaver (*Alice in Many Tongues*, pp. 75-108) in order to display the problems of rendering such a text into languages other than English. As might be expected, the verse-parodies and puns resist translation altogether in most cases, whereas turns of idiom and logical antics will usually transfer quite happily to Chinese, Swahili, and even French. Their intellectual basis is universal, as that of the linguistic and literary fooling is not.

10. Apart from upsetting his watch, and projecting himself and his colleagues into a Nietzschean cycle of eternal recurrence among the teacups, the quarrel with time has not done the Hatter much harm. Monotonous his world may be; static, in the Parmenidean sense, it obviously is not. Zeno's arrow became arrested in mid-air through the difficulty of finding any time in which to pass from time *t* to the next instant beyond it. The Hatter's problem is to get to any time other than tea-time. Perhaps because (unlike Zeno) he is far from disputing the reality of time as such, but more probably because tea-time is a period, rather than an instant, he is not deprived of change and movement within his specious present. His later appearances (still *t*-drinking) at the Trial (p. 107) and the battle between the Lion and the Unicorn (p. 205) suggest that although, like a relativistic astronaut, his local time is virtually stationary, it still moves on speedily enough from other people's point of view. (Gardner, p. 99, citing Eddington [12], p. 160, where the timeless tea-party is compared to similarly afflicted portions of De Sitter's model of the universe)

" *Up above the world you fly,*
Like a tea-tray in the sky.
Twinkle, twinkle —'"

Here the Dormouse shook itself, and began singing in its sleep '*Twinkle, twinkle, twinkle, twinkle* ——' and went on so long that they had to pinch it to make it stop.

'Well, I'd hardly finished the first verse,' said the Hatter, 'when the Queen jumped up and bawled out "He's murdering the time! Off with his head!"'

'How dreadfully savage!' exclaimed Alice.

'And ever since that,' the Hatter went on in a mournful tone, 'he won't do a thing I ask! It's always six o'clock now.'[10]

A bright idea came into Alice's head. 'Is that the reason so many tea-things are put out here?' she asked.

'Yes, that's it,' said the Hatter with a sigh: 'it's always

tea-time, and we've no time to wash the things between whiles.'

'Then you keep moving round, I suppose?' said Alice.

'Exactly so,' said the Hatter: 'as the things get used up.'

'But what happens when you come to the beginning again?' Alice ventured to ask.

'Suppose we change the subject,' the March Hare interrupted, yawning.[11] 'I'm getting tired of this. I vote the young lady tells us a story.'

'I'm afraid I don't know one,' said Alice, rather alarmed at the proposal.

'Then the Dormouse shall!' they both cried. 'Wake up, Dormouse!' And they pinched it on both sides at once.

The Dormouse slowly opened his eyes. 'I wasn't asleep,' he said in a hoarse, feeble voice: 'I heard every word you fellows were saying.'

'Tell us a story!' said the March Hare.

'Yes, please do!' pleaded Alice.

'And be quick about it,' added the Hatter, 'or you'll be asleep again before it's done.'

'Once upon a time there were three little sisters,' the Dormouse began in a great hurry; 'and their names were Elsie, Lacie, and Tillie; and they lived at the bottom of a well ——'

'What did they live on?' said Alice, who always took a great interest in questions of eating and drinking.

'They lived on treacle,' said the Dormouse, after thinking a minute or two.

'They couldn't have done that, you know,' Alice gently remarked; 'they'd have been ill.'

'So they were,' said the Dormouse; 'very ill.'

11. Alice's attempt to pry into the logistics of eternal recurrence is neatly sidetracked. For similar tactics, when a limiting question is reached, compare the later evasions of the Gryphon (p. 95) and the Red Queen (p. 224). (Shibles, p. 29)

12. 'Some more,' as Alice correctly surmises, means 'more than some'; she is therefore justified in complaining that the presuppositions of the March Hare's invitation have not been fulfilled. In stating her case, however, she bungles it by shifting its terms. 'More tea' presupposes 'tea' (which she has not had). 'More than nothing' presupposes 'nothing' (which she *has* had), and this lets the Hatter in to argue, legitimately, that she can easily do better than that. In treating 'nothing' as a quantity the Hatter practices what the mathematicians preach. But in making a difficulty about subtracting from zero he diverges (says Jourdain [p. 61]) from the orthodox view, though supported in his heresy by mathematical logicians and the White Queen (p. 227). (Sutherland, p. 168; Shibles, p. 29; Geach [19], p. 35, a pro-Hatter analysis; Monro [28], p. 48)

Alice tried to fancy to herself what such an extra-ordinary way of living would be like, but it puzzled her too much, so she went on: 'But why did they live at the bottom of a well?'

'Take some more tea,' the March Hare said to Alice, very earnestly.

'I've had nothing yet,' Alice replied in an offended tone, 'so I can't take more.'

'You mean you can't take *less*,' said the Hatter: 'it's very easy to take *more* than nothing.'[12]

'Nobody asked *your* opinion,' said Alice.

'Who's making personal remarks now?' the Hatter asked triumphantly.

Alice did not quite know what to say to this: so she helped herself to some tea and bread-and-butter, and then turned to the Dormouse, and repeated her question. 'Why did they live at the bottom of a well?'

The Dormouse again took a minute or two to think about it, and then said, 'It was a treacle-well.'

'There's no such thing!' Alice was beginning very angrily, but the Hatter and the March Hare went 'Sh! sh!' and the Dormouse sulkily remarked, 'If you can't be civil, you'd better finish the story for yourself.'

'No, please go on!' Alice said. 'I won't interrupt again. I dare say there may be *one*.'

'One, indeed!' said the Dormouse indignantly. How-ever, he consented to go on. 'And so these three little sisters — they were learning to draw, you know ——'

'What did they draw?' said Alice, quite forgetting her promise.

'Treacle,' said the Dormouse, without considering at all this time.

A Mad Tea-party

'I want a clean cup,' interrupted the Hatter: 'let's all move one place on.'

He moved on as he spoke, and the Dormouse followed him: the March Hare moved into the Dormouse's place, and Alice rather unwillingly took the place of the March Hare. The Hatter was the only one who got any advantage from the change: and Alice was a good deal worse off, as the March Hare had just upset the milk-jug into his plate.

Alice did not wish to offend the Dormouse again, so she began very cautiously: 'But I don't understand. Where did they draw the treacle from?'

'You can draw water out of a water-well,' said the Hatter; 'so I should think you could draw treacle out of a treacle-well — eh, stupid?'

'But they were *in* the well,' Alice said to the Dormouse, not choosing to notice this last remark.

'Of· course they were,' said the Dormouse; '— well in.'

This answer so confused poor Alice, that she let the Dormouse go on for some time without interrupting it.[13]

'They were learning to draw,' the Dormouse went on, yawning and rubbing its eyes, for it was getting very sleepy; 'and they drew all manner of things — everything that begins with an M ——,'[14]

'Why with an M?' said Alice.

'Why not?' said the March Hare.

Alice was silent.

The Dormouse had closed his eyes by this time, and was going off into a doze; but, on being pinched by the Hatter, it woke up again with a little shriek, and went on: '— that begins with an M, such as mouse-traps, and the moon, and memory, and muchness — you know you say things

13. To be ill in a well and be well in it, and to draw treacle in it as well as out of it, gets Alice well out of her depth. Contradictions, real or supposed, always arouse her anxiety; ambiguities never do. Her sense of logical impropriety in others is well-nigh infallible; her sense of humor, virtually nil.

14. Things, of course, do not begin with an *M*; it is their names that do. A class so defined is inevitably a hotch-potch of concrete and abstract, and if all its members are thought to be picturable, hypostatization or reification of the abstract items is bound to ensue. Portraits of such well-known abstractions as the Hegelian Absolute and the Kantian thing-in-itself have in fact been executed (*cf.* F. C. S. Schiller, *Mind*! [1901] and J. Bennett, *Kant's Analytic* [1966]), but it is hard to say if they are good likenesses or not. (Alexander, p. 563; Shibles, pp. 30-31; Holmes, p. 148)

15. A timely, though timeless, rebuke to Alice's indefatigable garrulity; but the Hatter now appears to have changed his opinion and to have come round to the March Hare's theory that speech is (or should be) preceded by a mental process of thinking, without which there is no 'meaning' for it to convey. Under the influence of Wittgenstein and Ryle, such views are now philosophically unfashionable, though still widely held by the vulgar (i.e., everyone else). (Shibles, p. 31)

Alice's Adventures in Wonderland

are 'much of a muchness' — did you ever see such a thing as a drawing of a muchness?'

'Really, now you ask me,' said Alice, very much confused, 'I don't think ——'

'Then you shouldn't talk,' said the Hatter.[15]

This piece of rudeness was more than Alice could bear: she got up in great disgust, and walked off; the Dormouse fell asleep instantly, and neither of the others took the least notice of her going, though she looked back once or twice, half hoping that they would call after her: the last time she saw them, they were trying to put the Dormouse into the teapot.

'At any rate I'll never go *there* again!' said Alice as she picked her way through the wood. 'It's the stupidest tea-party I ever was at in all my life!'

Just as she said this, she noticed that one of the trees

had a door leading right into it. 'That's very curious!' she thought. 'But everything's curious to-day. I think I may as well go in at once.' And in she went.

Once more she found herself in the long hall, and close to the little glass table. 'Now, I'll manage better this time,' she said to herself, and began by taking the little golden key, and unlocking the door that led into the garden. Then she set to work nibbling at the mushroom (she had kept a piece of it in her pocket) till she was about a foot high: then she walked down the little passage: and *then* — she found herself at last in the beautiful garden, among the bright flower-beds and the cool fountains.

CHAPTER VIII

THE QUEEN'S CROQUET-GROUND

A LARGE rose-tree stood near the entrance of the garden: the roses growing on it were white, but there were three gardeners at it, busily painting them red. Alice thought this a very curious thing, and she went nearer to watch them, and just as she came up to them she heard one of them say 'Look out now, Five! Don't go splashing paint over me like that!'

'I couldn't help it,' said Five, in a sulky tone. 'Seven jogged my elbow.'

On which Seven looked up and said, 'That's right, Five! Always lay the blame on others!'

'*You'd* better not talk!' said Five. 'I heard the Queen say only yesterday you deserved to be be-headed!'[1]

'What for?' said the one who had first spoken.

1. Five disclaims responsibility, on the ground that he did not originate the action objected to, and attempts to shift the blame to his colleague. When ironically accused of making a habit or principle of this, he resorts to *ignoratio elenchi*, arguing irrelevantly and *ad hominem* that his accuser already stands condemned for a totally different offense.

2. The gardeners' conspiracy is analysed by Sutherland (pp. 74 *ff*.) as an unsuccessful attempt to create a misleading, nonlinguistic sign. Their aim is not so much to alter the appearance of the rose-tree, as to deceive the Queen into believing, from this, that her orders have been obeyed.

'That's none of *your* business, Two!' said Seven.

'Yes, it *is* his business!' said Five. 'And I'll tell him — it was for bringing the cook tulip-roots instead of onions.'

Seven flung down his brush, and had just begun, 'Well, of all the unjust things ——' when his eye chanced to fall upon Alice, as she stood watching them, and he checked himself suddenly: the others looked round also, and all of them bowed low.

'Would you tell me,' said Alice, a little timidly, 'why you are painting those roses?'

Five and Seven said nothing, but looked at Two. Two began in a low voice, 'Why, the fact is, you see, Miss, this here ought to have been a *red* rose-tree, and we put a white one in by mistake; and if the Queen was to find it out, we should all have our heads cut off, you know. So you see, Miss, we're doing our best, afore she comes, to —'[2] At this moment, Five, who had been anxiously looking across the garden, called out, 'The Queen! The Queen!' and the three gardeners instantly threw themselves flat upon their faces. There was a sound of many footsteps, and Alice looked round, eager to see the Queen.

First came ten soldiers carrying clubs; these were all shaped like the three gardeners, oblong and flat, with their hands and feet at the corners; next the ten courtiers; these were ornamented all over with diamonds, and walked two and two, as the soldiers did. After these came the royal children; there were ten of them, and the little dears came jumping merrily along hand in hand, in couples: they were all ornamented with hearts. Next came the guests, mostly Kings and Queens, and among them Alice recognised the White Rabbit: it was talking in a hurried, nervous manner, smiling at everything that was said, and went by without noticing her. Then followed the Knave of Hearts, carrying the King's crown on a crimson velvet cushion; and, last of all this grand procession, came THE KING AND QUEEN OF HEARTS.

Alice was rather doubtful whether she ought not to lie down on her face like the three gardeners, but she could not remember ever having heard of such a rule at processions; 'and besides, what would be the use of a procession,' thought she, 'if people had all to lie down upon their faces, so that they couldn't see it?' So she stood still where she was, and waited.

When the procession came opposite to Alice, they all stopped and looked at her, and the Queen said severely, 'Who is this?' She said it to the Knave of Hearts, who only bowed and smiled in reply.

'Idiot!' said the Queen, tossing her head impatiently; and, turning to Alice, she went on, 'What's your name, child?'

'My name is Alice, so please your Majesty,' said Alice very politely; but she added, to herself, 'Why, they're only a pack of cards, after all. I needn't be afraid of them!'

'And who are *these*?' said the Queen, pointing to the three gardeners who were lying round the rose-tree; for, you see, as they were lying on their faces, and the pattern on their backs was the same as the rest of the pack, she could not tell whether they were gardeners, or soldiers, or courtiers, or three of her own children.

'How should *I* know?' said Alice, surprised at her own courage. 'It's no business of *mine*.'[3]

The Queen turned crimson with fury, and, after glaring at her for a moment like a wild beast, screamed 'Off with her head! Off ——'[4]

3. Alice's unwonted cunning is more surprising still. She knows the answer perfectly well, of course, but avoids telling a direct lie by denying it; instead, she casts doubt on her own credibility by denying that she is in any particular position to know. She thus leaves it to be inferred, wrongly, that she has no information to give. The Queen, unfortunately, has not read her Austin, and the attempted *suppressio veri* therefore fails to delude her.

4. The principle of government by decapitation scarcely ranks as a political theory, however popular its practice. The weakness of tyranny is that even its own agents are not safe under it, and thus have motives for evasion and/or revolt. The Hobbesian position, that government, though absolute, should not be oppressive if it wishes to survive, has a subscriber in the King of Hearts. Without his intervention, it is doubtful if the Wonderland monarchy would still have any subjects left to oppress. (Shibles, pp. 31-32)

'Nonsense!' said Alice, very loudly and decidedly, and the Queen was silent.

The King laid his hand upon her arm, and timidly said, 'Consider, my dear: she is only a child!'

The Queen turned angrily away from him, and said to the Knave, 'Turn them over!'

The Knave did so, very carefully, with one foot.

'Get up!' said the Queen, in a shrill, loud voice, and the three gardeners instantly jumped up, and began bowing to the King, the Queen, the royal children, and everybody else.

'Leave off that!' screamed the Queen. 'You make me giddy.' And then, turning to the rose-tree, she went on, 'What *have* you been doing here?'

'May it please your Majesty,' said Two, in a very humble tone, going down on one knee as he spoke, 'we were trying ——'

'*I* see!' said the Queen, who had meanwhile been examining the roses. 'Off with their heads!' and the procession moved on, three of the soldiers remaining behind to execute the unfortunate gardeners, who ran to Alice for protection.

'You shan't be beheaded!' said Alice, and she put them into a large flower-pot that stood near. The three soldiers wandered about for a minute or two, looking for them, and then quietly marched off after the others.

'Are their heads off?' shouted the Queen.

'Their heads are gone, if it please your Majesty!' the soldiers shouted in reply.[5]

'That's right!' shouted the Queen. 'Can you play croquet?'

The soldiers were silent, and looked at Alice, as the question was evidently meant for her.

'Yes!' shouted Alice.

'Come on, then!' roared the Queen, and Alice joined the procession, wondering very much what would happen next.

'It's — it's a very fine day!' said a timid voice at her

5. Alice's resort to *suppressio veri* by *suggestio falsi* (of her ignorance) is here put into reverse. In equivocating on 'gone,' the soldiers suggest falsely that they have done their duty, by a partial suppression of the truth. The heads are gone, indeed, but it is left undisclosed that their owners are gone too. (Sutherland, p. 180; Shibles, p. 32)

side. She was walking by the White Rabbit, who was peeping anxiously into her face.

'Very,' said Alice: '— where's the Duchess?'

'Hush! Hush!' said the Rabbit in a low hurried tone. He looked anxiously over his shoulder as he spoke, and then raised himself upon tiptoe, put his mouth close to her ear, and whispered, 'She's under sentence of execution.'

'What for?' said Alice.

'Did you say "What a pity!"?' the Rabbit asked.

'No, I didn't,' said Alice: 'I don't think it's at all a pity. I said "What for?"'

'She boxed the Queen's ears —' the Rabbit began. Alice gave a little scream of laughter. 'Oh, hush!' the Rabbit whispered in a frightened tone. 'The Queen will hear you! You see, she came rather late, and the Queen said —'

'Get to your places!' shouted the Queen in a voice of thunder, and people began running about in all directions tumbling up against each other; however, they got settled down in a minute or two, and the game began. Alice thought she had never seen such a curious croquet-ground in all her life; it was all ridges and furrows; the balls were live hedgehogs, the mallets live flamingoes, and the soldiers had to double themselves up and to stand upon their hands and feet, to make the arches.

The chief difficulty Alice found at first was in managing her flamingo: she succeeded in getting its body tucked away, comfortably enough, under her arm, with its legs hanging down, but generally, just as she had got its neck nicely straightened out, and was going to give the hedge-hog a blow with its head, it *would* twist itself round and look up in her face, with such a puzzled expression that she

could not help bursting out laughing: and when she had got its head down, and was going to begin again, it was very provoking to find that the hedgehog had unrolled itself, and was in the act of crawling away: besides all this, there was generally a ridge or a furrow in the way wherever she wanted to send the hedgehog to, and, as the doubled-up soldiers were always getting up and walking off to other parts of the ground, Alice soon came to the conclusion that it was a very difficult game indeed.

The players all played at once without waiting for turns, quarrelling all the while, and fighting for the hedgehogs; and in a very short time the Queen was in a furious passion, and went stamping about, and shouting 'Off with his head!' or 'Off with her head!' about once in a minute.

Alice began to feel very uneasy: to be sure she had not as yet had any dispute with the Queen, but she knew that it might happen any minute, 'and then,' thought she, 'what would become of me? They're dreadfully fond of beheading people here; the great wonder is that there's any one left alive!'

She was looking about for some way of escape, and

The Queen's Croquet-ground

wondering whether she could get away without being seen, when she noticed a curious appearance in the air: it puzzled her very much at first, but, after watching it a minute or two, she made it out to be a grin, and she said to herself, 'It's the Cheshire Cat: now I shall have somebody to talk to.'

'How are you getting on?' said the Cat, as soon as there was mouth enough for it to speak with.

Alice waited till the eyes appeared, and then nodded. 'It's no use speaking to it,' she thought, 'till its ears have come, or at least one of them.'[6] In another minute the whole head appeared, and then Alice put down her flamingo, and began an account of the game, feeling very glad she had some one to listen to her. The Cat seemed to think that there was enough of it now in sight, and no more of it appeared.

'I don't think they play at all fairly,' Alice began, in rather a complaining tone 'and they all quarrel so dreadfully one can't hear oneself speak — and they don't seem to have any rules in particular; at least, if there are, nobody attends to them[7] — and you've no idea how confusing it is all the things being alive; for instance, there's the arch I've got to go through next walking about at the other end of the ground — and I should have croqueted the Queen's hedgehog just now, only it ran away when it saw mine coming!'

'How do you like the Queen?' said the Cat in a low voice.

'Not at all,' said Alice: 'she's so extremely —' Just then she noticed that the Queen was close behind her listening: so she went on, '— likely to win, that it's hardly worth while finishing the game.'[8]

The
Philosopher's
Alice

82

6. Alice assumes that there can be no sense-impressions without sense-organs able to receive them, and does not stop to consider whether the Cat is coming into existence, or merely becoming visible to herself. She does not even ask if it is the *same* cat; and the question of how (if a physical object) it is able to defy gravity is left entirely in the air.

7. If there are no rules at all, even Alice ought to realize that it is impossible to play unfairly. Can it even be called a game? If rules there are but nobody attends to them, it is equally questionable whether anyone is playing *that* game. Wittgenstein asks more than once ([48] § 54; [49] p. 13) how an ignorant observer watching a game can discover the rules (rather than regularities) of play, and how he can tell if the players are obeying them and when they are making mistakes. Alice has the same problem, or a worse one, since in spite of her presumption that rules at least ought to exist, no regularities have yet become apparent that might count as an observance of them. For a recurrence of the difficulty, see p. 210. (Shibles, p. 33)

8. Alice's *savoir-faire* is improving; her veracity, alas, is not.

The Queen smiled and passed on.

'Who *are* you talking to?' said the King, coming up to Alice, and looking at the Cat's head with great curiosity.

'It's a friend of mine — a Cheshire Cat,' said Alice: 'allow me to introduce it.'

'I don't like the look of it at all,' said the King: 'however, it may kiss my hand if it likes.'

'I'd rather not,' the Cat remarked.

'Don't be impertinent,' said the King, 'and don't look at me like that!' He got behind Alice as he spoke.

'A cat may look at a king,' said Alice. 'I've read that in some book, but I don't remember where.'

'Well, it must be removed,' said the King very decidedly, and he called to the Queen, who was passing at the moment, 'My dear! I wish you would have this cat removed!'

The Queen had only one way of settling all difficulties, great or small. 'Off with his head!' she said, without even looking round.

'I'll fetch the executioner myself,' said the King eagerly, and he hurried off.

Alice thought she might as well go back and see how the game was going on, as she heard the Queen's voice in the distance, screaming with passion. She had already heard her sentence three of the players to be executed for having missed their turns, and she did not like the look of things at all, as the game was in such confusion that she never knew whether it was her turn or not. So she went in search of her hedgehog.

The hedgehog was engaged in a fight with another hedgehog, which seemed to Alice an excellent opportunity for croqueting one of them with the other: the only

The Philosopher's Alice

difficulty was, that her flamingo was gone across to the other side of the garden, where Alice could see it trying in a helpless sort of way to fly up into one of the trees.

By the time she had caught the flamingo and brought it back, the fight was over, and both the hedgehogs were out of sight: 'but it doesn't matter much,' thought Alice, 'as all the arches are gone from this side of the ground.' So she tucked it under her arm, that it might not escape again, and went back for a little more conversation with her friend.

When she got back to the Cheshire Cat, she was surprised to find quite a large crowd collected round it: there was a dispute going on between the executioner, the King, and the Queen, who were all talking at once, while all the rest were quite silent, and looked very uncomfortable.

The moment Alice appeared, she was appealed to by all three to settle the question, and they repeated their arguments to her, though, as they all spoke at once, she found it very hard indeed to make out exactly what they said.

The executioner's argument was, that you couldn't cut off a head unless there was a body to cut it off from: that he had never had to do such a thing before, and he wasn't going to begin at *his* time of life.

The King's argument was, that anything that had a head could be beheaded, and that you weren't to talk nonsense.

The Queen's argument was, that if something wasn't done about it in less than no time, she'd have everybody executed, all round. (It was this last remark that had made the whole party look so grave and anxious.)[9]

Alice could think of nothing else to say but 'It belongs to the Duchess: you'd better ask *her* about it.'

9. A head, in nearly all contexts, is by definition a distinguishable part of something. *To behead* is accordingly a relational verb, presupposing a whole having suitably identifiable and separable parts. There is no beheading a book, say, or a brick, and the reasons for this are conceptual, not practical, in nature. Presented with a head already enjoying an apparently detached existence, the executioner can find no employment for the concept of decapitation, and rightly declines the job.

The King knows that *head* is a part word, and can see that it applies to the object before him. He therefore concludes that this part must have a whole to which it belongs, or is connected, and from which detachment is possible. This is true enough in principle, but beside the point if detachment has already occurred. You cannot decapitate an already severed head.

The Queen relies, as usual, on an *argumentum ad baculum* (or irrelevant appeal to force), which would certainly give her the last word, if there was any (logical) possibility of carrying it out. (Sutherland, p. 145; Shibles, p. 32; Holmes, p. 142; Carney and Scheer [11], p. 5)

'She's in prison,' the Queen said to the executioner: 'fetch her here.' And the executioner went off like an arrow.

The Cat's head began fading away the moment he was gone, and, by the time he had come back with the Duchess, it had entirely disappeared; so the King and the executioner ran wildly up and down looking for it, while the rest of the party went back to the game.

CHAPTER IX

THE MOCK TURTLE'S STORY

'You can't think how glad I am to see you again, you dear old thing!' said the Duchess, as she tucked her arm affectionately into Alice's, and they walked off together.

Alice was very glad to find her in such a pleasant temper, and thought to herself that perhaps it was only the pepper that had made her so savage when they met in the kitchen.

'When *I'm* a Duchess,' she said to herself (not in a very hopeful tone though), 'I won't have any pepper in my kitchen *at all*. Soup does very well without — Maybe it's always pepper that makes people hot-tempered,' she went on, very much pleased at having found out a new kind of rule, 'and vinegar that makes them sour — and camomile that makes them bitter — and — and barley-sugar and such things that make children sweet-tempered.[1] I only wish people knew *that*: then they wouldn't be so stingy about it, you know ——'

She had quite forgotten the Duchess by this time, and was a little startled when she heard her voice close to her ear. 'You're thinking about something, my dear, and that makes you forget to talk.[2] I can't tell you just now what the moral of that is, but I shall remember it in a bit.'

'Perhaps it hasn't one,' Alice ventured to remark.

'Tut, tut, child!' said the Duchess. 'Everything's got a moral, if only you can find it.'[3] And she squeezed herself up closer to Alice's side as she spoke.

1. Another wild generalization from a single dubious case, which is at once elaborated into a universal rule. Alice's hypothesis of the influence of diet on character is reminiscent both of the magical belief that 'like causes like,' and of eighteenth-century theories about the similar influence of geography and climate. Outmoded in sociology, such theories still command some respect in medical circles, where the influence of diet on health, for example, is by now much more of a commonplace than it was in Carroll's day. (Shibles, p. 33)

2. The Duchess is evidently in agreement with the Hatter's second theory about thought and language, to the extent at least that she regards them as separate processes. But then she also implies that the one excludes the other (i.e., thinking entails not talking), whereas the Hatter's view was that not-thinking entails, if not not-talking, at least that you should not talk. (Shibles, pp. 33-34)

3. Everything, that is, can be seen as an illustration or special case of some more general principle—a sentiment that philosophers, of all people, should be the last to doubt, even though it risks a paradox in applying, presumably, to itself. (Sutherland, p. 13; Shibles, p. 34)

A quotation—doubtless from an inferior translation—of the well-known last line of Dante's *Paradiso*. Alice's counterquotation, from the Duchess herself, is met by the claim that the two statements express the same proposition, and by a reassertion of the principle that thought is not only prior to language, but also has primacy over it. The Duchess is clearing the way for Humpty Dumpty's later and more pungent expression of linguistic voluntarism (see p. 195). (Sutherland, pp. 185, 187-88; Pitcher [in Fann], p. 328)

Alice did not much like her keeping so close to her: first, because the Duchess was *very* ugly; and secondly, because she was exactly the right height to rest her chin upon Alice's shoulder, and it was an uncomfort-ably sharp chin. However, she did not like to be rude, so she bore it as well as she could. 'The game seems to be going on rather better now,' she said.

''Tis so,' said the Duchess: 'and the moral of it is — "Oh, 'tis love, 'tis love, that makes the world go round!"' [4]

'Somebody said,' whispered Alice, 'that it's done by everybody minding their own business!'

'Ah, well! It means much the same thing,' said the Duchess, digging her sharp little chin into Alice's shoulder as she added, 'and the moral of *that* is — "Take care of the sense, and the sounds will take care of themselves."'

'How fond she is of finding morals in things!' Alice thought to herself.

'I dare say you're wondering why I don't put my arm round your waist,' the Duchess said after a pause: 'the reason is, that I'm doubtful about the temper of your flamingo. Shall I try the experiment?'

'He might bite,' Alice cautiously replied, not feeling at all anxious to have the experiment tried.

'Very true,' said the Duchess: 'flamingoes and mustard both bite. And the moral of that is — "Birds of a feather flock together."'[5]

'Only mustard isn't a bird,' Alice remarked.

'Right as usual,' said the Duchess: 'what a clear way you have of putting things!'

'It's a mineral, I *think*,' said Alice.

'Of course it is,' said the Duchess, who seemed ready to agree to everything that Alice said: 'there's a large mustard-mine near here. And the moral of that is — "The more there is of mine, the less there is of yours."'[6]

'Oh, I know!' exclaimed Alice, who had not attended to this last remark. 'It's a vegetable. It doesn't look like one, but it is.'

'I quite agree with you,' said the Duchess; 'and the moral of that is — "Be what you would seem to be" — or if you'd like it put more simply — "Never imagine yourself not to be otherwise than what it might appear to others that what you were or might have been was not otherwise than what you had been would have appeared to them to be otherwise."'[7]

'I think I should understand that better,' Alice said very politely, 'if I had it written down: but I'm afraid I can't quite follow it as you say it.'

'That's nothing to what I could say if I chose,' the Duchess replied, in a pleased tone.

'Pray don't trouble yourself to say it any longer than that,' said Alice.

5. A somewhat reckless comparison, as even Alice can see. The Duchess, like most of her associates, is oblivious alike to homophonic ambiguity and to the dangers of classification based on an isolated point of resemblance. (Shibles, pp. 35-36)

6. An oracular reference, perhaps, to the ecological consequences of industrial overdevelopment.

7. The referential opacity of this restatement is a reflexive paradox in its own right, since it violates the very injunction it professes to formulate. Jourdain (p. 26) cites it as an example of the practical utility of logical symbolism; not that Alice would have been much the wiser for knowing that. (Sutherland, pp. 185, 188; Shibles, p. 36; Holmes, p. 134)

8. It is one thing to have a right; to be able to exercise it is quite another matter. The Duchess grants, apparently, that Alice is a rational being, but shares the same low view of her intelligence—or capacity to behave rationally—that is held by most other denizens of Wonderland. Alice has a right to, but does not and cannot, think, any more than pigs do or can fly; and hence the Duchess's original supposition that she *was* thinking must have been in error. Still, as the noble lady would probably say, it means much the same thing. Consistency is the vice of little minds, and neither she nor her protégée is in any danger of that.

'Oh, don't talk about trouble!' said the Duchess. 'I make you a present of everything I've said as yet.'

'A cheap sort of present!' thought Alice. 'I'm glad they don't give birthday presents like that!' But she did not venture to say it out loud.

'Thinking again?' the Duchess asked with another dig of her sharp little chin.

'I've a right to think,' said Alice sharply, for she was beginning to feel a little worried.

'Just about as much right,' said the Duchess, 'as pigs have to fly;[8] and the m ——'

But here, to Alice's great surprise, the Duchess's voice died away, even in the middle of her favourite word "moral", and the arm that was linked into hers began to tremble. Alice looked up, and there stood the Queen in front of them, with her arms folded, frowning like a thunderstorm.

'A fine day, your Majesty!' the Duchess began in a low, weak voice.

'Now, I give you fair warning,' shouted the Queen, stamping on the ground as she spoke; 'either you or your head must be off, and that in about half no time! Take your choice!'

The Duchess took her choice, and was gone in a moment.

'Let's get on with the game,' the Queen said to Alice; and Alice was too much frightened to say a word, but slowly followed her back to the croquet-ground.

The other guests had taken advantage of the Queen's absence, and were resting in the shade: however, the moment they saw her, they hurried back to the game, the Queen merely remarking that a moment's delay would cost them their lives.

All the time they were playing the Queen never left off quarrelling with the other players, and shouting 'Off with his head!' or 'Off with her head!' Those whom she sentenced were taken into custody by the soldiers, who of course had to leave off being arches to do this, so that by the end of half an hour or so there were no arches left, and all the players, except the King, the Queen, and Alice, were in custody and under sentence of execution.

Then the Queen left off, quite out of breath, and said to Alice, 'Have you seen the Mock Turtle yet?'

'No,' said Alice. 'I don't even know what a Mock Turtle is.'

'It's the thing Mock Turtle Soup is made from,' said the Queen.[9]

'I never saw one, or heard of one,' said Alice.

'Come on, then,' said the Queen, 'and he shall tell you his history.'

As they walked off together, Alice heard the King say in a low voice, to the company generally, 'You are all pardoned.' 'Come, *that's* a good thing!' she said to herself, for she had felt quite unhappy at the number of executions the Queen had ordered.

They very soon came upon a Gryphon, lying fast asleep in the sun. (If you don't know what a Gryphon is, look at the picture.) 'Up, lazy thing!' said the Queen, 'and take this young lady to see the Mock Turtle, and to hear his history. I must go back and see after some executions I have ordered,' and she walked off, leaving Alice alone with the Gryphon. Alice did not quite like the look of the creature, but on the whole she thought it would be quite as safe to stay with it as to go after that savage Queen: so she waited.

The Gryphon sat up and rubbed its eyes: then it watched

9. A Mock Turtle is, of course, no more a special kind of turtle than a March Hare is a special kind of hare. Much less so, in fact, for mock turtle soup is an imitation of turtle soup, not a soup made from an imitation turtle. The Queen and Alice are alike guilty of false hyphenation hereabouts, and between them generate an amphibolous monster, not an amphibious one.

10. It is appropriate enough that the Gryphon, himself a creature of fantasy (also taken from Dante, by the way; *cf.* Gardner, p. 124), should be earthily sceptical of the fantasies, paranoiac or melancholical, of the Queen of Hearts and the Mock Turtle. His cousin the Unicorn shows a similar strain of realism, later on, in doubting the existence of children in general, and Alice in particular (p. 206). (Shibles, p. 37)

the Queen till she was out of sight: then it chuckled. 'What fun!' said the Gryphon, half to itself, half to Alice.

'What *is* the fun?' said Alice.

'Why, *she,*' said the Gryphon. 'It's all her fancy, that: they never executes nobody, you know. Come on!'

'Everybody says "Come on!" here,' thought Alice, as she went slowly after it: 'I never was so ordered about in all my life, never!'

They had not gone far before they saw the Mock Turtle in the distance, sitting sad and lonely on a little ledge of rock, and, as they came nearer, Alice could hear him sighing as if his heart would break. She pitied him deeply. 'What is his sorrow?' she asked the Gryphon, and the Gryphon answered, very nearly in the same words as before, 'It's all his fancy, that: he hasn't got no sorrow, you know. Come on!'[10]

So they went up to the Mock Turtle, who looked at them with large eyes full of tears, but said nothing.

'This here young lady,' said the Gryphon, 'she wants for to know your history, she do.'

'I'll tell it her,' said the Mock Turtle in a deep, hollow tone: 'sit down, both of you, and don't speak a word till I've finished.'

So they sat down, and nobody spoke for some minutes. Alice thought to herself, 'I don't see how he can *ever* finish, if he doesn't begin.'[11] But she waited patiently.

'Once,' said the Mock Turtle at last, with a deep sigh, 'I was a real Turtle.'

These words were followed by a very long silence, broken only by an occasional exclamation of 'Hjckrrh!' from the Gryphon, and the constant heavy sobbing of the Mock Turtle. Alice was very nearly getting up and saying, 'Thank you, sir, for your interesting story,' but she could not help thinking there *must* be more to come, so she sat still and said nothing.

'When we were little,' the Mock Turtle went on at last, more calmly, though still sobbing a little now and then, 'we went to school in the sea. The master was an old Turtle — we used to call him Tortoise ——'

'Why did you call him Tortoise, if he wasn't one?' Alice asked.

'We called him Tortoise because he taught us,' said the Mock Turtle angrily: 'really you are very dull!'[12]

'You ought to be ashamed of yourself for asking such a simple question,' added the Gryphon; and then they both sat silent and looked at poor Alice, who felt ready to sink into the earth. At last the Gryphon said to the Mock Turtle, 'Drive on, old fellow! Don't be all day about it!' and he went on in these words:

11. A reasonable comment in the circumstances, but the principle involved has exceptions. The series of negative integers has an end but no beginning, just as the positive integers have a beginning but no end. Many philosophers, however, have had trouble in seeing how the world could have even a present, let alone an end, if, as has been contended, it had no beginning in time. For in that case an infinite series must seemingly have elapsed already, which is thought to be impossible. An attempted solution of the difficulty is given in Kant's discussion of his First Antinomy (*Critique of Pure Reason*, A 426-34*ff.*).

Shibles (p. 38) sees Kantian allusions everywhere in this chapter; but the eye of faith—or an intellectual understanding—is needed to discern most of them, or, once found, to suppose them intended by Carroll himself.

12. Wittgenstein, believe it or not, thought this a 'good grammatical joke' (Pitcher [in Fann], p. 316*n*). Carroll himself thought sufficiently well of it, alas, to revive it in his 'What the Tortoise said to Achilles,' a logical article published in *Mind* (April 1895, quoted by Gardner, pp. 127-28).

The remainder of this chapter, and the next, contain what is probably the direst collection of bad puns and false etymologies since Plato's *Cratylus*. A more probable source, however, is Horne Tooke's once-famous *Diversions of Purley*, which Carroll was reading in 1855. Tooke believed the meanings of words to be contained in their etymologies, a theory now utterly refuted, but still quite popular in Carroll's day.

13. She has now, at all events. A reverse variant of the trap later successfully laid for Alice by Humpty Dumpty (p. 190).

'Yes, we went to school in the sea, though you mayn't believe it ——'

'I never said I didn't!' interrupted Alice.

'You did,' said the Mock Turtle.[13]

'Hold your tongue!' added the Gryphon, before Alice could speak again. The Mock Turtle went on: —

'We had the best of educations — in fact, we went to school every day ——'

'*I've* been to a day-school, too,' said Alice; 'you needn't be so proud as all that.'

'With extras?' asked the Mock Turtle a little anxiously.

'Yes,' said Alice, 'we learned French and music.'

'And washing?' said the Mock Turtle.

'Certainly not!' said Alice indignantly.

'Ah! then yours wasn't a really good school,' said the Mock Turtle in a tone of great relief. 'Now at *ours* they had at the end of the bill, "French, music, *and washing* — extra."'[14]

'You couldn't have wanted it much,' said Alice; 'living at the bottom of the sea.'

'I couldn't afford to learn it,' said the Mock Turtle with a sigh. 'I only took the regular course.'

'What was that?' inquired Alice.

'Reeling and Writhing, of course, to begin with,' the Mock Turtle replied; 'and then the different branches of Arithmetic — Ambition, Distraction, Uglification, and Derision.'

'I never heard of "Uglification",' Alice ventured to say. 'What is it?'

The Gryphon lifted up both its paws in surprise. 'What! Never heard of uglifying!' it exclaimed. 'You know what to beautify is, I suppose?'

'Yes,' said Alice doubtfully: 'it means — to — make — anything — prettier.'

'Well, then,' the Gryphon went on, 'if you don't know what to uglify is, you *must* be a simpleton.'[15]

Alice did not feel encouraged to ask any more questions about it, so she turned to the Mock Turtle, and said 'What else had you to learn?'

14. The Mock Turtle has succumbed to a type fallacy. Generic similarity as an 'extra' offers no presumption of specific resemblance as an extra subject of instruction. (Gardner, p. 128)

15. A typical example of Socratic method. The meaning of an unknown term is conveyed by first eliciting a definition of its opposite, and then leaving it to the respondent to arrive at the new definition by immediate inference *per contradictionem*.

16. Alice, having grasped the rule governing the series, pursues the latter to its limit, beyond which it yields impossible negative values of the variable. Like the March Hare (p. 72) and the Red Queen (p. 224), the Gryphon astutely blocks the awkward question. Jourdain (p. 77) unkindly compares him to mathematicians who relegate paradoxes in their subject to 'philosophy.'

'Well, there was Mystery,' the Mock Turtle replied, counting off the subjects on his flappers, '— Mystery, ancient and modern, with Seaography: then Drawling — the Drawling-master was an old conger-eel, that used to come once a week: *he* taught us Drawling, Stretching, and Fainting in Coils.'

'What was *that* like?' said Alice.

'Well, I can't show it you myself,' the Mock Turtle said: 'I'm too stiff. And the Gryphon never learnt it.'

'Hadn't time,' said the Gryphon: 'I went to the Classical master, though. He was an old crab, *he* was.'

'I never went to him,' the Mock Turtle said with a sigh: 'he taught Laughing and Grief, they used to say.'

'So he did, so he did,' said the Gryphon, sighing in his turn; and both creatures hid their faces in their paws.

'And how many hours a day did you do lessons?' said Alice, in a hurry to change the subject.

'Ten hours the first day,' said the Mock Turtle: 'nine the next, and so on.'

'What a curious plan!' exclaimed Alice.

'That's the reason they're called lessons,' the Gryphon remarked: 'because they lessen from day to day.'

This was quite a new idea to Alice, and she thought it over a little before she made her next remark. 'Then the eleventh day must have been a holiday?'

'Of course it was,' said the Mock Turtle.

'And how did you manage on the twelfth?' Alice went on eagerly.[16]

'That's enough about lessons,' the Gryphon interrupted in a very decided tone: 'tell her something about the games now.'

CHAPTER X

THE LOBSTER QUADRILLE

THE Mock Turtle sighed deeply, and drew the back of one flapper across his eyes. He looked at Alice, and tried to speak, but, for a minute or two, sobs choked his voice. 'Same as if he had a bone in his throat,' said the Gryphon: and it set to work shaking him and punching him in the back. At last the Mock Turtle recovered his voice, and, with tears running down his cheeks, went on again: —

'You may not have lived much under the sea —' ('I haven't,' said Alice) 'and perhaps you were never even introduced to a lobster —' (Alice began to say 'I once tasted ——' but checked herself hastily, and said 'No, never') '— so you can have no idea what a delightful thing a Lobster Quadrille is!'

'No, indeed,' said Alice. 'What sort of a dance is it?'

'Why,' said the Gryphon, 'you first form into a line along the sea-shore ——'

'Two lines!' cried the Mock Turtle. 'Seals, turtles, and so on; then, when you've cleared the jelly-fish out of the way ——'

'*That* generally takes some time,' interrupted the Gryphon.

'— you advance twice ——'

'Each with a lobster as a partner!' cried the Gryphon.

'Of course,' the Mock Turtle said: 'advance twice, set to partners ——'

'— change lobsters, and retire in same order,' continued the Gryphon.

'Then, you know,' the Mock Turtle went on, 'you throw the ——'

'The lobsters!' shouted the Gryphon, with a bound into the air.

'— as far out to sea as you can ——'

'Swim after them!' screamed the Gryphon.

'Turn a somersault in the sea!' cried the Mock Turtle, capering wildly about.

'Change lobsters again!' yelled the Gryphon.

'Back to land again, and — that's all the first figure,' said the Mock Turtle, suddenly dropping his voice: and the two creatures, who had been jumping about like mad things, sat down again very sadly and quietly, and looked at Alice.

'It must be a very pretty dance,' said Alice, timidly.

'Would you like to see a little of it?' said the Mock Turtle.

'Very much indeed,' said Alice.

'Let's try the first figure!' said the Mock Turtle to the Gryphon. 'We can do without lobsters, you know. Which shall sing?'

'Oh, *you* sing,' said the Gryphon. 'I've forgotten the words.'

So they began solemnly dancing round and round Alice, every now and then treading on her toes when they passed too close, and waving their forepaws to mark the time, while the Mock Turtle sang this, very slowly and sadly: —

'*Will you walk a little faster?*' *said a whiting to a snail.*
'*There's a porpoise close behind us, and he's treading on my tail.*
See how eagerly the lobsters and the turtles all advance!
They are waiting on the shingle—will you come and join the
  dance?
  Will you, won't you, will you, won't you, will you join the
    dance?
  Will you, won't you, will you, won't you, won't you join the
    dance?

'*You can really have no notion how delightful it will be,*
When they take us up and throw us, with the lobsters, out to sea!'
But the snail replied 'Too far, too far!' and gave a look askance —
Said he thanked the whiting kindly, but he would not join the
  dance.
  Would not, could not, would not, could not, would not join the
    dance.
  Would not, could not, would not, could not, could not join the
    dance.

'*What matters it how far we go?' his scaly friend replied.*
'*There is another shore, you know, upon the other side.*
The further off from England the nearer is to France —
Then turn not pale, beloved snail, but come and join the dance.
  Will you, won't you, will you, won't you, will you join the
    dance?
  Will you, won't you, will you, won't you, won't you join the
    dance?'

'Thank you, it's a very interesting dance to watch,' said Alice, feeling very glad that it was over at last: 'and I do so like that curious song about the whiting!'

'Oh, as to the whiting,' said the Mock Turtle, 'they — you've seen them, of course?'

'Yes,' said Alice, 'I've often seen them at dinn ——' she checked herself hastily.

'I don't know where Dinn may be,' said the Mock Turtle, 'but if you've seen them so often, of course you know what they're like.'

'I believe so,' Alice replied thoughtfully. 'They have their tails in their mouths — and they're all over crumbs.'[1]

'You're wrong about the crumbs,' said the Mock Turtle: 'crumbs would all wash off in the sea. But they *have* their

1. Alice and the Mock Turtle are at cross porpoises, so to speak. Her range of experience with whiting (cooked) is altogether different from his (live), and it is only *per accidens* (or rather by the author's contrivance) that they find a common characteristic to agree on. The same characteristic happens also to be shared after a fashion by Alice herself, for whom foot-in-the-mouth trouble is a fairly frequent social disaster throughout the book.

2. The explanation given appeals to a principle of contrariety governing the terrestrial and aquatic worlds, not unlike the Aristotelian belief in a similar opposition between the unchanging perfection of the celestial order and the vulgar mutability prevailing in the sublunary sphere.

tails in their mouths; and the reason is —' here the Mock Turtle yawned and shut his eyes. 'Tell her about the reason and all that,' he said to the Gryphon.

'The reason is,' said the Gryphon, 'that they *would* go with the lobsters to the dance. So they got thrown out to sea. So they had to fall a long way. So they got their tails fast in their mouths. So they couldn't get them out again. That's all.'

'Thank you,' said Alice, 'it's very interesting. I never knew so much about a whiting before.'

'I can tell you more than that, if you like,' said the Gryphon. 'Do you know why it's called a whiting?'

'I never thought about it,' said Alice. 'Why?'

'*It does the boots and shoes*,' the Gryphon replied very solemnly.

Alice was thoroughly puzzled. 'Does the boots and shoes!' she repeated in a wondering tone.

'Why, what are *your* shoes done with?' said the Gryphon. 'I mean, what makes them so shiny?'

Alice looked down at them, and considered a little before she gave her answer. 'They're done with blacking, I believe.'

'Boots and shoes under the sea,' the Gryphon went on in a deep voice, 'are done with whiting.[2] Now you know.'

'And what are they made of?' Alice asked in a tone of great curiosity.

'Soles and eels, of course,' the Gryphon replied rather impatiently: 'any shrimp could have told you that.'

'If I'd been the whiting,' said Alice, whose thoughts were still running on the song, 'I'd have said to the porpoise, "Keep back, please: we don't want *you* with us!"'

'They were obliged to have him with them,' the Mock

Turtle said: 'no wise fish would go anywhere without a porpoise.'

'Wouldn't it really?' said Alice in a tone of great surprise.

'Of course not,' said the Mock Turtle: 'why, if a fish came to *me*, and told me he was going a journey, I should say "With what porpoise?"'

'Don't you mean "purpose"?' said Alice.[3]

'I mean what I say,' the Mock Turtle replied in an offended tone. And the Gryphon added, 'Come, let's hear some of *your* adventures.'

'I could tell you my adventures — beginning from this morning,' said Alice a little timidly: 'but it's no use going back to yesterday, because I was a different person then.'[4]

'Explain all that,' said the Mock Turtle.

'No, no! The adventures first,' said the Gryphon in an impatient tone: 'explanations take such a dreadful time.'

So Alice began telling them her adventures from the time when she first saw the White Rabbit. She was a little nervous about it just at

3. Alice, at long last, actually recognizes a possible case of homophonic ambiguity. The Mock Turtle rebuts any suggestion of a *lapsus linguae* by an open espousal of nominalism. What he means is determined by what he says, and not vice versa, an attitude shared by the Hatter (before he changed his views) and by many modern philosophers. (Holmes, p. 142)

4. Alice's identity problem has still not been exorcised, yet it is hard to have much patience with it. If she knows who she was yesterday, and remembers events of that period as *her* experiences, her refusal to discuss or admit ownership of them is both philosophically unreasonable and socially perverse. How is she even to complain that her memory is treacherous, if it is not *her* memories that she is trying to recall?

first, the two creatures got so close to her, one on each side, and opened their eyes and mouths so *very* wide, but she gained courage as she went on. Her listeners were perfectly quiet till she got to the part about her repeating '*You are old, Father William*' to the Caterpillar, and the words all coming different, and then the Mock Turtle drew a long breath, and said, 'That's very curious.'

'It's all about as curious as it can be,' said the Gryphon.

'It all came different!' the Mock Turtle repeated thoughtfully. 'I should like to hear her repeat something now. Tell her to begin,' He looked at the Gryphon as if he thought it had some kind of authority over Alice.

'Stand up and repeat "'*Tis the voice of the sluggard*",' said the Gryphon.

'How the creatures order one about, and make one repeat lessons!' thought Alice. 'I might as well be at school at once.' However, she got up, and began to repeat it, but her head was so full of the Lobster Quadrille, that she hardly knew what she was saying, and the words came very queer indeed: —

> '*'Tis the voice of the Lobster; I heard him declare,*
> "*You have baked me too brown, I must sugar my hair.*"
> *As a duck with its eyelids, so he with his nose*
> *Trims his belt and his buttons, and turns out his toes.*
> *When the sands are all dry, he is gay as a lark,*
> *And will talk in contemptuous tones of the Shark:*
> *But, when the tide rises and sharks are around,*
> *His voice has a timid and tremulous sound.*'

'That's different from what *I* used to say when I was a child,' said the Gryphon.

The Philosopher's Alice

———

101

'Well, I never heard it before,' said the Mock Turtle; 'but it sounds uncommon nonsense.'

Alice said nothing; she had sat down with her face in her hands, wondering if anything would *ever* happen in a natural way again.

'I should like to have it explained,' said the Mock Turtle.

'She can't explain it,' hastily said the Gryphon. 'Go on to the next verse.'

'But about his toes?' the Mock Turtle persisted. 'How *could* he turn them out with his nose, you know?'[5]

'It's the first position in dancing,' Alice said; but was dreadfully puzzled by it all, and longed to change the subject.

'Go on with the next verse,' the Gryphon repeated: 'it begins with the words "*I passed by his garden*".'

Alice did not dare to disobey, though she felt sure it would all come wrong, and she went on in a trembling voice: —

> *'I passed by his garden, and marked, with one eye,*
> *How the Owl and the Panther were sharing a pie:*
> *The Panther took pie-crust, and gravy, and meat,*
> *While the Owl had the dish as its share of the treat.*
> *When the pie was all finished, the Owl, as a boon,*
> *Was kindly permitted to pocket the spoon:*
> *While the Panther received knife and fork with a growl,*
> *And concluded the banquet ——'*

The Philosopher's Alice

102

'What *is* the use of repeating all that stuff,' the Mock Turtle interrupted, 'if you don't explain it as you go on? It's by far the most confusing thing *I* ever heard!'

'Yes, I think you'd better leave off,' said the Gryphon: and Alice was only too glad to do so.

5. His common sense affronted by Alice's vagaries, the Mock Turtle is quite properly persistent in his demands for further explanation. What he requires is not so much a law to cover the alleged facts, as an elucidation that will enable him to reconcile apparent inconsistencies and to fill in causal gaps in her story. What he gets is an irrelevant redescription of the lobster's stance, which may explain why he adopted it, but throws no light at all on how it was arrived at. (Shibles, pp. 39-40)

'Shall we try another figure of the Lobster Quadrille?' the Gryphon went on. 'Or would you like the Mock Turtle to sing you a song?'

'Oh, a song, please, if the Mock Turtle would be so kind,' Alice replied, so eagerly that the Gryphon said, in a rather offended tone. 'Hm! No accounting for tastes! Sing her "*Turtle Soup*", will you, old fellow?'

The Mock Turtle sighed deeply, and began, in a voice sometimes choked with sobs, to sing this: —

> *'Beautiful Soup, so rich and green,*
> *Waiting in a hot tureen!*
> *Who for such dainties would not stoop?*
> *Soup of the evening, beautiful Soup!*
> *Soup of the evening, beautiful Soup!*
> *   Beau—ootiful Soo—oop!*
> *   Beau—ootiful Soo—oop!*
> *Soo—oop of the e—e—evening.*
> *   Beautiful, beautiful Soup!*

> *'Beautiful Soup! Who cares for fish,*
> *Game, or any other dish?*
> *Who would not give all else for two p*
> *ennyworth only of beautiful Soup?*
> *Pennyworth only of beautiful Soup?*
> *   Beau—ootiful Soo—oop!*
> *   Beau—ootiful Soo—oop!*
> *Soo—oop of the e—e—evening,*
> *   Beautiful, beauti—FUL SOUP!'*

'Chorus again!' cried the Gryphon, and the Mock Turtle had just begun to repeat it, when a cry of 'The trial's beginning!' was heard in the distance.

'Come on!' cried the Gryphon, and, taking Alice by the hand, it hurried off, without waiting for the end of the song.

'What trial is it?' Alice panted as she ran; but the Gryphon only answered 'Come on!' and ran the faster, while more and more faintly came, carried on the breeze that followed them, the melancholy words: —

> *'Soo—oop of the e—e—evening,*
> *   Beautiful, beautiful Soup!'*

The
Philosopher's
Alice

——————

CHAPTER XI

WHO STOLE THE TARTS?

1. Since Alice's conception of legal procedure is confined to 'knowledge by description' (Russell), she can identify the contents of the courtroom only by discovering nonlinguistic features which assign these objects to the names already known to her—a kind of reversed ostensive definition. Her inferences from the judge's wig and the number of the jurymen are successful, but, not having heard the indictment yet, her nonrecognition of the tarts as the *corpus delicti* is a predictable, though pardonable, mistake. (Sutherland, pp. 78, 220)

THE King and Queen of Hearts were seated on their throne when they arrived, with a great crowd assembled about them — all sorts of little birds and beasts, as well as the whole pack of cards: the Knave was standing before them, in chains, with a soldier on each side to guard him; and near the King was the White Rabbit, with a trumpet in one hand, and a scroll of parchment in the other. In the very middle of the court was a table, with a large dish of tarts upon it: they looked so good, that it made Alice quite hungry to look at them — 'I wish they'd get the trial done,' she thought, 'and hand round the refreshments!' But there seemed to be no chance of this, so she began looking about her, to pass away the time.

Alice had never been in a court of justice before, but she had read about them in books, and she was quite pleased to find that she knew the name of nearly everything there. 'That's the judge,' she said to herself, 'because of his great wig.'[1]

The judge, by the way, was the King; and as he wore his crown, over the wig, (look at the frontispiece if you want to see how he did it,) he did not look at all comfortable, and it was certainly not becoming.

'And that's the jury-box,' thought Alice, 'and those twelve creatures,' (she was obliged to say 'creatures', you see, because some of them were animals, and some were birds,) 'I suppose they are the jurors.' She said this last

2. A. J. Ayer, in his phenomenalist period, having lost his fountain pen under similarly mysterious circumstances, is said to have tried to account for its disappearance as simply a 'favorable run of sense-data come to an end'; but could not get himself to believe it. No such explanation occurs to Bill; but at least he follows Kant (and anticipates Prichard and Ross) in believing that duty requires him not actually to achieve anything, but only to try to do so.

word two or three times over to herself, being rather proud of it: for she thought, and rightly too, that very few little girls of her age knew the meaning of it at all. However, 'jurymen' would have done just as well.

The twelve jurors were all writing very busily on slates. 'What are they all doing?' Alice whispered to the Gryphon. 'They can't have anything to put down yet, before the trial's begun.'

'They're putting down their names,' the Gryphon whispered in reply, 'for fear they should forget them before the end of the trial.'

'Stupid things!' Alice began in a loud, indignant voice, but she stopped hastily, for the White Rabbit cried out 'Silence in the court!' and the King put on his spectacles and looked anxiously round, to see who was talking.

Alice could see, as well as if she were looking over their shoulders, that all the jurors were writing down 'Stupid things!' on their slates, and she could even make out that one of them didn't know how to spell 'stupid,' and that he had to ask his neighbour to tell him. 'A nice muddle their slates will be in before the trial's over!' thought Alice.

One of the jurors had a pencil that squeaked. This, of course, Alice could *not* stand, and she went round the court and got behind him, and very soon found an opportunity of taking it away. She did it so quickly that the poor little juror (it was Bill, the Lizard) could not make out at all what had become of it; so, after hunting all about for it, he was obliged to write with one finger for the rest of the day; and this was of very little use, as it left no mark on the slate.[2]

'Herald, read the accusation!' said the King.

On this the White Rabbit blew three blasts on the

Who Stole the Tarts?

3. The concept of 'due process' and the presumption of 'innocent until proved guilty' are as much a mystery to the King of Hearts as they are to his imbecile jury. His notion of evidence, when he remembers to call any, is that it should explain how the crime was committed; that it is a crime, and was committed, and who committed it are questions begged against the accused from the start.

trumpet, and then unrolled the parchment scroll, and read as follows: —

> 'The Queen of Hearts, she made some tarts,
>   All on a summer day:
> The Knave of Hearts, he stole those tarts,
>   And took them quite away!'

'Consider your verdict,' the King said to the jury.[3]
'Not yet, not yet!' the Rabbit hastily interrupted. 'There's a great deal to come before that!'
'Call the first witness,' said the King; and the White

4. Assuming, as a suppressed premise, that a hat either belongs to its wearer or has been dishonestly appropriated from another, the King reasons validly by *modus tollendo ponens* (i.e., denying one alternative in order to affirm the other) to the Hatter's supposed larceny. But the premise and conclusion are both false. The Hatter has invited trouble by using the word *mine* to cover personal possessions only, not his stock-in-trade, and by refusing to recognize that 'your hat' obviously refers to the one he is wearing, regardless of who its real owner may be. (Sutherland, pp. 105*ff*.; Shibles, p. 44)

5. In faint reminiscence, perhaps, of Dr. Johnson's *mot* concerning the beneficial effects of being hanged in a fortnight: it concentrates the mind wonderfully. A less effective sedative than that proposed it would, however, be difficult to discover.

Rabbit blew three blasts on the trumpet, and called out 'First witness!'

The first witness was the Hatter. He came in with a teacup in one hand and a piece of bread-and-butter in the other. 'I beg pardon, your Majesty,' he began, 'for bringing these in: but I hadn't quite finished my tea when I was sent for.'

'You ought to have finished,' said the King. 'When did you begin?'

The Hatter looked at the March Hare, who had followed him into the court, arm-in-arm with the Dormouse. 'Fourteenth of March, I *think* it was,' he said.

'Fifteenth,' said the March Hare.

'Sixteenth,' added the Dormouse.

'Write that down,' the King said to the jury, and the jury eagerly wrote down all three dates on their slates, and then added them up, and reduced the answer to shillings and pence.

'Take off your hat,' the King said to the Hatter.

'It isn't mine,' said the Hatter.

'*Stolen!*' the King exclaimed, turning to the jury, who instantly made a memorandum of the fact.[4]

'I keep them to sell,' the Hatter added as an explanation: 'I've none of my own. I'm a hatter.'

Here the Queen put on her spectacles, and began staring hard at the Hatter, who turned pale and fidgeted.

'Give your evidence,' said the King; 'and don't be nervous, or I'll have you executed on the spot.[5]

This did not seem to encourage the witness at all: he kept shifting from one foot to the other, looking uneasily at the Queen, and in his confusion he bit a large piece out of his teacup instead of the bread-and-butter.

Who Stole the Tarts?

Just at this moment Alice felt a very curious sensation, which puzzled her a good deal until she made out what it was: she was beginning to grow larger again, and she thought at first she would get up and leave the court; but on second thoughts she decided to remain where she was as long as there was room for her.

'I wish you wouldn't squeeze so,' said the Dormouse, who was sitting next to her. 'I can hardly breathe.'

'I can't help it,' said Alice very meekly: 'I'm growing.'

'You've no right to grow here,' said the Dormouse.

'Don't talk nonsense,' said Alice more boldly: 'you know you're growing too.'[6]

'Yes, but I grow at a reasonable pace,' said the Dormouse: 'not in that ridiculous fashion.' And he got up very sulkily and crossed over to the other side of the court.

All this time the Queen had never left off staring at the Hatter, and, just as the Dormouse crossed the court, she said to one of the officers of the court, 'Bring me the list of the singers in the last concert!' on which the wretched Hatter trembled so, that he shook both his shoes off.

'Give your evidence,' the King repeated angrily, 'or I'll have you executed, whether you're nervous or not.'

6. Another example of *argumentum ad glirem* (*tu quoque*, or 'same to you' variety), rebutted by pointing out that the cases are not alike.

7. Homophonic ambiguity once more. (Sutherland, p. 175)

8. An effective sarcasm, but a bad argument (if so intended). The lexical ambiguity of *poor* here (between 'poor absolutely' and 'poor of its kind') is obvious enough, though the parallel inferences to the effect that a good man will necessarily make a good politician, or a bad man a bad one, still regularly impose on the unsophisticated at election-time.

'I'm a poor man, your Majesty,' the Hatter began, in a trembling voice, '— and I hadn't begun my tea — not above a week or so — and what with the bread-and-butter getting so thin — and the twinkling of the tea ——'

'The twinkling of the *what*?' said the King.

'It *began* with the tea,' the Hatter replied.

'Of course twinkling begins with a T!'[7] said the King sharply. 'Do you take me for a dunce? Go on!'

'I'm a poor man,' the Hatter went on, 'and most things twinkled after that — only the March Hare said ——'

'I didn't!' the March Hare interrupted in a great hurry.

'You did!' said the Hatter.

'I deny it!' said the March Hare.

'He denies it,' said the King: 'leave out that part.'

'Well, at any rate, the Dormouse said ——' the Hatter went on, looking anxiously round to see if he would deny it too: but the Dormouse denied nothing, being fast asleep.

'After that,' continued the Hatter, 'I cut some more bread-and-butter ——'

'But what did the Dormouse say?' one of the jury asked.

'That I can't remember,' said the Hatter.

'You *must* remember,' remarked the King, 'or I'll have you executed.'

The miserable Hatter dropped his teacup and bread-and-butter, and went down on one knee. 'I'm a poor man, your Majesty,' he began.

'You're a *very* poor *speaker*,' said the King.[8]

Here one of the guinea-pigs cheered, and was immediately suppressed by the officers of the court. (As that is rather a hard word, I will just explain to you how it was done. They had a large canvas bag which tied up at the mouth with strings: into this they slipped the guinea-pig, head first, and then sat upon it.)

'I'm glad I've seen that done,' thought Alice. 'I've so often read in the newspapers, at the end of trials, "There was some attempt at applause, which was immediately suppressed by the officers of the court," and I never understood what it meant till now.'[9]

'If that's all you know about it, you may stand down,' continued the King.

'I can't go no lower,' said the Hatter: 'I'm on the floor, as it is.'[10]

'Then you may *sit* down,' the King replied.

Here the other guinea-pig cheered, and was suppressed.

'Come, that finishes the guinea-pigs!' thought Alice. 'Now we shall get on better.'

'I'd rather finish my tea,' said the Hatter, with an anxious look at the Queen, who was reading the list of singers.

9. Cited by Pitcher (in Fann, p. 322) as an illustration of Wittgenstein's claim that an ostensive definition is always liable to be misunderstood. Alice takes the treatment of the guinea-pig to be a classic or paradigm instance of courtroom suppression, and so gets a somewhat distorted impression of the term's meaning as a description of proceedings in other and less eccentric tribunals than that depicted here.

10. The King's idiom is interpreted literally and in terms that make obedience impossible, since wherever the Hatter may happen to be standing he is in immediate contact with what is beneath him, and can 'go no lower' than he is already.

'You may go,' said the King; and the Hatter hurriedly left the court, without even waiting to put his shoes on.

'— and just take his head off outside,' the Queen added to one of the officers; but the Hatter was out of sight before the officer could get to the door.

'Call the next witness!' said the King.

The next witness was the Duchess's cook. She carried the pepper-box in her hand, and Alice guessed who it was, even before she got into the court, by the way the people near the door began sneezing all at once.

'Give your evidence,' said the King.

'Shan't,' said the cook.

The King looked anxiously at the White Rabbit, who said in a low voice, 'Your Majesty must cross-examine *this* witness.'

'Well, if I must, I must,' the King said with a melancholy air, and, after folding his arms and frowning at the cook till his eyes were nearly out of sight, he said in a deep voice, 'What are tarts made of?'

'Pepper, mostly,' said the cook.

'Treacle,' said a sleepy voice behind her.

'Collar that Dormouse,' the Queen shrieked out. 'Behead that Dormouse! Turn that Dormouse out of court! Suppress him! Pinch him! Off with his whiskers!'

For some minutes the whole court was in confusion, getting the Dormouse turned out, and, by the time they had settled down again, the cook had disappeared.

'Never mind!' said the King, with an air of great relief. 'Call the next witness.' And, he added in an undertone to the Queen, 'Really, my dear, *you* must cross-examine the next witness. It quite makes my forehead ache!'

Alice watched the White Rabbit as he fumbled over the list, feeling very curious to see what the next witness would be like, '— for they haven't got much evidence *yet*,' she said to herself. Imagine her surprise, when the White Rabbit read out, at the top of his shrill little voice, the name 'Alice!'

CHAPTER XII

ALICE'S EVIDENCE

'HERE!' cried Alice, quite forgetting in the flurry of the moment how large she had grown in the last few minutes, and she jumped up in such a hurry that she tipped over the jury-box with the edge of her skirt, upsetting all the jury-men on to the heads of the crowd below, and there they lay sprawling about, reminding her very much of a globe of gold-fish she had accidentally upset the week before.

'Oh, I *beg* your pardon!' she exclaimed in a tone of great dismay, and began picking them up again as quickly as she could, for the accident of the gold-fish kept running in her head, and she had a vague sort of idea that they must be collected at once and put back into the jury-box, or they would die.[1]

'The trial cannot proceed,' said the King in a very grave voice, 'until all the jurymen are back in their proper places — *all*,' he repeated with great emphasis, looking hard at Alice as he said so.

Alice looked at the jury-box, and saw that, in her haste, she had put the Lizard in head downwards, and the poor little thing was waving its tail about in a melancholy way, being quite unable to move. She soon got it out again, and put it right; 'not that it signifies much,' she said to herself; 'I should think it would be *quite* as much use in the trial one way up as the other.'[2]

As soon as the jury had a little recovered from the shock of being upset, and their slates and pencils had been found

1. A clear case of the association of ideas by resemblance, leading, as it often does, to a less than rational course of conduct, from the strictly causal point of view.

2. In other words, $0 = 0$. The irony is uncharacteristic, but Alice's *Weltanschauung* is already growing markedly more sceptical and sophisticated, as she reverts to normal size.

and handed back to them, they set to work very diligently to write out a history of the accident, all except the Lizard, who seemed too much overcome to do anything but sit with its mouth open, gazing up into the roof of the court.

'What do you know about this business?' the King said to Alice.

'Nothing,' said Alice.

'Nothing *whatever*?' persisted the King.

'Nothing whatever,' said Alice.

'That's very important,' the King said, turning to the jury. They were just beginning to write this down on their slates, when the White Rabbit interrupted: '*Un*important, your Majesty means, of course,' he said in a very respectful tone, but frowning and making faces at him as he spoke.

'*Un*important, of course, I meant,' the King hastily said, and went on to himself in an undertone, 'important — unimportant — unimportant — important ——' as if he were trying which word sounded best.

Some of the jury wrote it down 'important', and some 'unimportant'.[3] Alice could see this, as she was near enough to look over their slates; 'but it doesn't matter a bit,' she thought to herself.

At this moment the King, who had been for some time busily writing in his note-book, called out 'Silence!' and read out from his book, 'Rule Forty-two. *All persons more than a mile high to leave the court.*'

Everybody looked at Alice.

'*I'm* not a mile high,' said Alice.

'You are,' said the King.

'Nearly two miles high,' added the Queen.

'Well, I shan't go, at any rate,' said Alice: 'besides, that's not a regular rule: you invented it just now.'

'It's the oldest rule in the book,' said the King.

'Then it ought to be Number One,' said Alice.[4]

The King turned pale, and shut his note-book hastily. 'Consider your verdict,' he said to the jury, in a low trembling voice.

'There's more evidence to come yet, please your

3. Obedient slaves to the law of excluded middle, the jury presume that it must be one or the other. The King's vacillations are more creditable, though their causes are beyond him. If Alice knows nothing whatever of the business, her evidence can have no relevance, let alone importance, to the case. But the *fact* of her ignorance, like the alibi of a suspect, might well be of crucial importance in removing her from the proceedings or redirecting the course of enquiry, however little it may contribute to the solution of the crime. (Sutherland, pp. 127*ff*.; Shibles, p. 44)

4. Alice begins by denying that she is a case under the rule; then refuses to obey it; then contests its validity as a piece of retrospective legislation; and finally demolishes its claim to be anything else. A compelling argument, much above her usual standard, and its success is gratifyingly complete. The King, outmaneuvered, collapses, and Rule 42 is strangled at birth.

5. The King of Hearts, like the White King, has endured much ridicule from philosophers for treating nobody as a person, and thus hypostatizing the null class. But the cases are slightly different. Seeing 'nobody on the road,' which the White King supposes Alice to do (p. 200), commits him to the existence of a walking and visible nonentity for her to see. But anyone can write a letter to nobody by forgetting to address the envelope, or by directing it hopefully to Santa Claus or Prester John, without being thereby committed to the existence of any, or no, such addressee. (Sutherland, p. 199)

6. The King begs the question of authorship by assuming the paper to be a Knavish forgery. When informed that the document is unsigned, he continues on the same assumption, and construes nonsignature as further evidence of guilt, much as a Baconian supposes Bacon's failure to make mention of Shakespeare's plays to be sure evidence that he wrote them himself. The formal argument relied on is this: if the Knave writes anything, and is honest, he signs it; he has not signed the present document; therefore (by *modus tollens*), he is not both the writer and honest. But this allows him to be either not honest or not the writer (or both), and only on the prior assumption that he *is* the writer does it follow (by a disjunctive argument) that he is not honest. (Alexander, pp. 560-61; Shibles, p. 44)

Majesty,' said the White Rabbit, jumping up in a great hurry: 'this paper has just been picked up.'

'What's in it?' said the Queen.

'I haven't opened it yet,' said the White Rabbit, 'but it seems to be a letter, written by the prisoner to — to somebody.'

'It must have been that,' said the King, 'unless it was written to nobody, which isn't usual, you know.'[5]

'Who is it directed to?' said one of the jurymen.

'It isn't directed at all,' said the White Rabbit; 'in fact, there's nothing written on the *outside*.' He unfolded the paper as he spoke, and added, 'It isn't a letter, after all: it's a set of verses.'

'Are they in the prisoner's handwriting?' asked another of the jurymen.

'No, they're not,' said the White Rabbit, 'and that's the queerest thing about it.' (The jury all looked puzzled.)

'He must have imitated somebody else's hand,' said the King. (The jury all brightened up again.)

'Please your Majesty,' said the Knave, 'I didn't write it, and they can't prove I did: there's no name signed at the end.'

'If you didn't sign it,' said the King, 'that only makes the matter worse. You *must* have meant some mischief, or else you'd have signed your name like an honest man.'[6]

There was a general clapping of hands at this: it was the first really clever thing the King had said that day.

'That *proves* his guilt,' said the Queen.

'It proves nothing of the sort!' said Alice. 'Why, you don't even know what they're about!'

'Read them,' said the King.

The White Rabbit put on his spectacles. 'Where shall I begin, please your Majesty?' he asked.

'Begin at the beginning,' the King said gravely, 'and go on till you come to the end: then stop.'[7]

These were the verses the White Rabbit read: —

> *'They told me you had been to her,*
> *And mentioned me to him:*
> *She gave me a good character,*
> *But said I could not swim.*
>
> *He sent them word I had not gone,*
> *(We know it to be true):*
> *If she should push the matter on,*
> *What would become of you?*
>
> *I gave her one, they gave him two,*
> *You gave us three or more;*
> *They all returned from him to you,*
> *Though they were mine before.*
>
> *If I or she should chance to be*
> *Involved in this affair,*
> *He trusts to you to set them free,*
> *Exactly as we were.*
>
> *My notion was that you had been*
> *(Before she had this fit)*
> *An obstacle that came between*
> *Him, and ourselves, and it.*
>
> *Don't let him know she liked them best,*
> *For this must ever be*
> *A secret, kept from all the rest,*
> *Between yourself and me.'*

7. An early example of an algorithm, or instruction for programing a modern computer. Since the wits of these machines, though speedy, are approximately those of a rabbit, it will be seen that there is nothing at all odd about the use of such an instruction in the present case. (Hoffman [22], p. 9; Kemeny [24], p. 259)

8. Alice belongs to that self-denying school of literary criticism for which a poem is just a heap of words to be interpreted as they stand without regard to the author's intention. Given the limitations of her method, her scepticism is natural, though needlessly extreme, for the verses plainly record an intrigue of some kind, even if the details are too complex and uncoordinated to be readily understood. The primary difficulty is to find suitable referents for the various pronouns, and this, in fact, is precisely what the King attempts to do. There is no real lack of atomic propositions in the text; it is their molecular arrangement and the cash value of their 'egocentric particulars' (to use Russell's terminology for personal pronouns and the like), which still continue in doubt.

9. The King seems to be reasoning on the Kantian principle that 'ought implies can.' If this is so, then (by *modus tollens*) there can be no obligation to try to do the impossible. Nobody (and he alone) is required to find the solution to a pseudo-problem. The only difficulty, as the King recognizes, is to be perfectly sure that the problem is not a real one. (Kemeny [24], p. 187)

'That's the most important piece of evidence we've heard yet,' said the King, rubbing his hands; 'so now let the jury ——'

'If any one of them can explain it,' said Alice, (she had grown so large in the last few minutes that she wasn't a bit afraid of interrupting him,) 'I'll give him sixpence. *I* don't believe there's an atom of meaning in it.'[8]

The jury all wrote down on their slates, '*She* doesn't believe there's an atom of meaning in it,' but none of them attempted to explain the paper.

'If there's no meaning in it,' said the King, 'that saves a world of trouble, you know, as we needn't try to find any.[9] And yet I don't know,' he went on, spreading out the verses on his knee, and looking at them with one eye;

'I seem to see some meaning in them, after all. "— *said I could not swim —*" you can't swim, can you?' he added, turning to the Knave.

The Knave shook his head sadly. 'Do I look like it?' he said. (Which he certainly did *not*, being made entirely of cardboard.)

'All right, so far,' said the King, and he went on muttering over the verses to himself: '"*We know it to be true —*" that's the jury, of course —"*I gave her one, they gave him two —*" why, that must be what he did with the tarts, you know ——'

'But it goes on "*they all returned from him to you*",' said Alice.

'Why, there they are!' said the King triumphantly, pointing to the tarts on the table. 'Nothing can be clearer than *that*. Then again — "*before she had this fit —*" you never had fits, my dear, I think?' he said to the Queen.

'Never!' said the Queen furiously, throwing an inkstand at the Lizard as she spoke. (The unfortunate little Bill had left off writing on his slate with one finger, as he found it made no mark, but he now hastily began again, using the ink, that was trickling down his face, as long as it lasted.)

'Then the words don't *fit* you,' said the King, looking round the court with a smile. There was a dead silence.

'It's a pun!' the King added in an offended tone, and everybody laughed.[10]

'Let the jury consider their verdict,' the King said, for about the twentieth time that day.

'No, no!' said the Queen. 'Sentence first — verdict afterwards.'[11]

'Stuff and nonsense!' said Alice loudly. 'The idea of having the sentence first!'

10. The only recorded instance in Wonderland of a declared and deliberate pun, and even then it has to be pointed out before anyone is able to recognize it. The concept itself is not unknown, but the inability to apply it to any actual cases makes it well-nigh useless in practice.

11. A hysteron-proteron (or 'cart before the horse' type of utterance) which defies all recognized authority on the matter, and provokes Alice, for the second time, into a grave contempt of court. The White Queen, an unrecognized authority, agrees with and even outdoes the Queen of Hearts, since in her view punishment should come first of all (p. 178). But then the world she inhabits is hysterico-proterous throughout, whereas the temporal order in Wonderland, when there is any at all, is directed 'forward,' just as it is elsewhere.

'Hold your tongue!' said the Queen, turning purple.

'I won't!' said Alice.

'Off with her head!' the Queen shouted at the top of her voice. Nobody moved.

'Who cares for you?' said Alice, (she had grown to her full size by this time). 'You're nothing but a pack of cards!'

At this the whole pack rose up into the air, and came flying down upon her: she gave a little scream, half of fright and half of anger, and tried to beat them off, and found herself lying on the bank, with her head in the lap of her sister, who was gently brushing away some dead leaves that had fluttered down from the trees upon her face.

'Wake up, Alice dear!' said her sister. 'Why, what a long sleep you've had!'

'Oh, I've had such a curious dream!' said Alice, and she told her sister, as well as she could remember them, all these strange Adventures of hers that you have just been reading about; and when she had finished, her sister kissed her, and said 'It *was* a curious dream, dear, certainly: but now run in to your tea; it's getting late.' So Alice got up and ran off, thinking while she ran, as well she might, what a wonderful dream it had been.

———

The
Philosopher's
Alice

———

But her sister sat still just as she left her, leaning her head on her hand, watching the setting sun, and thinking of little Alice and all her wonderful Adventures, till she too began dreaming after a fashion, and this was her dream: —[12]

First, she dreamed of little Alice herself, and once again the tiny hands were clasped upon her knee, and the bright eager eyes were looking up into hers — she could hear the very tones of her voice, and see that queer little toss of her head to keep back the wandering hair that *would* always get into her eyes — and still as she listened, or seemed to listen, the whole place around her became alive with the strange creatures of her little sister's dream.

The long grass rustled at her feet as the White Rabbit hurried by — the frightened Mouse splashed his way through the neighbouring pool — she could hear the rattle of the teacups as the March Hare and his friends shared their never-ending meal, and the shrill voice of the Queen ordering off her unfortunate guests to execution — once more the pig-baby was sneezing on the Duchess' knee, while plates and dishes crashed around it — once more the shriek of the Gryphon, the squeaking of the Lizard's slate-pencil, and the choking of the suppressed guinea-pigs, filled the air, mixed up with the distant sobs of the miserable Mock Turtle.

So she sat on with closed eyes, and half believed herself in Wonderland, though she knew she had but to open them again, and all would change to dull reality — the grass would be only rustling in the wind, and the pool rippling to the waving of the reeds — the rattling teacups would change to the tinkling sheep-bells, and the Queen's shrill cries to the voice of the shepherd boy — and the

12. Misled, perhaps, by a phrase in Carroll's earlier version of the story, Gardner (p. 163) refers to this passage as a dream-within-a-dream, though this is at once amended to the more accurate description of it as a dream of (or about) a dream. More exactly still (as Carroll is careful to explain) it is a reverie ('dreaming after a fashion'), in which a thoroughly naturalistic explanation is offered for the incidents of Alice's dream, which are thereby reduced, with considerable banality, to mere unconscious elaborations of subliminally perceived field and farmyard noises. The sources of this theory (which Carroll perhaps accepted) should be looked for in Hobbes (*Leviathan*, Bk. I, Ch. 2) rather than in Freud.

sneeze of the baby, the shriek of the Gryphon, and all the other queer noises, would change (she knew) to the confused clamour of the busy farm-yard — while the lowing of the cattle in the distance would take the place of the Mock Turtle's heavy sobs.

Lastly, she pictured to herself how this same little sister of hers would, in the after-time, be herself a grown woman; and how she would keep, through all her riper years, the simple and loving heart of her childhood: and how she would gather about her other little children, and make *their* eyes bright and eager with many a strange tale, perhaps even with the dream of Wonderland of long ago: and how she would feel with all their simple sorrows, and find a pleasure in all their simple joys, remembering her own child-life, and the happy summer days.

THE END

Part II

Through The Looking-Glass

AND WHAT ALICE FOUND THERE

CHILD of the pure unclouded brow
    And dreaming eyes of wonder!
Though time be fleet, and I and thou
    Are half a life asunder,
Thy loving smile will surely hail
The love-gift of a fairy-tale.

I have not seen thy sunny face,
    Nor heard thy silver laughter;
No thought of me shall find a place
    In thy young life's hereafter —
Enough that now thou wilt not fail
To listen to my fairy-tale.

A tale begun in other days,
    When summer suns were glowing —
A simple chime, that served to time
    The rhythm of our rowing —
Whose echoes live in memory yet,
Though envious years would say 'forget'.

Come, hearken then, ere voice of dread,
    With bitter tidings laden,
Shall summon to unwelcome bed
    A melancholy maiden!
We are but older children, dear,
Who fret to find our bedtime near.

Without, the frost, the blinding snow,
   The storm-wind's moody madness —
Within, the firelight's ruddy glow
   And childhood's nest of gladness.
The magic words shall hold thee fast:
Thou shalt not heed the raving blast.

And though the shadow of a sigh
   May tremble through the story,
For 'happy summer days' gone by,
   And vanish'd summer glory —
It shall not touch with breath of bale
The pleasance of our fairy-tale.

DRAMATIS PERSONÆ

(As arranged before commencement of game.)

WHITE		RED	
PIECES	PAWNS	PAWNS	PIECES
Tweedledee	Daisy	Daisy . .	Humpty Dumpty
Unicorn	Haigha	Messenger .	Carpenter
Sheep	Oyster	Oyster . .	Walrus
W. Queen	'Lily'	Tiger-lily .	R. Queen
W. King.	Fawn	Rose . . .	R. King
Aged man	Oyster	Oyster . .	Crow
W. Knight	Hatta	Frog . . .	R. Knight
Tweedledum . . .	Daisy	Daisy . .	Lion

White Pawn (Alice) to play, and win in eleven moves.

The Philosopher's Alice

126

PREFACE

As the chess problem has puzzled some of my readers, it may be well to explain that it is correctly worked out, so far as the *moves* are concerned.[1] The *alternation* of Red and White is perhaps not so strictly observed as it might be, and the 'castling' of the three Queens is merely a way of saying that they entered the palace: but the 'check' of the White King at move 6, the capture of the Red Knight at move 7, and the final 'checkmate' of the Red King, will be found, by any one who will take the trouble to set the pieces and play the moves as directed, to be strictly in accordance with the laws of the game.

The new words, in the poem 'Jabberwocky' (see p. 154), have given rise to some differences of opinion as to their pronunciation: so it may be as well to give instructions on *that* point also. Pronounce 'slithy' as if it were two words 'sly, the': make the 'g' *hard* in 'gyre' and 'gimble': and pronounce 'rath' to rhyme with 'bath'.

Christmas, 1896.

---

1. A full discussion of the moves in this game and of their relation to the plot will be found in Gardner, pp. 170*ff.*, and *passim.*

CHAPTER I

LOOKING-GLASS HOUSE

ONE thing was certain, that the *white* kitten had had nothing to do with it: — it was the black kitten's fault entirely. For the white kitten had been having its face washed by the old cat for the last quarter of an hour (and bearing it pretty well, considering); so you see that it *couldn't* have had any hand in the mischief.

The way Dinah washed her children's faces was this: first she held the poor thing down by its ear with one paw, and then with the other paw she rubbed its face all over, the wrong way, beginning at the nose: and just now, as I said, she was hard at work on the white kitten, which was lying quite still and trying to purr — no doubt feeling that it was all meant for its good.

But the black kitten had been finished with earlier in the afternoon, and so, while Alice was sitting curled up in a corner of the great arm-chair, half talking to herself and half asleep, the kitten had been having a grand game of romps with the ball of worsted Alice had been trying to wind up, and had been rolling it up and down till it had all come undone again; and there it was, spread over the hearthrug, all knots and tangles, with the kitten running after its own tail in the middle.

'Oh, you wicked wicked little thing!' cried Alice, catching up the kitten, and giving it a little kiss to make it understand that it was in disgrace. 'Really, Dinah ought to have taught you better manners! You *ought*, Dinah, you know you ought!' she added, looking reproachfully at the old cat, and speaking in as cross a voice as she could manage — and then she scrambled back into the arm-chair, taking the kitten and worsted with her, and began winding up the ball again. But she didn't get on very fast, as she was talking all the time, sometimes to the kitten, and sometimes to herself. Kitty sat very demurely on her knee, pretending to watch the progress of the winding, and now and then putting out one paw and gently touching the ball, as if it would be glad to help if it might.

'Do you know what to-morrow is, Kitty?' Alice began. 'You'd have guessed if you'd been up in the window with me —— only Dinah was making you tidy, so you couldn't. I was watching the boys getting in sticks for the bonfire — — and it wants plenty of sticks, Kitty! Only it got so cold, and it snowed so, they had to leave off. Never mind, Kitty, we'll go and see the bonfire to-morrow.' Here Alice wound two or three turns of the worsted round the kitten's neck, just to see how it would look: this led to a scramble, in which the ball rolled down upon the floor, and yards and yards of it got unwound again.

'Do you know, I was so angry, Kitty,' Alice went on, as soon as they were comfortably settled again, 'when I saw all the mischief you had been doing, I was very nearly opening the window, and putting you out into the snow! And you'd have deserved it, you little mischievous darling! What have you got to say for yourself? Now don't interrupt me!' she went on, holding up one finger. 'I'm going to tell you all your faults. Number one: you squeaked twice while Dinah was washing your face this morning. Now you can't deny it, Kitty, for I heard you! What's that you say?' (pretending that the kitten was speaking). 'Her paw went into your eye? Well, that's *your* fault, for keeping your eyes open — if you'd shut them tight up, it wouldn't have happened. Now don't make any more excuses, but listen! Number two: you pulled Snowdrop away by the tail just as I had put down the saucer of milk before her! What, you were thirsty, were you? How do you know she wasn't thirsty too? Now for number three: you unwound every bit of the worsted while I wasn't looking!

'That's three faults, Kitty, and you've not been punished for any of them yet. You know I'm saving up all your punishments for Wednesday week — Suppose they had saved up all *my* punishments!' she went on, talking more to herself than the kitten. 'What *would* they do at the end of a year? I should be sent off to prison, I suppose, when the day came. Or — let me see — suppose each punishment was to be going without a dinner: then, when the miserable day came, I should have to go without fifty dinners at once! Well, I shouldn't mind *that* much! I'd far rather go without them than eat them!' [1]

'Do you hear the snow against the window-panes, Kitty? How nice and soft it sounds! Just as if some one was kissing the window all over outside. I wonder if the snow *loves* the trees and fields, that it kisses them so gently? And then it covers them up snug, you know, with a white quilt; and perhaps it says "Go to sleep, darlings, till the summer comes again." And when they wake up in the summer, Kitty, they dress themselves all in green, and dance about —— whenever the wind blows ——oh,

1. A self-administered sophism, arrived at by way of a fallacy of composition. A property true of each individual member of a class is not necessarily true of them all, taken together. As Alice herself sees, a sequence of consecutive privations would be no privation at all if made to run concurrently. This would not be true, for example, of an accumulation of monetary fines, for there the inconvenience of a single large payment might well be greater than that of a number of small ones. But the inelastic nature of Alice's daily demand for dinners is such that the marginal utility of further dinners on a given day becomes negative almost at once, so that it is a positive boon to go without them.

that's very pretty!' cried Alice, dropping the ball of worsted to clap her hands. 'And I do so *wish* it was true! I'm sure the woods look sleepy in the autumn, when the leaves are getting brown.

'Kitty, can you play chess? Now, don't smile, my dear, I'm asking it seriously. Because, when we were playing just now, you watched just as if you understood it:[2] and when I said "Check!" you purred! Well, it *was* a nice check, Kitty, and really I might have won, if it hadn't been for that nasty Knight, that came wriggling down among my pieces. Kitty, dear, let's pretend ——' And here I wish I could tell you half the things Alice used to say, beginning with her favourite phrase 'Let's pretend.'[3] She had had quite a long argument with her sister only the day before — all because Alice had begun with 'Let's pretend we're kings and queens'; and her sister, who liked being very exact, had argued that they couldn't, because there were only two of them, and Alice had been reduced at last to say 'Well, *you* can be one of them then, and *I'll* be all the rest.' And once she had really frightened her old nurse by shouting suddenly in her ear, 'Nurse! Do let's pretend that I'm a hungry hyæna, and you're a bone!'

But this is taking us away from Alice's speech to the kitten. 'Let's pretend that you're the Red Queen, Kitty! Do you know, I think, if you sat up and folded your arms, you'd look exactly like her. Now do try, there's a dear!' And Alice got the Red Queen off the table, and set it up before the kitten as a model for it to imitate: however, the thing didn't succeed, principally, Alice said, because the kitten wouldn't fold its arms properly. So, to punish it, she held it up to the Looking-glass, that it might see how sulky it was '— and if you're not good directly,' she

2. The kitten has shown apparent interest in the game by watching the moves and making more-or-less appropriate noises. But this is a far cry from knowing that it is a game, that they are moves, and what game it is, let alone being able to make such moves correctly for oneself. The spectator's problem, of discovering the rules of a game by observation, and the converse difficulty of knowing of such a spectator whether his interest is intelligent, and whether he can or has been able to grasp the rules correctly, are favorite Wittgensteinian themes that here occur in combination.

3. 'Pretending' is another typically Wittgensteinian problem-concept, whose analysis has since been debated at length by Ryle, Austin, and many others. Alice is not actually pretending, in any strict sense, since she is not out to deceive anyone, even herself. 'Let's pretend,' as she uses it, is an invitation not to play-acting, daydreaming, or conspiracy to defraud, but rather to an act of fanciful supposition or make-believe whose only object is pleasure. The range of such supposition is very wide, but Alice's sister is probably right in thinking that it must have categorial limits and that the unity of consciousness would preclude imaginative identification with more than one other subject at a time.

4. The themes of mirror-image reversal and of corresponding inversions in the time-sequence are, of course, repeatedly if not very consistently employed throughout the narrative. The whole question of spatio-temporal asymmetry is a very curious one with ramifications in many fields of science, which Alice has often been called on to illustrate. The best-known philosophical discussions are those of Kant, who refers more than once to the phenomenon of 'incongruous counterparts' (pairs of objects with right-left asymmetry), and at one time thought it a proof of Newtonian absolute space. Later, however, he took it to justify his own celebrated thesis that spatiality is not a characteristic of things-in-themselves, but only of things as we perceive them (*Prolegomena to Any Future Metaphysics*, Sect. 13). (Further references and a good discussion are to be found in Gardner, pp. 180-84; the same author's *The Ambidextrous Universe* [rev. ed., 1969] is an excellent popular introduction to the 'ramifications' mentioned above.)

5. This would be a case of pretending in the fraudulent or deceptive sense, in which (maliciously or otherwise) there is at least an intention of creating in others a false expectation or belief.

6. On the probable composition and predictably disastrous effects of this beverage, see Gardner, p. 183.

added, 'I'll put you through into Looking-glass House. How would you like *that*?'

'Now, if you'll only attend, Kitty, and not talk so much, I'll tell you all my ideas about Looking-Glass House. First, there's the room you can see through the glass — that's just the same as our drawing-room, only the things go the other way.[4] I can see all of it when I get upon a chair — all but the bit just behind the fire-place. Oh! I do so wish I could see *that* bit! I want so much to know whether they've a fire in the winter: you never *can* tell, you know, unless our fire smokes, and then smoke comes up in that room too — but that may be only pretence, just to make it look as if they had a fire.[5] Well then, the books are something like our books, only the words go the wrong way; I know that, because I've held up one of our books to the glass, and then they hold up one in the other room.

'How would you like to live in Looking-glass House, Kitty? I wonder if they'd give you milk, there? Perhaps Looking-glass milk isn't good to drink [6]— But oh, Kitty! now we come to the passage. You can just see a little *peep* of the passage in Looking-glass House, if you leave the door of our drawing-room wide open: and it's very like our passage as far as you can see, only you know it may be quite different on beyond. Oh, Kitty! how nice it would be if we could only get through into Looking-glass House! I'm sure it's got, oh! such beautiful things in it! Let's pretend there's a way of getting through into it somehow, Kitty. Let's pretend the glass has got soft like gauze, so that we can get through. Why, it's turning into a sort of mist now, I declare! It'll be easy enough to get through ——' She was up on the chimney-piece while she said this, though she hardly knew how she had got there.

And certainly the glass *was* beginning to melt away, just like a bright silvery mist.

a fire in the fireplace, and she was quite pleased to find that there was a real one, and blazing away as brightly as

In another moment Alice was through the glass, and had jumped lightly down into the Looking-glass room. The very first thing she did was to look whether there was

the one she had left behind. 'So I shall be as warm here as I was in the old room,' thought Alice: 'warmer, in fact, because there'll be no one here to scold me away from the fire. Oh, what fun it'll be, when they see me through the glass in here, and can't get at me!'

Then she began looking about, and noticed that what could be seen from the old room was quite common and uninteresting, but that all the rest was as different as possible. For instance, the pictures on the wall next the fire seemed to be all alive, and the very clock on the chimney-piece (you know you can only see the back of it in the Looking-glass) had got the face of a little old man, and grinned at her.

'They don't keep this room so tidy as the other,' Alice thought to herself, as she noticed several of the chessmen down in the hearth among the cinders: but in another moment, with a little 'Oh!' of surprise, she was down on her hands and knees watching them. The chessmen were walking about, two and two!

'Here are the Red King and the Red Queen,' Alice said (in a whisper, for fear of frightening them), 'and there are the White King and the White Queen sitting on the edge of the shovel — and here are two Castles walking arm in arm — I don't think they can hear me,' she went on, as she put her head closer down, 'and I'm nearly sure they can't see me. I feel as if I were invisible ——'

Here something began squeaking on the table, and made Alice turn her head just in time to see one of the White Pawns roll over and begin kicking: she watched it with great curiosity to see what would happen next.

'It is the voice of my child!' the White Queen cried out, as she rushed past the King, so violently that she knocked him over among the cinders. 'My precious Lily! My imperial kitten!' and she began scrambling wildly up the side of the fender.

'Imperial fiddlestick!' said the King, rubbing his nose, which had been hurt by the fall. He had a right to be a *little* annoyed, for he was covered with ashes from head to foot.

Alice was very anxious to be of use, and, as the poor little Lily was nearly screaming herself into a fit, she hastily picked up the Queen and set her upon the table by the side of her noisy little daughter.

The Queen gasped, and sat down: the rapid journey through the air had quite taken away her breath, and for a minute or two she could do nothing but hug the little Lily in silence. As soon as she had recovered her breath a little, she called out to the White King, who was sitting sulkily among the ashes. 'Mind the volcano!'[7]

7. The White Queen's sudden levitation is just what she wanted, but it never occurs to her to suspect an intelligent agency behind it. Instead, she credits her arrival to a hastily invented (and none too likely) force of nature. The King, soon afterwards, does much the same in attributing his unintended memoranda not to another person, but to his own pencil. What seems on the face of it to be crass materialism is in fact more plausibly interpreted as a form of primitive animism. Looking-glass objects, like chessmen themselves, are quite commonly found to be animate; the normally sharp distinction between things and persons is therefore much less in evidence than it would otherwise tend to be.

'What volcano?' said the King, looking up anxiously into the fire, as if he thought that was the most likely place to find one.

'Blew —— me —— up,' panted the Queen, who was still a little out of breath. 'Mind you come up —— the regular way —— don't get blown up!'

Alice watched the White King as he slowly struggled up from bar to bar, till at last she said, 'Why, you'll be hours and hours getting to the table, at that rate. I'd far better help you, hadn't I?' But the King took no notice of the question: it was quite clear that he could neither hear her nor see her.

So Alice picked him up very gently, and lifted him across more slowly than she had lifted the Queen, that she mightn't take his breath away: but, before she put him on the table, she thought she might as well dust him a little, he was so covered with ashes.

She said afterwards that she had never seen in all her life such a face as the King made, when he found himself held in the air by an invisible hand, and being dusted: he was far too much astonished to cry out, but his eyes and his mouth went on getting larger and larger, and rounder and rounder, till her hand shook so with laughing that she nearly let him drop upon the floor.

'Oh! *please* don't make such faces, my dear!' she cried out, quite forgetting that the King couldn't hear her. 'You make me laugh so that I can hardly hold you! And don't keep your mouth so wide open! All the ashes will get into it — there, now I think you're tidy enough!' she added, as she smoothed his hair, and set him down very carefully upon the table near the Queen.

The Philosopher's Alice

Through the Looking-glass

8. The White King's statement is closely analogous to Russell's well-known allegation that the present King of France is bald. Merely to deny it will hardly do, since (in the White King's instance) that would imply that, although he *has* whiskers, he did not turn cold to the very ends of them. Russell's theory of descriptions was devised for just such a situation as this, but the White Queen will have none of it. Taking a leaf from Strawson's 'On Referring' (*Mind*, July 1950), she simply denies the suppressed premise that her consort has any whiskers to turn cold to the ends of. Hence the question of how far along them he did turn cold is a question that does not arise.

The Philosopher's Alice

136

The King immediately fell flat on his back, and lay perfectly still: and Alice was a little alarmed at what she had done, and went round the room to see if she could find any water to throw over him. However, she could find nothing but a bottle of ink, and when she got back with it she found he had recovered, and he and the Queen were talking together in a frightened whisper — so low, that Alice could hardly hear what they said.

The King was saying 'I assure you, my dear, I turned cold to the very ends of my whiskers!'

To which the Queen replied, 'You haven't got any whiskers.'[8]

'The horror of that moment,' the King went on, 'I shall never, *never* forget!'

9. Unforgettable feelings should need no recording; persuaded, however, that they *are* forgettable, the King takes steps to record them, though his effort is not a success. Whether it would have helped him if he *had* succeeded, is a sentiment open to doubt. Wittgenstein ([48] § 258*ff.*) has a man who keeps similar records in his diary of the recurrence of a particular sensation, but then has the puzzle of telling (since he cannot compare them) that the sensations are in fact the same. The King would be no better off. For how is he to know, on consulting his memorandum, that what he now remembers feeling is in any way like what he originally felt? The Queen can tell that his attempted memorandum is all wrong. But can *anyone* tell, even of a better memorandum, that it is all right? (Sutherland, p. 54; Purtill [35], p. 21)

'You will, though,' the Queen said, 'if you don't make a memorandum of it.'

Alice looked on with great interest as the King took an enormous memorandum-book out of his pocket, and began writing.[9] A sudden thought struck her, and she took hold of the end of the pencil, which came some way over his shoulder, and began writing for him.

The poor King looked puzzled and unhappy, and struggled with the pencil for some time without saying anything; but Alice was too strong for him, and at last he panted out, 'My dear! I really *must* get a thinner pencil. I can't manage this one a bit; it writes all manner of things that I don't intend ——'

'What manner of things?' said the Queen, looking over the book (in which Alice had put "*The White Knight is sliding down the poker. He balances very badly*"). 'That's not a memorandum of *your* feelings!'

There was a book lying near Alice on the table, and while she sat watching the White King (for she was still a little anxious about him, and had the ink all ready to

throw over him, in case he fainted again), she turned over the leaves, to find some part that she could read, '— for it's all in some language I don't know,' she said to herself.

It was like this.

JABBERWOCKY.

'Twas brillig, and the slithy toves
Did gyre and gimble in the wabe;
All mimsy were the borogoves,
And the mome raths outgrabe.

She puzzled over this for some time, but at last a bright thought struck her. 'Why, it's a Looking-glass book, of course! And if I hold it up to a glass, the words will all go the right way again.'

This was the poem that Alice read.

JABBERWOCKY.

'Twas brillig, and the slithy toves
Did gyre and gimble in the wabe;
All mimsy were the borogoves,
And the mome raths outgrabe.

'Beware the Jabberwock, my son!
The jaws that bite, the claws that catch!
Beware the Jubjub bird, and shun
The frumious Bandersnatch!'

He took his vorpal sword in hand:
Long time the manxome foe he sought —
So rested he by the Tumtum tree,
And stood awhile in thought.

The
Philosopher's
Alice

———

138

10. The most curious thing about this poem is that, though everybody agrees that it is great nonsense, nobody is prepared to leave it that way. Carroll himself, Humpty Dumpty, and a host of succeeding commentators, have labored diligently to invent or discover meanings for its unfamiliar terms. (Gardner gives all the details, pp. 191-97). Once this is done, of course, it ceases to be nonsense (a point well made by Spacks, p. 95), and becomes a mere philological puzzle. Apart from the obscure first stanza, there is in fact no difficulty in following out the events of the poem—a sorry tale of the destruction of innocent wildlife. Alice's aesthetic reaction to it is deplorable, but at least she responds appropriately to the combination of clear structure with defective elements of reference and description. Unlike the critics, she does not attempt to supply the missing images, but indulges instead in a bout of 'imageless thought.'

It is significant, also, that of all the many translations, the German *Der Jammerwoch* (Gardner, pp. 193-94) is easily the best. In no other language is elaboration of structure so readily compatible with entire absence of meaning. (Sutherland, pp. 208*ff*.; Holmes, p. 136; Carney and Scheer [11], p. 129; Eddington [13], pp. 280-81; [14], pp. 255-56; High [21], p. 52)

Through the Looking-glass

And as in uffish thought he stood,
   The Jabberwock, with eyes of flame,
Came whiffling through the tulgey wood,
   And burbled as it came!

One, two! One, two! And through and through
   The vorpal blade went snicker-snack!
He left it dead, and with its head
   He went galumphing back.

'And hast thou slain the Jabberwock?
   Come to my arms, my beamish boy!
O frabjous day! Callooh! Callay!'
   He chortled in his joy.

'Twas brillig, and the slithy toves
   Did gyre and gimble in the wabe;
All mimsy were the borogoves,
   And the mome raths outgrabe.

'It seems very pretty,' she said when she had finished it, 'but it's *rather* hard to understand!' (You see, she didn't like to confess even to herself, that she couldn't make it out at all). 'Somehow it seems to fill my head with ideas — only I don't exactly know what they are! However, *somebody* killed *something*: that's clear, at any rate ——'[10]

'But oh!' thought Alice, suddenly jumping up, 'if I don't make haste I shall have to go back through the Looking-glass, before I've seen what the rest of the house is like! Let's have a look at the garden first!' She was out of the room in a moment, and ran downstairs — or, at least, it wasn't exactly running, but a new invention for getting downstairs quickly and easily, as Alice said to herself. She just kept the tips of her fingers on the hand-rail, and floated gently down without even touching the stairs with her feet; then she floated on through the hall, and would have gone straight out at the door in the same way, if she hadn't caught hold of the door-post. She was getting a little giddy with so much floating in the air, and was rather glad to find herself walking again in the natural way.

CHAPTER II

THE GARDEN OF LIVE FLOWERS

'I SHOULD see the garden far better,' said Alice to herself, 'if I could get to the top of that hill: and here's a path that leads straight to it — at least, no, it doesn't do that ——' (after going a few yards along the path, and turning several sharp corners), 'but I suppose it will at last. But how curiously it twists! It's more like a cork-screw than a path! Well, *this* turn goes to the hill, I suppose — no, it doesn't! This goes straight back to the house! Well then, I'll try it the other way.'[1]

And so she did: wandering up and down, and trying turn after turn, but always coming back to the house, do what she would. Indeed, once, when she turned a corner rather more quickly than usual, she ran against it before she could stop herself.

'It's no use talking about it,' Alice said, looking up at the house and pretending it was arguing with her. 'I'm *not* going in again yet. I know I should have to get through the Looking-glass again — back into the old room — and there'd be an end of all my adventures!'

So, resolutely turning her back upon the house, she set out once more down the path, determined to keep straight on till she got to the hill. For a few minutes all went on well, and she was just saying, 'I really *shall* do it this time ——' when the path gave a sudden twist and shook itself (as she described it afterwards), and the next moment she found herself actually walking in at the door.

1. Alice's frustrations, like those of Kafka's heroes, spring not from errors of performance, but from a faulty method of approach. Philosophical and scientific perplexities are often attributable to the same cause. When all roads lead away from the objective and end in a common obstacle, it is generally time to start asking methodological questions and to reconsider the terms of the problem itself. What seems insoluble from one angle may be no problem at all from another, as Alice finds out in due course. (Kemeny [24], p. 85)

2. Alice shows surprise at a rational vegetable; the flowers show none at a mobile one, though they doubt its rationality. The reason, no doubt, is that, having only one category of organism to operate with (namely the vegetable), they are less inhibited by Aristotelian prejudices. Mobility and rationality, as they see it, are not essential differences that mark off new categories, but merely accidental properties, of which a flower may have either or both or neither without ceasing to be a flower.

'Oh, it's too bad!' she cried. 'I never saw such a house for getting in the way! Never!'

However, there was the hill full in sight, so there was nothing to be done but start again. This time she came upon a large flower-bed, with a border of daisies, and a willow-tree growing in the middle.

'O Tiger-lily,' said Alice, addressing herself to one that was waving gracefully about in the wind, 'I *wish* you could talk!'

'We *can* talk,' said the Tiger-lily: 'when there's anybody worth talking to.'

Alice was so astonished that she couldn't speak for a minute: it quite seemed to take her breath away.[2] At length, as the Tiger-lily only went on waving about, she spoke again, in a timid voice — almost in a whisper. 'And can *all* the flowers talk?'

'As well as *you* can,' said the Tiger-lily. 'And a great deal louder.'

'It isn't manners for us to begin, you know,' said the Rose, 'and I really was wondering when you'd speak! Said I to myself, "Her face has got *some* sense in it, though it's not a clever one!" Still, you're the right colour, and that goes a long way.'

'I don't care about the colour,' the Tiger-lily remarked. 'If only her petals curled up a little more, she'd be all right.'

Alice didn't like being criticised, so she began asking questions: 'Aren't you sometimes frightened at being planted out here, with nobody to take care of you?'

'There's the tree in the middle,' said the Rose. 'What else is it good for?'

'But what could it do, if any danger came?' Alice asked.

'It could bark,' said the Rose.

'It says "Bough-wough!"' cried a Daisy: 'that's why its branches are called boughs!"[3]

3. Another piece of false etymologizing. As in the 'tortoise' case (p. 92), the name *bough* is made to derive from an alleged activity (barking), itself punningly misinferred from the *bona fide* name of a standard feature of trees. (Sutherland, p. 143; Spacks, p. 93)

'Didn't you know *that*?' cried another Daisy, and here they all began shouting together, till the air seemed quite full of little shrill voices. 'Silence, every one of you!' cried the Tiger-lily, waving itself passionately from side to side, and trembling with excitement. 'They know I can't get at

4. Needless to say, it is not. Alice has been taken in as usual, this time by a false analogy based on the lexical ambiguity of *bed*, and has been induced to accept a Leibnizian theory of subliminal plant-consciousness. The Rose, like the Duchess, holds exactly the opposite view about Alice; and one has to admit that it is uncomfortably close to the truth.

them!' it panted, bending its quivering head towards Alice, 'or they wouldn't dare do it!'

'Never mind!' Alice said in a soothing tone, and stooping down to the daisies, who were just beginning again, she whispered 'If you don't hold your tongues, I'll pick you!'

There was silence in a moment, and several of the pink daisies turned white.

'That's right!' said the Tiger-lily. 'The daisies are worst of all. When one speaks, they all begin together, and it's enough to make one wither to hear the way they go on!'

'How is it you can all talk so nicely?' Alice said, hoping to get it into a better temper by a compliment. 'I've been in many gardens before, but none of the flowers could talk.'

'Put your hand down, and feel the ground,' said the Tiger-lily. 'Then you'll know why.'

Alice did so. 'It's very hard,' she said, 'but I don't see what that has to do with it.'

'In most gardens,' the Tiger-lily said, 'they make the beds too soft — so that the flowers are always asleep.'

This sounded a very good reason, and Alice was quite pleased to know it.[4] 'I never thought of that before!' she said.

'It's *my* opinion you never think *at all*,' the Rose said in a rather severe tone.

'I never saw anybody that looked stupider,' a Violet said, so suddenly that Alice quite jumped: for it hadn't spoken before.

'Hold *your* tongue!' cried the Tiger-lily. 'As if *you* ever saw anybody! You keep your head under the leaves, and snore away there till you know no more what's going on in the world than if you were a bud!'

*The
Philosopher's
Alice*

143

'Are there any more people in the garden besides me?' Alice said, not choosing to notice the Rose's last remark.

'There's one other flower in the garden that can move about like you,' said the Rose.[5] 'I wonder how you do it —' ('You're always wondering,' said the Tiger-lily), 'but she's more bushy than you are.'

'Is she like me?' Alice asked eagerly, for the thought crossed her mind, 'There's another little girl in the garden somewhere!'

'Well, she has the same awkward shape as you,' the Rose said: 'but she's redder — and her petals are shorter, I think.'

'Her petals are done up close, almost like a dahlia,' the Tiger-lily interrupted: 'not tumbled about anyhow, like yours.'

'But that's not *your* fault,' the Rose added kindly: 'you're beginning to fade, you know — and then one can't help one's petals getting a little untidy.'

Alice didn't like this idea at all: so, to change the subject, she asked 'Does she ever come out here?'

'I daresay you'll see her soon,' said the Rose. 'She's one of the thorny kind.'

'Where does she wear the thorns?' Alice asked with some curiosity.

'Why, all round her head, of course,' the Rose replied. 'I was wondering *you* hadn't got some too. I thought it was the regular rule.'

'She's coming!' cried the Larkspur. 'I hear her footstep, thump, thump, along the gravel-walk!'

Alice looked round eagerly, and found that it was the Red Queen. 'She's grown a good deal!' was her first remark. She had indeed: when Alice first found her in the

5. Possessing only a single category, the flowers see everything in the garden as vegetable, and consequently describe everything, including Alice, in botanical terms. Sutherland (p. 103) calls this misclassification, which is not entirely fair. The flowers must overwork the limited stock of concepts available to them, and so treat as alike things that are really different; their vocabulary is inadequate, but they do not blunder in the use of it, any more than children or primitives do.

ashes, she had been only three inches high — and here she was, half a head taller than Alice herself!

'It's the fresh air that does it,' said the Rose: 'wonderfully fine air it is, out here.'

'I think I'll go and meet her,' said Alice, for, though the flowers were very interesting, she felt that it would be far grander to have a talk with a real Queen.

'You can't possibly do that,' said the Rose: '*I* should advise you to walk the other way.'

This sounded nonsense to Alice, so she said nothing, but set off at once towards the Red Queen. To her surprise, she lost sight of her in a moment, and found herself walking in at the front door again.

A little provoked, she drew back and, after looking everywhere for the Queen (whom she spied out at last, a long way off), she thought she would try the plan, this time, of walking in the opposite direction.

It succeeded beautifully. She had not been walking a minute before she found herself face to face with the Red Queen, and full in sight of the hill she had been so long aiming at.

'Where do you come from?' said the Red Queen. 'And where are you going? Look up, speak nicely, and don't twiddle your fingers all the time.'

Alice attended to all these directions, and explained, as well as she could, that she had lost her way.

'I don't know what you mean by *your* way,' said the Queen: 'all the ways about here belong to *me* — but why did you come out here at all?' she added in a kinder tone. 'Curtsey while you're thinking what to say. It saves time.'

Alice wondered a little at this, but she was too much in awe of the Queen to disbelieve it. 'I'll try it when I go

home,' she thought to herself, 'the next time I'm a little late for dinner.'

'It's time for you to answer now,' the Queen said, looking at her watch: 'open your mouth a *little* wider when you speak, and always say "your Majesty".'

'I only wanted to see what the garden was like, your Majesty ——'

'That's right,' said the Queen, patting her on the head, which Alice didn't like at all: 'though, when you say "garden", *I've* seen gardens, compared with which this would be a wilderness.'

Alice didn't dare to argue the point, but went on: '— and I thought I'd try and find my way to the top of that hill ——'

'When you say "hill",' the Queen interrupted, '*I* could show you hills, in comparison with which you'd call that a valley.'

'No, I shouldn't,' said Alice, surprised into contradicting her at last: 'a hill *can't* be a valley, you know.[6] That would be nonsense ——'

The Red Queen shook her head. 'You may call it "nonsense" if you like,' she said, 'but *I've* heard nonsense, compared with which that would be as sensible as a dictionary!'[7]

Alice curtseyed again, as she was afraid from the Queen's tone that she was a *little* offended: and they walked on in silence till they got to the top of the little hill.

For some minutes Alice stood without speaking, looking out in all directions over the country — and a most curious country it was. There were a number of little brooks running across from side to side, and the ground between was divided up into squares by a number of hedges, that reached from brook to brook.

'I declare it's marked out just like a large chess-board!' Alice said at last. 'There ought to be some men moving about somewhere — and so there are!' she added in a tone of delight, and her heart began to beat quick with excitement as she went on. 'It's a great game of chess that's being played — all over the world — if this *is* the world at all, you know. Oh, what fun it is! How I *wish* I was one of them! I wouldn't mind being a Pawn, if only I might join — though of course I should *like* to be a Queen, best.'

6. The terms *garden* and *wilderness* imply a contrast in degree of tidiness, yet the same plot could be described as either, depending on the horticultural standards employed. *Hill* and *valley*, though logically related, provide no such relative contrast in degree of hilliness (as *mountain* and *molehill* do); they are antithetical and mutually exclusive concepts, which no variation of standards could ever make applicable to the same thing. (Sutherland, pp. 177-78)

7. Alice, scenting a contradiction, calls it 'nonsense,' presumably in an absolute sense. The Red Queen, however, treats this, too, as an adjustable and relative term. Here she has more of a case, since various kinds of nonsense can be and have been distinguished, of which some might be considered more nonsensical than others. Compared with utter gibberish, a mere verbal contradiction might still make a modicum of sense. Much depends, therefore, on the criteria for nonsense employed. Alexander (p. 562) sees the Queen as engaging in stipulative (i.e., arbitrary) definition of the term, to give sense to her previous observation; whereas Alice has rejected it, in logical positivist fashion, as empirically unverifiable and therefore without meaning. If so, however, her case is no stronger than the Queen's, for if anyone ever indulged in stipulative definition of the word *nonsense*, it was surely the logical positivists. There is more to be said for Alexander's alternative view that Alice is not a positivist, and that her agonized '*can't* be a valley' protests not merely (as with treacle-wells) that 'there's no such thing,' but rather that the combination is a logically impossible one, which no manipulation of nonsense-standards could ever redeem into sense. (Sutherland, p. 128; Eddington [13], p. 330; Purtill [35], p. 21)

8. By begging her way into the game, Alice casts aside her free will. From now on she is involved as a Presbyterian pawn in a Calvinistic scheme of predestination, or, if preferred, as a proletarian one in a Marxian pilgrimage toward the classless society, whose necessary stages will shortly be expounded by the (significantly titled) Red Queen. Luckily for her, Alice is one of the elect, and can look forward to a saints' or workers' paradise, where all is feasting and fun.

9. An early taste of the implications of determinism. Salvation is not to be achieved by works. The revolution comes by historical necessity, and cannot be hastened by premature activism. Running will get you nowhere, either in Calvin's universe or Marx's. The same is true on the chessboard (which is all the author probably had in mind here). A piece may have the illusion of moving when it pleases, but cannot in fact leave its square until its moment has come and the decision to move it has been taken elsewhere.

She glanced rather shyly at the real Queen as she said this, but her companion only smiled pleasantly, and said 'That's easily managed. You can be the White Queen's Pawn, if you like, as Lily's too young to play; and you're in the Second Square to begin with: when you get into the Eighth Square you'll be a Queen ——'[8] Just at this moment, somehow or other, they began to run.

Alice never could quite make out, in thinking it over afterwards, how it was that they began: all she remembers is, that they were running hand in hand, and the Queen went so fast that it was all she could do to keep up with her: and still the Queen kept crying 'Faster!' but Alice felt she *could not* go faster, though she had no breath to say so.

The most curious part of the thing was that the trees and the other things round them never changed their places at all: however fast they went, they never seemed to pass anything.[9] 'I wonder if all the things move along

10. (Hoffman [22], p. 159; Kemeny [24], p. 174 [chapter headings])

with us?' thought poor puzzled Alice. And the Queen seemed to guess her thoughts, for she cried 'Faster! Don't try to talk!'

Not that Alice had any idea of doing *that*. She felt as if she would never be able to talk again, she was getting so out of breath: and still the Queen cried 'Faster! Faster!' and dragged her along. 'Are we nearly there?' Alice managed to pant out at last.

'Nearly there!' the Queen repeated. 'Why, we passed it ten minutes ago! Faster!' And they ran on for a time in silence, with the wind whistling in Alice's ears, and almost blowing her hair off her head, she fancied.

'Now! Now!' cried the Queen. 'Faster! Faster!' And they went so fast that at last they seemed to skim through the air, hardly touching the ground with their feet, till suddenly, just as Alice was getting quite exhausted, they stopped, and she found herself sitting on the ground, breathless and giddy.

11. In Gardner's opinion, the most frequently quoted passage in either book. Of especial value to all, such as politicians and businessmen, in whom professions of energy are unaccompanied by any tendency to progress. (Eddington [14], p. 219, in allusion to the problems of circumnavigating an expanding universe)

The Queen propped her against a tree, and said kindly, 'You may rest a little now.'

Alice looked round her in great surprise. 'Why, I do believe we've been under this tree all the time! Everything's just as it was!'

'Of course it is,' said the Queen: 'what would you have it?'

'Well, in *our* country,' said Alice, still panting a little, 'you'd generally get to somewhere else — if you ran very fast for a long time, as we've been doing.'

'A slow sort of country!' said the Queen. 'Now, *here*, you see, it takes all the running *you* can do, to keep in the same place. If you want to get somewhere else, you must run at least twice as fast as that!'[11]

'I'd rather not try, please!' said Alice. 'I'm quite content to stay here — only I *am* so hot and thirsty!'

'I know what *you'd* like!' the Queen said good-naturedly, taking a little box out of her pocket. 'Have a biscuit?'

Alice thought it would not be civil to say 'No,' though it wasn't at all what she wanted. So she took it, and ate it as well as she could: and it was *very* dry; and she thought she had never been so nearly choked in all her life.

'While you're refreshing yourself,' said the Queen, 'I'll just take the measurements.' And she took a ribbon out of her pocket, marked in inches, and began measuring out the ground, and sticking little pegs in here and there.

'At the end of two yards,' she said, putting in a peg to mark the distance, 'I shall give you your directions — have another biscuit?'

'No, thank you,' said Alice: 'one's *quite* enough!'

'Thirst quenched, I hope?' said the Queen.

The Philosopher's Alice

Alice did not know what to say to this, but luckily the Queen did not wait for an answer, but went on. 'At the end of *three* yards I shall repeat them — for fear of your forgetting them. At the end of *four*, I shall say good-bye. And at the end of *five*, I shall go!'

She had got all the pegs put in by this time, and Alice looked on with great interest as she returned to the tree, and then began slowly walking down the row.

At the two-yard peg she faced round, and said 'A pawn goes two squares in its first move. So you'll go *very* quickly through the Third Square — by railway, I should think — and you'll find yourself in the Fourth Square in no time. Well, *that* square belongs to Tweedledum and Tweedledee — the Fifth is mostly water — the Sixth belongs to Humpty Dumpty — But you make no remark?'

'I — I didn't know I had to make one — just then,' Alice faltered out.

'You *should* have said,' the Queen went on in a tone of grave reproof, '"It's extremely kind of you to tell me all this" — however, we'll suppose it said — the Seventh Square is all forest — however, one of the Knights will show you the way — and in the Eighth Square we shall be Queens together, and it's all feasting and fun!' Alice got up and curtseyed, and sat down again.

At the next peg the Queen turned again, and said 'Speak in French, when you can't think of the English for a thing — turn out your toes as you walk — and remember who you are!' She did not wait for Alice to curtsey this time, but walked on quickly to the next peg, where she turned to say 'good-bye', and then hurried on to the last.

How it happened, Alice never knew, but exactly as she came to the last peg, she was gone. Whether she vanished into the air, or ran quickly into the wood ('and she *can* run very fast!' thought Alice), there was no way of guessing, but she was gone, and Alice began to remember that she was a Pawn, and that it would soon be time to move.

CHAPTER III

LOOKING-GLASS INSECTS

OF course the first thing to do was to make a grand survey of the country she was going to travel through. 'It's something very like learning geography,' thought Alice, as she stood on tiptoe in hopes of being able to see a little further. 'Principal rivers — there *are* none. Principal mountains — I'm on the only one, but I don't think it's got any name. Principal towns — why, what *are* those creatures, making honey down there? They can't be bees — nobody ever saw bees a mile off, you know ——' and for some minutes, she stood silent, watching one of them that was bustling about among the flowers, poking its proboscis into them, 'just as if it was a regular bee', thought Alice.

However, this was anything but a regular bee: in fact, it was an elephant — as Alice soon found out, though the idea quite took her breath away at first. 'And what enormous flowers they must be!' was her next idea. 'Something like cottages with the roofs taken off, and stalks put to them — and what quantities of honey they must make! I think I'll go down and — no, I won't go *just* yet,' she went on, checking herself just as she was beginning to run down the hill, and trying to find some excuse for turning shy so suddenly. 'It'll never do to go down among them without a good long branch to brush them away — and what fun it'll be when they ask me how I liked my walk. I shall say — "Oh, I liked it well enough ——" (here

came the favourite little toss of the head), "only it was so dusty and hot, and the elephants did tease so!"'

'I think I'll go down the other way,' she said after a pause: 'and perhaps I may visit the elephants later on. Besides, I do so want to get into the Third Square!'

So with this excuse she ran down the hill and jumped over the first of the six little brooks.

*   *   *   *   *

    *   *   *   *

*   *   *   *   *

'Tickets, please!' said the Guard, putting his head in at at the window. In a moment everybody was holding out a ticket: they were about the same size as the people, and quite seemed to fill the carriage.

'Now then! Show your ticket, child!' the Guard went on, looking angrily at Alice. And a great many voices all said together ('like the chorus of a song,' thought Alice), 'Don't keep him waiting, child! Why, his time is worth a thousand pounds a minute!'

'I'm afraid I haven't got one,' Alice said in a frightened tone: 'there wasn't a ticket-office where I came from.' And again the chorus of voices went on. 'There wasn't room for one where she came from. The land there is worth a thousand pounds an inch!'

'Don't make excuses,' said the Guard: 'you should have bought one from the engine-driver.' And once more the chorus of voices went on with 'The man that drives the engine. Why, the smoke alone is worth a thousand pounds a puff!'

Alice thought to herself, 'Then there's no use in speaking.' The voices didn't join in this time, as she hadn't spoken, but, to her great surprise, they all *thought* in

1. Thinking in chorus is a practice common, indeed universal, among Leibnizian monads, the miniature 'minds' which together make up the substance of his universe. Since monads can do nothing *but* 'think,' after their fashion, and since each is preprogramed by God to do so in harmony with all the others, the analogy of a chorus is perfectly apt, and was actually so used (in 1687) by Leibniz himself (*Correspondence with Arnauld*, ed. H. T. Mason [1967], p. 119). Even without help from Leibniz, it is not so very surprising that a number of minds should entertain, simultaneously, the same commercial thought. What *is* surprising is that Alice should suddenly develop the extrasensory capacity to perceive it.

chorus (I hope you understand what *thinking in chorus* means — for I must confess that *I* don't), 'Better say nothing at all. Language is worth a thousand pounds a word!'[1]

'I shall dream about a thousand pounds to-night, I know I shall!' thought Alice.

All this time the Guard was looking at her, first through a telescope, then through a microscope, and then through an opera-glass. At last he said 'You're travelling the wrong way,' and shut up the window and went away.

'So young a child,' said the gentleman sitting opposite to her, (he was dressed in white paper,) 'ought to know which way she's going, even if she doesn't know her own name!'

A Goat, that was sitting next to the gentleman in white, shut his eyes and said in a loud voice, 'She ought to know her way to the ticket-office, even if she doesn't know her alphabet!'

There was a Beetle sitting next to the Goat (it was a very queer set of passengers altogether), and, as the rule seemed to be that they should all speak in turn, *he* went on with 'She'll have to go back from here as luggage!'

Alice couldn't see who was sitting beyond the Beetle, but a hoarse voice spoke next. 'Change engines ——' it said, and there it choked and was obliged to leave off.

'It sounds like a horse,' Alice thought to herself. And an extremely small voice, close to her ear, said 'You might make a joke on that—something about "horse" and "hoarse", you know.'

Then a very gentle voice in the distance said 'She must be labelled "Lass, with care", you know ——'

And after that other voices went on ('What a number of people there are in the carriage!' thought Alice), saying 'She must go by post, as she's got a head on her ——' 'She must be sent as a message by the telegraph ——' 'She must draw the train herself the rest of the way ——,' and so on.

But the gentleman dressed in white paper leaned forwards and whispered in her ear, 'Never mind what they all say, my dear, but take a return-ticket every time the train stops.'

'Indeed I shan't!' Alice said rather impatiently. 'I don't belong to this railway journey at all — I was in a wood just now — and I wish I could get back there!'

'You might make a joke on *that*,' said the little voice close to her ear: 'something about "you *would* if you could", you know.'

'Don't tease so,' said Alice, looking about in vain to see where the voice came from; 'if you're so anxious to have a joke made, why don't you make one yourself?'[2]

2. The Gnat is unusual in recognizing that a pun can be made the basis of a joke. But his attempts in this direction are so feeble that his anxiety to transfer responsibility for them is not to be wondered at.

The little voice sighed deeply: it was *very* unhappy, evidently, and Alice would have said something pitying to comfort it, 'if it would only sigh like other people!' she thought. But this was such a wonderfully small sigh, that she wouldn't have heard it at all, if it hadn't come *quite* close to her ear. The consequence of this was that it tickled her ear very much, and quite took off her thoughts from the unhappiness of the poor little creature.

'I know you are a friend,' the little voice went on; 'a dear friend, and an old friend. And you won't hurt me, though I *am* an insect.'

'What kind of insect?' Alice inquired a little anxiously. What she really wanted to know was, whether it could sting or not, but she thought this wouldn't be quite a civil question to ask.

'What, then you don't——' the little voice began, when it was drowned by a shrill scream from the engine, and everybody jumped up in alarm, Alice among the rest.

The Horse, who had put his head out of the window, quietly drew it in and said 'It's only a brook we have to jump over.' Everybody seemed satisfied with this, though Alice felt a little nervous at the idea of trains jumping at all. 'However, it'll take us into the Fourth Square, that's some comfort!' she said to herself. In another moment she felt the carriage rise straight up into the air, and in her fright she caught at the thing nearest to her hand, which happened to be the Goat's beard.

```
        *       *       *       *       *
            *       *       *       *
        *       *       *       *       *
```

But the beard seemed to melt away as she touched it, and she found herself sitting quietly under a tree — while

3. The literal interpretation of idiom in a sense not intended by the speaker is a trick more commonly played on Alice than practiced by herself. It has a certain affinity with the ancient but ill-defined fallacy of *secundum quid*, whereby a statement is taken up in a wider or more restricted sense than was originally meant, in order to impose an unwelcome or absurd conclusion. (Purtill [35], p. 21)

4. The subject of names and naming is here introduced, with a probable passing reference to the well-known discussion in John Stuart Mill's *Logic* (Bk. I, Ch. II, Sect. 5). Both Alice and the Gnat omit to observe a necessary distinction between proper and general names. Of the former, some (like *Dash*) can be used either to address or to summon their individual owners, or else to refer to them. Others (e.g., place names) are used only to refer. Since it takes a comparatively intelligent and mobile nominee to answer to his proper name, and a comparatively important one to call for mention as an individual, the vast majority of inert, unintelligent, or unimportant things do not have proper names, and are referred to by means of general names, suitably qualified by articles or demonstratives, whereby it is possible either to single out individuals as one of a class (the Gnat), or to allude to the class as a whole (gnats). There is no reason why those so referred to should know anything of these names, or be able to respond to them. A language-user, by contrast, *can* always be summoned by use of his general name or, as Alice points out to the Gnat, by other modes of address. (Sutherland, pp. 129, 132; Holmes, p. 136; Kemeny [24], p. 122)

5. The majority of general names do not describe or define their nominees: *automobile* does, for example, but *horse-fly* and *butterfly* do not. The looking-glass insects, however, do have names that genuinely describe them, and thus do answer, in the sense of corresponding, to them. So interpreted, the Gnat's original query seems reasonable enough. (Sutherland, p. 143; Spacks, p. 93)

the Gnat (for that was the insect she had been talking to) was balancing itself on a twig just over her head, and fanning her with its wings.

It certainly was a *very* large Gnat: 'about the size of a chicken,' Alice thought. Still, she couldn't feel nervous with it, after they had been talking together so long.

'— then you don't like all insects?' the Gnat went on, as quietly as if nothing had happened.

'I like them when they can talk,' Alice said. 'None of them ever talk, where *I* come from.'

'What sort of insects do you rejoice in, where *you* come from?' the Gnat inquired.

'I don't *rejoice* in insects at all,' Alice explained,[3] 'because I'm rather afraid of them — at least the large kinds. But I can tell you the names of some of them.'

'Of course they answer to their names?' the Gnat remarked carelessly.[4]

'I never knew them do it.'

'What's the use of their having names,' the Gnat said, 'if they won't answer to them?'

'No use to *them*,' said Alice; 'but it's useful to the people that name them, I suppose. If not, why do things have names at all?'

'I can't say,' said the Gnat. 'In the wood down there, they've got no names — however, go on with your list of insects.'

'Well, there's the Horse-fly,' Alice began, counting off the names on her fingers.

'All right,' said the Gnat: 'half way up that bush, you'll see a Rocking-horse-fly, if you look. It's made entirely of wood, and gets about by swinging itself from branch to branch.'[5]

'What does it live on?' Alice asked, with great curiosity.

'Sap and sawdust,' said the Gnat. 'Go on with the list.'

Alice looked at the Rocking-horse-fly with great interest and made up her mind that it must have been just re-painted, it looked so bright and sticky; and then she went on.

'And there's the Dragon-fly.'

'Look on the branch above your head,' said the Gnat, 'and there you'll find a Snap-dragon-fly. Its body is made of plum-pudding, its wings of holly-leaves, and its head is a raisin burning in brandy.'

'And what does it live on?' Alice asked, as before.

'Frumenty and mince-pie,' the Gnat replied; 'and it makes its nest in a Christmas-box.'

'And then there's the Butterfly,' Alice went on, after she had taken a good look at the insect with its head on fire, and had thought to herself, 'I wonder if that's the reason insects are so fond of flying into candles — because they want to turn into Snap-dragon-flies!'

'Crawling at your feet,' said the Gnat (Alice drew her feet back in some alarm), 'you may observe a Bread-and-butter-fly. Its wings are thin slices of bread-and-butter, its body is a crust, and its head is a lump of sugar.'

'And what does *it* live on?'

'Weak tea with cream in it.'

A new difficulty came into Alice's head. 'Supposing it couldn't find any?' she suggested.

'Then it would die, of course.'

'But that must happen very often,' Alice remarked thoughtfully.

'It always happens,' said the Gnat.[6]

After this, Alice was silent for a minute or two, pondering. The Gnat amused itself meanwhile by humming round and round her head: at last it settled again and remarked, 'I suppose you don't want to lose your name?'

'No, indeed,' Alice said, a little anxiously.

'And yet I don't know,' the Gnat went on in a careless tone: 'only think how convenient it would be if you could

6. Jourdain remarks (p. 36) that if the Gnat had refrained from pointing out an instance of the species, his statement that its members always die would still have been valid, in virtue of the doctrine that universal propositions have no existential import; that is, they do not assert that the class referred to has any actual members. In defense of the Gnat, it could be urged that all he is asserting is that Bread-and-butter-flies (like Socrates and the Duke of Wellington) are *mortal*, and so does not contradict himself by first exhibiting a living specimen and then denying that there can be any such thing.

7. The Gnat is mistaken in supposing that a loss of personal name makes the victim unaddressable. The Snark-hunting Baker, for instance, who had suffered this misfortune, would respond to *Hi!* and a number of other appellatives, and readily acquired nicknames as well. Alice rightly discounts the argument—but she still has problems to come. (Sutherland, p. 130)

manage to go home without it! For instance, if the governess wanted to call you to your lessons, she would call out "Come here —," and there she would have to leave off, because there wouldn't be any name for her to call, and of course you wouldn't have to go, you know.'[7]

'That would never do, I'm sure,' said Alice: 'the governess would never think of excusing me lessons for that. If she couldn't remember my name, she'd call me "Miss!" as the servants do.'

'Well, if she said "Miss", and didn't say anything more,' the Gnat remarked, 'of course you'd miss your lessons. That's a joke. I wish *you* had made it.'

'Why do you wish *I* had made it?' Alice asked. 'It's a very bad one.'

But the Gnat only sighed deeply, while two large tears came rolling down its cheeks.

'You shouldn't make jokes,' Alice said, 'if it makes you so unhappy.'

Then came another of those melancholy little sighs, and

this time the poor Gnat really seemed to have sighed itself away, for, when Alice looked up, there was nothing whatever to be seen on the twig, and, as she was getting quite chilly with sitting still so long, she got up and walked on.

She very soon came to an open field, with a wood on the other side of it: it looked much darker than the last wood, and Alice felt a *little* timid about going into it. However, on second thoughts, she made up her mind to go on: 'for I certainly won't go *back*,' she thought to herself, and this was the only way to the Eighth Square.

'This must be the wood,' she said thoughtfully to herself, 'where things have no names. I wonder what'll become of *my* name when I go in? I shouldn't like to lose it at all — because they'd have to give me another, and it would be almost certain to be an ugly one. But then the fun would be, trying to find the creature that had got my old name!⁸ That's just like the advertisements, you know, when people lose dogs — "*answers to the name of 'Dash'*: *had on a brass collar*" — just fancy calling everything you met "Alice", till one of them answered! Only they wouldn't answer at all, if they were wise.'

She was rambling on in this way when she reached the wood: it looked very cool and shady. 'Well, at any rate it's a great comfort,' she said as she stepped under the trees, 'after being so hot, to get into the — into the — into *what*?' she went on, rather surprised at not being able to think of the word. 'I mean to get under the — under the — under *this*, you know!' putting her hand on the trunk of the tree. 'What *does* it call itself? I do believe it's got no name — why, to be sure it hasn't!'

She stood silent for a minute, thinking: then she suddenly began again. 'Then it really *has* happened, after all!

8. Alice assumes that if she loses her name, it will have to be replaced by a new one, and that the old one will have been acquired by someone else. She also forgets that personal names have other functions besides those of issuing and answering to a summons. The nameless wood is not in fact a place where things have no names; it is a place where visitors forget the names that *they* customarily give to things. Alice, on entering it, finds nothing out of the way there, and her prattle continues unabated. All that happens is that she forgets her own personal name, and the general names of objects, and has to make do with demonstratives, or 'logically proper names' (e.g., *this*), as Russell called them. She thus has trouble in referring to things, and is obliged to talk in 'protocols' (*this here now*), like an early logical positivist; but the things themselves remain unaltered. (Sutherland, pp. 133*ff.*; Gardner, p. 227; Holmes, p. 136; Spacks, pp. 96-97)

9. So far from being a justified claim to knowledge, this is a necessary falsehood. The *L* may be a jocular reference to Alice *Liddell*, but since the fictional Alice's name begins with an *A*, it is impossible that she should *know* it to begin with anything else. (Purtill [35], p. 21)

And now, who am I? I *will* remember, if I can! I'm determined to do it!' But being determined didn't help her much, and all she could say, after a great deal of puzzling, was, 'L, I *know* it begins with L!'[9]

Just then a Fawn came wandering by: it looked at Alice with its large gentle eyes, but didn't seem at all frightened. 'Here then! Here then!' Alice said, as she held out her hand and tried to stroke it; but it only started back a little, and then stood looking at her again.

'What do you call yourself?' the Fawn said at last. Such a soft sweet voice it had!

'I wish I knew!' thought poor Alice. She answered, rather sadly, 'Nothing, just now.'

'Think again,' it said: 'that won't do.'

Alice thought, but nothing came of it. 'Please, would you tell me what *you* call yourself?' she said timidly. 'I think that might help a little.'

'I'll tell you, if you'll come a little further on,' the Fawn said. 'I can't remember here.'

So they walked on together through the wood, Alice with her arms clasped lovingly round the soft neck of the Fawn, till they came out into another open field, and here the Fawn gave a sudden bound into the air, and shook itself free from Alice's arms. 'I'm a Fawn!' it cried out in a voice of delight. 'And, dear me, you're a human child!' A sudden look of alarm came into its beautiful brown eyes, and in another moment it had darted away at full speed.[10]

Alice stood looking after it, almost ready to cry with vexation at having lost her dear little fellow-traveller so suddenly. 'However, I know my name now,' she said: 'that's *some* comfort. Alice — Alice — I won't forget it again. And now, which of these finger-posts ought I to follow, I wonder?'

It was not a difficult question to answer, as there was only one road, and the finger-posts both pointed along it. 'I'll settle it,' Alice said to herself, 'when the road divides and they point different ways.'

But this did not seem likely to happen. She went on and on, a long way, but wherever the road divided there were sure to be two finger-posts pointing the same way, one marked "TO TWEEDLEDUM'S HOUSE", and the other "TO THE HOUSE OF TWEEDLEDEE".

'I do believe,' said Alice at last, 'that they live in the same house![11] I wonder I never thought of that before — But I can't stay there long. I'll just call and say "How

10. The Fawn reacts not to Alice as such, but to what it takes her to be, in virtue of the affective connotation (i.e., the emotional meaning) of the general name describing her. That this is mere word magic can be seen from the fact that if it had simply discovered her name to be *Alice*, no such response would have followed. Proper names, as Mill put it, have no connotation; they designate their owners, but have no meaning of their own, and hence, unlike general names, convey little or no information as to the nature of the object denoted by them. Pitcher (in Fann, p. 325) regards the Fawn's behavior as exhibiting the opposite absurdity to that of the Cheshire Cat's 'call it what you like' (p. 64): the supposition that the nature of a thing is completely dependent on what it is called. But in fact it is the Fawn's *belief* that is affected, and the case is one of 'seeing as' (Wittgenstein), mediated through the assignment of a general name. To learn what a thing is called is often to see it suddenly in a new light, and thus to entertain a variety of new beliefs, expectations, and emotions about it, although *what is seen* remains (in a sense) exactly as before. (Sutherland, p. 215)

11. The credit for Alice's discovery (first noted by Jourdain, p. 53), that two expressions may have different meanings but the same denotation, has somehow been appropriated by Gottlob Frege. His celebrated distinction between *Sinn* and *Bedeutung* (meaning and reference) is not only a carbon copy of Alice's, but is founded on a precisely similar example, that of the morning and evening star. For a further instance of unacknowledged borrowing by Frege, see p. 218. (Sutherland, pp. 79*ff*., thinks the inference unwarranted, since there may be two houses, but recognizes [pp. 190-91] that the distinction itself is sound.)

d'ye do?" and ask them the way out of the wood. If I could only get to the Eighth Square before it gets dark!' So she wandered on, talking to herself as she went, till, on turning a sharp corner, she came upon two fat little men, so suddenly that she could not help starting back, but in another moment she recovered herself, feeling sure that they must be ——

CHAPTER IV

TWEEDLEDUM AND TWEEDLEDEE

THEY were standing under a tree, each with an arm round the other's neck, and Alice knew which was which in a moment, because one of them had "DUM" embroidered on his collar, and the other "DEE". 'I suppose they've each got "TWEEDLE" round at the back of the collar,' she said to herself.[1]

They stood so still that she quite forgot they were alive, and she was just looking round to see if the word "TWEEDLE" was written at the back of each collar, when she was startled by a voice coming from the one marked "DUM".

'If you think we're wax-works,' he said, 'you ought to pay, you know.[2] Wax-works weren't made to be looked at for nothing. Nohow!'

'Contrariwise,' added the one marked "DEE", 'if you think we're alive, you ought to speak.'

'I'm sure I'm very sorry,' was all Alice could say; for the words of the old song kept ringing through her head like the ticking of a clock, and she could hardly help saying them out loud: —

'*Tweedledum and Tweedledee*
Agreed to have a battle;
For Tweedledum said Tweedledee
Had spoiled his nice new rattle.

1. Failing these labels, Alice might well have had trouble over the identity of indiscernibles, since her later attempt at serial ordering is not accepted. The Tweedle brothers, as Gardner observes (p. 231) are enantiomorphs, or mirror-images of each other, and though asymmetric in gesture are physically symmetrical and indistinguishable. The likeness has betrayed even the usually infallible Tenniel, whose battle-scene illustration (p. 173) departs from the text by giving both bolster and saucepan-helmet to the same twin, who, if he is Tweedledum, should also have had the sword as well. (Sutherland, pp. 120*ff.*; Barnes [5], p. 66)

2. Tweedledum reactivates the problem of other minds—the difficulty of proving of a body other than one's own that it is animate. In raising it, however, he supplies, if not an answer to scepticism, at least a strong presumption in favor of the orthodox view. (Kemeny [24], p. 195)

3. These statements enunciate a cardinal principle of modal inference (if '*p*' then '*p* is possible'), followed by a formalized version of *modus tollens* (if *p* then *p*; not-*p*; therefore not-*p*). The view, says Jourdain (p. 11), that logic consists solely of the law of identity, is held by Leibniz, Drobitsch, Ueberweg, and Tweedledee. Professor Quine ([36] p. xi) has lately added his name to this list, at least as an endorser of Tweedledee's implied restriction of logic to the domain of formal truth. (Purtill [35], p. 21)

Tweedledum and Tweedledee

'*Just then flew down a monstrous crow,*
As black as a tar-barrel;
Which frightened both the heroes so,
They quite forgot their quarrel.'

'I know what you're thinking about,' said Tweedledum: 'but it isn't so, nohow.'

'Contrariwise,' continued Tweedledee, 'if it was so, it might be; and if it were so, it would be: but as it isn't, it ain't. That's logic.'[3]

'I was thinking,' Alice said very politely, 'which is the best way out of this wood: it's getting so dark. Would you tell me, please?'

But the fat little men only looked at each other and grinned.

They looked so exactly like a couple of great schoolboys, that Alice couldn't help pointing her finger at Tweedledum, and saying 'First Boy!'

'Nohow!' Tweedledum cried out briskly, and instantly shut his mouth up again with a snap.

'Next Boy!' said Alice, passing on to Tweedledee, though she felt quite certain he would only shout out 'Contrariwise!' and so he did.

'You've begun wrong!' cried Tweedledum. 'The first thing in a visit is to say "How d'ye do?" and shake hands!' And here the two brothers gave each other a hug, and then they held out the two hands that were free, to shake hands with her.

Alice did not like shaking hands with either of them first, for fear of hurting the other one's feelings; so, as the best way out of the difficulty, she took hold of both hands at once: the next moment they were dancing round in a ring. This seemed quite natural (she remembered afterwards), and she was not even surprised to hear music playing: it seemed to come from the tree under which they were dancing, and it was done (as well as she could make it out) by the branches rubbing one across the other, like fiddles and fiddle-sticks.

'But it certainly *was* funny,' (Alice said afterwards, when she was telling her sister the history of all this,) 'to find myself singing "*Here we go round the mulberry bush*". I don't know when I began it, but somehow I felt as if I'd been singing it a long, long time!'

The other two dancers were fat, and very soon out of breath. 'Four times round is enough for one dance,'

Tweedledum panted out, and they left off dancing as suddenly as they had begun: the music stopped at the same moment.

Then they let go of Alice's hands, and stood looking at her for a minute: there was a rather awkward pause, as Alice didn't know how to begin a conversation with people she had just been dancing with. 'It would never do to say "How d'ye do?" *now*,' she said to herself: 'we seem to have got beyond that, somehow!'

'I hope you're not much tired?' she said at last.

'Nohow. And thank you *very* much for asking,' said Tweedledum.

'So *much* obliged!' added Tweedledee. 'You like poetry?'

'Ye-es, pretty well — *some* poetry,' Alice said doubtfully. 'Would you tell me which road leads out of the wood?'

'What shall I repeat to her?' said Tweedledee, looking round at Tweedledum with great solemn eyes, and not noticing Alice's question.

'"*The Walrus and the Carpenter*" is the longest,' Tweedledum replied, giving his brother an affectionate hug.

Tweedledee began instantly:

'*The sun was shining —*'

Here Alice ventured to interrupt. 'If it's *very* long,' she said as politely as she could, 'would you tell me first which road ——'

Tweedledee smiled gently, and began again:

4. Odd but not impossible; in high latitudes it seems, at times, to be the regular thing. And why should the moon complain, when she frequently appears in broad daylight herself? (Carney and Scheer [11], p. 137)

Through the Looking-glass

'The sun was shining on the sea,
   Shining with all his might:
He did his very best to make
   The billows smooth and bright —
And this was odd, because it was
   The middle of the night.[4]

The moon was shining sulkily,
   Because she thought the sun
Had got no business to be there
   After the day was done —
"It's very rude of him," she said,
   "To come and spoil the fun!"

The sea was wet as wet could be,
   The sands were dry as dry.
You could not see a cloud, because
   No cloud was in the sky:
No birds were flying overhead —
   There were no birds to fly.

The Walrus and the Carpenter
   Were walking close at hand;
They wept like anything to see
   Such quantities of sand:
"If this were only cleared away,"
   They said, "it would be grand!"

"If seven maids with seven mops
   Swept it for half a year,
Do you suppose," the Walrus said,
   "That they could get it clear?"
"I doubt it," said the Carpenter,
   And shed a bitter tear.

Tweedledum and Tweedledee

"O Oysters, come and walk with us!"
  The Walrus did beseech.
"A pleasant walk, a pleasant talk,
  Along the briny beach:
We cannot do with more than four,
  To give a hand to each."

The eldest Oyster looked at him,
  But never a word he said:
The eldest Oyster winked his eye,
  And shook his heavy head —
Meaning to say he did not choose
  To leave the oyster-bed.

Through the Looking-glass

But four young Oysters hurried up,
  All eager for the treat:
Their coats were brushed, their faces washed,
  Their shoes were clean and neat —
And this was odd, because, you know,
  They hadn't any feet.

Four other Oysters followed them,
  And yet another four;
And thick and fast they came at last,
  And more, and more, and more —
All hopping through the frothy waves,
  And scrambling to the shore.

The Walrus and the Carpenter
  Walked on a mile or so,
And then they rested on a rock
  Conveniently low:
And all the little Oysters stood
  And waited in a row.

"The time has come," the Walrus said,
  "To talk of many things:
Of shoes — and ships — and sealing-wax —
  Of cabbages —and kings —
And why the sea is boiling hot —
  And whether pigs have wings." 5

"But, wait a bit," the Oysters cried,
  "Before we have our chat;
For some of us are out of breath,
  And all of us are fat!"
"No hurry!" said the Carpenter.
  They thanked him much for that.

5. This old-fashioned list of *quaestiones disputatae* identifies the Walrus as an adherent of scholastic natural philosophy, as a disciple of Bacon and Montaigne, or at best as one of those who will some day publish his philosophical essays for posterity to leave unread.

Tweedledum and Tweedledee

" *A loaf of bread," the Walrus said,*
  " *Is what we chiefly need:*
Pepper and vinegar besides
  Are very good indeed —
Now if you're ready, Oysters dear,
  We can begin to feed."

" *But not on us!" the Oysters cried,*
  Turning a little blue.
" *After such kindness, that would be*
  A dismal thing to do!"
" *The night is fine,' the Walrus said.*
  " *Do you admire the view?*

"I weep for you," the Walrus said:
    "I deeply sympathize."
With sobs and tears he sorted out
    Those of the largest size
Holding his pocket-handkerchief
    Before his streaming eyes.

"O Oysters," said the Carpenter,
    "You've had a pleasant run!
Shall we be trotting home again?"
    But answer came there none —
And this was scarcely odd, because
    They'd eaten every one.'

'I like the Walrus best,' said Alice: 'because, you see, he was a *little* sorry for the poor oysters.'

'He ate more than the Carpenter, though,' said Tweedledee. 'You see, he held his handkerchief in front, so that the Carpenter couldn't count how many he took: contrariwise.'

'That was mean!' Alice said indignantly. 'Then I like the Carpenter best — if he didn't eat so many as the Walrus.'

'But he ate as many as he could get,' said Tweedledum.

This was a puzzler. After a pause, Alice began, 'Well! They were *both* very unpleasant characters —'[6] Here she checked herself in some alarm, at hearing something that sounded to her like the puffing of a large steam-engine in the wood near them, though she feared it was more likely to be a wild beast. 'Are there any lions or tigers about here?' she asked timidly.

'It's only the Red King snoring,' said Tweedledee.

'Come and look at him!' the brothers cried, and they

"It was so kind of you to come!
    And you are very nice!"
The Carpenter said nothing but
    "Cut us another slice:
I wish you were not quite so deaf —
    I've had to ask you twice!"

"It seems a shame," the Walrus said,
    "To play them such a trick,
After we've brought them out so far,
    And made them trot so quick!"
The Carpenter said nothing but
    "The butter's spread too thick!"

6. Alienated by the duplicity of the Walrus, rather than by his greed or hypocrisy, Alice switches her vote to the underachieving Carpenter. Once it is pointed out that his aims are no better for his partial failure to fulfill them, she becomes uncertain whether to judge by intentions or by consequences, and so wavers ethically between a deontological standpoint and a utilitarian one. (Gardner, p. 237)

each took one of Alice's hands, and led her up to where the King was sleeping.

'Isn't he a *lovely* sight?' said Tweedledum.

Alice couldn't say honestly that he was. He had a tall red night-cap on, with a tassel, and he was lying crumpled up into a sort of untidy heap, and snoring loud — 'fit to snore his head off!' as Tweedledum remarked.

'I'm afraid he'll catch cold with lying on the damp grass,' said Alice, who was a very thoughtful little girl.

'He's dreaming now,' said Tweedledee: 'and what do you think he's dreaming about?'

Alice said 'Nobody can guess that.'

'Why, about *you*!' Tweedledee exclaimed, clapping his hands triumphantly. 'And if he left off dreaming about you, where do you suppose you'd be?'

'Where I am now, of course,' said Alice.

'Not you!' Tweedledee retorted contemptuously. 'You'd be nowhere. Why, you're only a sort of thing in his dream!'

The Philosopher's Alice

'If that there King was to wake,' added Tweedledum, 'you'd go out — bang! — just like a candle!'

'I shouldn't!' Alice exclaimed indignantly. 'Besides, if *I'm* only a sort of thing in his dream, what are *you*, I should like to know?'

'Ditto,' said Tweedledum.

'Ditto, ditto!' cried Tweedledee.

He shouted this so loud that Alice couldn't help saying, 'Hush! You'll be waking him, I'm afraid, if you make so much noise.'

'Well, it's no use *your* talking about waking him,' said Tweedledum, 'when you're only one of the things in his dream. You know very well you're not real.'

'I *am* real!' said Alice, and began to cry.

'You won't make yourself a bit realer by crying,' Tweedledee remarked: 'there's nothing to cry about.'

'If I wasn't real,' Alice said — half laughing through her tears, it all seemed so ridiculous — 'I shouldn't be able to cry.'

'I hope you don't suppose those are real tears?' Tweedledum interrupted in a tone of great contempt.[7]

'I know they're talking nonsense,' Alice thought to herself: 'and it's foolish to cry about it.' So she brushed away her tears, and went on as cheerfully as she could, 'At any rate I'd better be getting out of the wood, for really it's coming on very dark. Do you think it's going to rain?'

Tweedledum spread a large umbrella over himself and his brother, and looked up into it. 'No, I don't think it is,' he said: 'at least — not under *here*. Nohow.'

'But it may rain *outside*?'

'It may — if it chooses,' said Tweedledee: 'we've no objection. Contrariwise.'[8]

7. Most commentators (e.g., Alexander, p. 561; Gardner, p. 238; Holmes, pp. 143*ff.*) see allusion here to Dr. Johnson's common-sense reaction to Berkeleian idealism. Johnson professed to refute Berkeley by kicking a stone, but failed, since in doing so he merely confirmed the presence of those very sensory qualities, or 'ideas,' on whose empirical reality Berkeley was anxious to insist. Alice falls into the same error. Her alleged unreality would not alter the appearances of her world, though it robs her of true causal efficacy, for example, in waking the Red King; the allegation refers to her metaphysical status, not to the perceived content of her experience.

However, there are complications. If the Tweedle brothers are right, the Red King is equivalent to Berkeley's God, on whose entertainment of ideas the 'choir of heaven and furniture of the earth' depend for their existence. But Berkeley did not, as they do, include in this inventory the 'finite spirits' who also at times perceive these ideas. They are God's creatures, but have, in perceiving, a real existence that the merely perceived does not. Berkeley would never have taunted Alice with being unreal, though he would no more have thought her tears a proof of her reality than Tweedledum.

But now Alice, as it later transpires, is herself, for Carroll—a Berkeleian God, or Goddess, or perhaps a Fichtean Ego. The episode under discussion is part of *her* dream, which includes the Red King. So we have a dreamer, a dreamed dreamer, and the dreamer dreaming that she is (perhaps) being dreamed by the dreamer she is dreaming of. So whose is the 'real' dream? This is the puzzle left to tantalize the reader on p. 209 and at the end of the book. But it is (literally) not quite the whole story, since *both* the rival dreamers are themselves characters in fiction, dreamed or imagined by Carroll, and on *this* level their contest is therefore as unreal as Alice's tears are from the standpoint of Tweedledum. Even if his standpoint is a false one (which if he is correct it very likely is, for how is a dreamed character to know that he is *being* dreamed?), his statement is nonetheless true, *per accidens*. Alice's tears are *not* real. They are fictional, and fictionally dreamed by her, even if they are not fictionally dreamed by her to be dreamed by the fictionally dreamed, and dreaming, Red King. (Russell, p. 216; Spacks, p. 98; Hoffman [22], p. 80; Kemeny [24], p. 217; Moore [30], p. 311; [31], p. 123)

8. The proposition that 'it is raining' is apt to worry philosophers, since, unlike the more eternal verities, its truth or falsity seems to depend on when and where it is uttered. Such 'fugitive propositions' make it necessary to distinguish between propositions and statements. The statement that it is raining will then be true if it is in fact raining at the time and place of utterance, and otherwise false; whereas the proposition so expressed has no determinate truth value. Tweedledum creates an additional difficulty by arbitrarily restricting the scope of Alice's question to the prospect of rain in his own very immediate neighborhood, under the umbrella. The elasticity of the term *here* allows him to abuse her confidence by an obvious resort to *secundum quid*. Tweedledee, for his part, seems to accept the view propounded on p. 30, that there is an 'it' that does the raining, and can choose to do so, be dissuaded by objections, or the like.

'Selfish things!' thought Alice, and she was just going to say 'Good-night' and leave them, when Tweedledum sprang out from under the umbrella, and seized her by the wrist.

'Do you see *that*?' he said, in a voice choking with passion, and his eyes grew large and yellow all in a moment, as he pointed with a trembling finger at a small white thing lying under the tree.

'It's only a rattle,' Alice said, after a careful examination of the little white thing. 'Not a rattle-*snake*, you know,' she added hastily, thinking that he was frightened: 'only an old rattle — quite old and broken.'

'I knew it was!' cried Tweedledum, beginning to stamp about wildly and tear his hair. 'It's spoilt, of course!' Here he looked at Tweedledee, who immediately sat down on the ground, and tried to hide himself under the umbrella.

Alice laid her hand upon his arm, and said in a soothing tone, 'You needn't be so angry about an old rattle.'

'But it isn't old!' Tweedledum cried, in a greater fury than ever. 'It's new, I tell you — I bought it yesterday — my nice NEW RATTLE!' and his voice rose to a perfect scream.

All this time Tweedledee was trying his best to fold up the umbrella, with himself in it: which was such an extraordinary thing to do, that it quite took off Alice's attention from the angry brother. But he couldn't quite succeed, and it ended in his rolling over, bundled up in the umbrella, with only his head out: and there he lay, opening and shutting his mouth and his large eyes — 'looking more like a fish than anything else,' Alice thought.

'Of course you agree to have a battle?' Tweedledum said in a calmer tone.[9]

'I suppose so,' the other sulkily replied, as he crawled out of the umbrella: 'only *she* must help us to dress up, you know.'

So the two brothers went off hand-in-hand into the wood, and returned in a minute with their arms full of things — such as bolsters, blankets, hearthrugs, table-cloths, dish-covers, and coal-scuttles. 'I hope you're a good hand at pinning and tying strings?' Tweedledum remarked. 'Every one of these things has got to go on, somehow or other.'

Alice said afterwards she had never seen such a fuss made about anything in all her life — the way those two bustled about — and the quantity of things they put on — and the trouble they gave her in tying strings and fastening buttons — 'Really they'll be more like bundles of old clothes than anything else, by the time they're ready!' she

9. Determinism, indeed fatalism, rears its head once more. Alice, Cassandra-like, has already prophesied the doom of the house of Tweedle, as she is later to forecast the fall of Humpty Dumpty. Her claims go rejected, of course, but in each case the march of events proceeds with Aeschylean inevitability, as she and the rhymes predict. (Spacks, p. 98)

10. The old joke of naive understatement about death, familiar alike to Shakespeare (*Antony and Cleopatra*, Act V. Sc. ii, l. 247) and Damon Runyon. Death, being an absolute, does not admit of degrees. Tweedledee, who appears (with some justice) to regard his head as a limb, merely, has not asked himself what could be *more*, or even equally serious, and still happen to *him*.

11. It undeniably *was* a saucepan, in the sense, at least, of having the shape and physical properties normally required of a thing before it is called a saucepan or used as such. But to call it a helmet is not, under the circumstances, a metaphor, misnomer, or mistake of any kind, since it does legitimately describe the present use of the object. Artifacts constructed for one purpose can often be employed for another, and may then have temporarily bestowed on them the name of the object they are used to replace, and which would have been the proper thing to use, had it been available. (Sutherland, pp. 127-28)

said to herself, as she arranged a bolster round the neck of Tweedledee, 'to keep his head from being cut off,' as he said.

'You know,' he added very gravely, 'it's one of the most serious things that can possibly happen to one in a battle — to get one's head cut off.'[10]

Alice laughed loud, but managed to turn it into a cough, for fear of hurting his feelings.

'Do I look very pale?' said Tweedledum, coming up to have his helmet tied on. (He *called* it a helmet, though it certainly looked much more like a saucepan.)[11]

'Well — yes — a *little*,' Alice replied gently.

'I'm very brave generally,' he went on in a low voice: 'only to-day I happen to have a headache.'

'And *I've* got a toothache!' said Tweedledee, who had overheard the remark. 'I'm far worse than you!'

'Then you'd better not fight to-day,' said Alice, thinking it a good opportunity to make peace.

'We *must* have a bit of a fight, but I don't care about going on long,' said Tweedledum. 'What's the time now?'

Tweedledee looked at his watch, and said 'Half-past four.'

'Let's fight till six, and then have dinner,' said Tweedledum.

'Very well,' the other said, rather sadly: 'and *she* can watch us — only you'd better not come *very* close,' he added: 'I generally hit everything I can see — when I get really excited.'

'And *I* hit everything within reach,' cried Tweedledum, 'whether I can see it or not!'

Alice laughed. 'You must hit the *trees* pretty often, I should think,' she said.

Tweedledum looked round him with a satisfied smile. 'I don't suppose,' he said, 'there'll be a tree left standing, for ever so far round, by the time we've finished!'

'And all about a rattle!' said Alice, still hoping to make them a *little* ashamed of fighting for such a trifle.

'I shouldn't have minded it so much,' said Tweedledum, 'if it hadn't been a new one.'

'I wish the monstrous crow would come!' thought Alice.

'There's only one sword, you know,' Tweedledum said to his brother: 'but you can have the umbrella — it's quite as sharp. Only we must begin quick. It's getting as dark as it can.'

'And darker,' said Tweedledee.[12]

It was getting dark so suddenly that Alice thought there must be a thunderstorm coming on. 'What a thick black cloud that is!' she said. 'And how fast it comes! Why, I do believe it's got wings!'

'It's the crow!' Tweedledum cried out in a shrill voice of alarm: and the two brothers took to their heels and were out of sight in a moment.

Alice ran a little way into the wood, and stopped under a large tree. 'It can never get at me *here*,' she thought: 'it's far too large to squeeze itself in among the trees. But I wish it wouldn't flap its wings so—it makes quite a hurricane in the wood — here's somebody's shawl being blown away!'

12. The ad-man's paradox (or rather, absurdity) of 'whiter than white' is here prefigured by Tweedledee, who is again oblivious to the fact that you cannot outdo a superlative, absolute, or limiting expression. Martial excitement is perhaps responsible for these errors, as it also was, no doubt, in the case of the famous, if ungrammatical, general who 'got thar' fustest with the mostest men.'

1. A praiseworthy display of semantic tolerance by both parties. The Queen would not herself describe shawl-arranging as 'dressing,' but if Alice wishes to, that is her affair. Alice, in return, obligingly covers up for the misreading of her original query. It is easier and politer to accept the error than to try to put it right.

CHAPTER V

WOOL AND WATER

SHE caught the shawl as she spoke, and looked about for the owner: in another moment the White Queen came running wildly through the wood, with both arms stretched out wide, as if she were flying, and Alice very civilly went to meet her with the shawl.

'I'm very glad I happened to be in the way,' Alice said, as she helped her to put on her shawl again.

The White Queen only looked at her in a helpless frightened sort of way, and kept repeating something in a whisper to herself that sounded like 'Bread-and-butter, bread-and-butter,' and Alice felt that if there was to be any conversation at all, she must manage it herself. So she began rather timidly: 'Am I addressing the White Queen?'

'Well, yes, if you call that a-dressing,' the Queen said. 'It isn't *my* notion of the thing, at all.'

Alice thought it would never do to have an argument at the very beginning of their conversation, so she smiled and said 'If your Majesty will only tell me the right way to begin, I'll do it as well as I can.'[1]

'But I don't want it done at all!' groaned the poor Queen. 'I've been a-dressing myself for the last two hours.'

It would have been all the better, as it seemed to Alice, if only she had got someone else to dress her, she was so dreadfully untidy. 'Every single thing's crooked,' Alice thought to herself, 'and she's all over pins! — May I put your shawl a little more straight for you?' she added aloud.

'I don't know what's the matter with it!' the Queen said, in a melancholy voice. 'It's out of temper, I think. I've pinned it here, and I've pinned it there, but there's no pleasing it!'

'It *can't* go straight, you know, if you pin it all on one side,' Alice said, as she gently put it right for her; 'and, dear me, what a state your hair is in!'

'The hairbrush has got entangled in it!' the Queen said with a sigh. 'And I lost the comb yesterday.'

Alice carefully released the brush, and did her best to get the hair into order. 'Come, you look rather better now!' she said, after altering most of the pins. 'But really you should have a lady's-maid!'

'I'm sure I'll take you with pleasure!' the Queen said. 'Twopence a week, and jam every other day.'

Alice couldn't help laughing, as she said 'I don't want you to hire *me* — and I don't care for jam.'

'It's very good jam,' said the Queen.

'Well, I don't want any *to-day*, at any rate.'

'You couldn't have it if you *did* want it,' the Queen said. 'The rule is, jam to-morrow and jam yesterday — but never jam to-day.'

2. This famous proof—for the special case of jam, at least —that (contrary to Hume) the future necessarily *will* resemble the past, if not the present, has endeared the White Queen to philosophers and politicians alike. There is no chance, at any rate, of producing an exception to her rule, since, as she uses them, the words *every other day* equivocate between 'alternate days' and 'every day other than today.' On the first interpretation, as Alice says, it must come sometimes to 'jam today,' but then this is ruled out by the second. The Queen does not, as is sometimes said, treat *today, tomorrow,* and so forth as the fixed and unchangeable names of particular days, thereby implying that time stands still. On the contrary, she uses these terms with systematic ambiguity of reference, so that the rules always specify jam on a day ahead of, or behind, any given day on which jam might be demanded. *Tomorrow* is never allowed to become *today,* and thus retires continually into the future, holding out an eternal prospect of jam, whose realization is forever being postponed by the passage of time itself. As Pitcher notes, it is a moot point whether the Queen does not know the game she is up to, or knows it only too well. (Alexander, p. 559; Holmes, pp. 147-48; Pitcher [in Fann], p. 334, citing Wittgenstein [49], p. 108; Spacks, pp. 93-94; Terrell and Baker [46], p. 75)

3. Alice seems merely to regret her mnemonic deficiency as an empirical limitation, and so fails to perceive, says Pitcher (in Fann, p. 332), that it is a matter of logical or conceptual necessity. The Queen makes a similar error in speaking of Alice's memory as a poor one; but Pitcher's belief that the Queen's memory works forward only is not supported by the text. (Shibles, p. 46; Flew [18], p. 61; Moore [30], p. 319; Pears [34], p. 247)

4. The second sight of Sir John Tenniel is every bit as remarkable as that of the White Queen. Who else can this possibly be in the picture but a late eminent philosopher, languishing in custody *circa* 1918, and there composing *An Introduction to Mathematical Philosophy*?

'It *must* come sometimes to "jam to-day",' Alice objected.

'No, it can't,' said the Queen. 'It's jam every *other* day: to-day isn't any *other* day, you know.'[2]

'I don't understand you,' said Alice. 'It's dreadfully confusing!'

'That's the effect of living backwards,' the Queen said kindly: 'it always makes one a little giddy at first ——'

'Living backwards!' Alice repeated in great astonishment. 'I never heard of such a thing!'

'—— but there's one great advantage in it, that one's memory works both ways.'

'I'm sure *mine* only works one way,' Alice remarked. "I can't remember things before they happen.'

'It's a poor sort of memory that only works backwards,' the Queen remarked.[3]

'What sort of things do *you* remember best?' Alice ventured to ask.

'Oh, things that happened the week after next,' the Queen replied in a careless tone. 'For instance, now,' she went on, sticking a large piece of plaster on her finger as she spoke, 'there's the King's Messenger. He's in prison now, being punished:[4] and the trial doesn't even begin till

next Wednesday: and of course the crime comes last of all.'

'Suppose he never commits the crime?' said Alice.

'That would be all the better, wouldn't it?' the Queen said, as she bound the plaster round her finger with a bit of ribbon.

Alice felt there was no denying *that*. 'Of course it would be all the better,' she said: 'but it wouldn't be all the better his being punished.'

'You're wrong *there*, at any rate,' said the Queen: 'were *you* ever punished?'

'Only for faults,' said Alice.

'And you were all the better for it, I know!' the Queen said triumphantly.

'Yes, but then I *had* done the things I was punished for,' said Alice: 'that makes all the difference.'

'But if you *hadn't* done them,' the Queen said, 'that would have been better still; better, and better, and better!'⁵ Her voice went higher with each 'better', till it got quite to a squeak at last.

Alice was just beginning to say 'There's a mistake somewhere ——,' when the Queen began screaming, so loud that she had to leave the sentence unfinished. 'Oh, oh, oh!' shouted the Queen, shaking her hand about as if she wanted to shake it off. 'My finger's bleeding! Oh, oh, oh, oh!'

Her screams were so exactly like the whistle of a steam-engine, that Alice had to hold both her hands over her ears.

'What *is* the matter?' she said, as soon as there was a chance of making herself heard. 'Have you pricked your finger?'

5. Critics of utilitarianism have argued that its aim of maximizing general happiness would permit sending criminals in secret to luxurious holiday resorts, while deterring imitators by publishing tales of the fearsome severity of the law. The White Queen's policy is the exact opposite, and coincides with the 'ideal utilitarianism' of G. E. Moore. The object of right action is to maximize goodness, and the aim of punishment is to reform and improve. If punishment is beneficial, therefore, the way to do most good is evidently to punish the innocent rather than the guilty. As Alice says, there's a mistake somewhere. It consists in supposing that punishment still is, or does, good—or is even punishment—when it is no longer related to crime. (Holmes, p. 145; Bradbury [7], pp. 57-58; Carney and Scheer [11], p. 5)

6. The impression conveyed here is that events are occurring in reverse order. But if so, the pricking should precede the clutching, and the clutching the opening of the brooch, which is not what happens. It is simpler to assume, as before, that the order of events, though normal, is predestined, and known in advance to the Queen, who then reacts to this knowledge with hysteria, psychosomatic bleeding, etc., before the arrival of the foreseen event. Emotional catharsis achieved, the catastrophe, when it comes, is reduced to anticlimax, and can thus be accepted with composure. (Holmes, pp. 146-47; Pitcher [in Fann], p. 330)

7. Recipes for happiness, though unreliable, are not inherently absurd, and the Queen's rules for dispelling melancholy are actually not foolish at all. Since the focus of attention is restricted, it is at least difficult to *concentrate* on two things at once; and hence, by adverting to something else, unwanted feelings may be made to disappear. Why, then, does a rule for gladness seem out of the question? The short answer is doubtless that moods and feelings are essentially spontaneous responses, and cannot be mechanically created, though they may be artificially suppressed.

'I haven't pricked it *yet*,' the Queen said, 'but I soon shall — oh, oh, oh!'

'When do you expect to do it?' Alice asked, feeling very much inclined to laugh.

'When I fasten my shawl again,' the poor Queen groaned out: 'the brooch will come undone directly. Oh, oh!' As she said the words the brooch flew open, and the Queen clutched wildly at it, and tried to clasp it again.

'Take care!' cried Alice. 'You're holding it all crooked!' And she caught at the brooch; but it was too late: the pin had slipped, and the Queen had pricked her finger.

'That accounts for the bleeding, you see,' she said to Alice with a smile. 'Now you understand the way things happen here.'[6]

'But why don't you scream now?' Alice asked, holding her hands ready to put over her ears again.

'Why, I've done all the screaming already,' said the Queen. 'What would be the good of having it all over again?'

By this time it was getting light. 'The crow must have flown away, I think,' said Alice: 'I'm so glad it's gone. I thought it was the night coming on.'

'I wish *I* could manage to be glad!' the Queen said. 'Only I never can remember the rule.[7] You must be very happy, living in this wood, and being glad whenever you like!'

'Only it is so *very* lonely here!' Alice said in a melancholy voice; and at the thought of her loneliness two large tears came rolling down her cheeks.

'Oh, don't go on like that!' cried the poor Queen, wringing her hands in despair. 'Consider what a great girl you are. Consider what a long way you've come to-day. Consider what o'clock it is. Consider anything, only don't cry!'

Alice could not help laughing at this, even in the midst of her tears. 'Can *you* keep from crying by considering things?' she asked.

'That's the way it's done,' the Queen said with great decision: 'nobody can do two things at once, you know. Let's consider your age to begin with — how old are you?'

'I'm seven and a half exactly.'

'You needn't say "exactually",' the Queen remarked: 'I can believe it without that. Now I'll give *you* something to believe. I'm just one hundred and one, five months and a day.'

'I can't believe *that*!' said Alice.

'Can't you?' the Queen said in a pitying tone. 'Try again: draw a long breath, and shut your eyes.'

Alice laughed. 'There's no use trying,' she said: 'one *can't* believe impossible things.'

'I daresay you haven't had much practice,' said the Queen. 'When I was your age, I always did it for half-an-hour a day. Why, sometimes I've believed as many as six impossible things before breakfast.[8] There goes the shawl again!'

The brooch had come undone as she spoke, and a sudden gust of wind blew her shawl across a little brook. The Queen spread out her arms again, and went flying after it, and this time succeeded in catching it for herself. 'I've got it!' she cried in a triumphant tone. 'Now you shall see me pin it on again, all by myself!'

'Then I hope your finger is better now?' Alice said very politely, as she crossed the little brook after the Queen.

```
    *       *       *       *       *
        *       *       *       *
    *       *       *       *       *
```

8. Gardner (p. 251) considers the Queen an exponent of Tertullian's *credo quia absurdum*—'I believe *because* it is absurd'—(Christianity, if it were reasonable, would not require faith), while Jourdain (p. 88) proclaims her a pioneer of the *Gedankenexperiment*. Alice's sceptical position is all very well in principle, but she carries it too far in practice. There is nothing *logically* impossible about the royal age-claim; it merely seems factually unlikely. Yet only logical impossibilities can be claimed with any plausibility to be a priori beyond belief. Jourdain (p. 56) reckons Alice among the opponents of Meinong, who (so his detractors claim) was willing to tolerate as objects of belief a wide variety of logical and factual absurdities—round squares, unicorns, golden mountains, and the like. But when Alice later meets the Unicorn (p. 206), she has to change her views, though at the price of falling foul of Lord Russell, a lifelong objector to unicorns in logic or anywhere else ('Logic . . . must no more admit a unicorn than zoology can,' *An Introduction to Mathematical Philosophy* [1919], p. 169). The grounds of Russell's prejudice are, however, obscure. The nonexistence of unicorns is, on the face of it, an empirical matter, not a logical necessity, and if so it should be no more impossible for a logician to believe in them than it is for Alice to believe that the White Queen is 101. (Holmes, p. 140)

'Oh, much better!' cried the Queen, her voice rising into a squeak as she went on. 'Much be-etter! Be-etter! Be-e-e-etter! Be-e-ehh!' The last word ended in a long bleat, so like a sheep that Alice quite started.

She looked at the Queen, who seemed to have suddenly wrapped herself up in wool. Alice rubbed her eyes, and looked again. She couldn't make out what had happened at all. Was she in a shop? And was that really — was it really a *sheep* that was sitting on the other side of the counter? Rub as she would, she could make nothing more of it: she was in a little dark shop, leaning with her elbows on the counter, and opposite to her was an old Sheep, sitting in an arm-chair knitting, and every now and then leaving off to look at her through a great pair of spectacles.

'What is it you want to buy?' the Sheep said at last, looking up for a moment from her knitting.

'I don't *quite* know yet,' Alice said very gently. 'I should like to look all round me first, if I might.'

'You may look in front of you, and on both sides, if you like,' said the Sheep; 'but you can't look *all* round you — unless you've got eyes at the back of your head.'

But these, as it happened, Alice had *not* got; so she contented herself with turning round, looking at the shelves as she came to them.

The shop seemed to be full of all manner of curious things — but the oddest part of it all was, that whenever she looked hard at any shelf, to make out exactly what it had on it, that particular shelf was always quite empty: though the others round it were crowded as full as they could hold.

'Things flow about so here!' she said at last in a plaintive tone, after she had spent a minute or so in vainly pursuing a large bright thing, that looked sometimes like a

The Philosopher's Alice

181

9. It is naturally difficult to affix more than a provisional name to a 'thing' that is either subject to difficulties of observation or itself indulges in protean behavior. When it finally ceases to behave even as a material object, by going through the ceiling, there is no knowing what to say of it. It is not an ambiguous or borderline case of anything, but simply an enigma. (Sutherland, pp. 109*ff.*)

The Philosopher's Alice

182

doll and sometimes like a work-box, and was always in the shelf next above the one she was looking at. 'And this one is the most provoking of all — but I'll tell you what ——' she added, as a sudden thought struck her, 'I'll follow it up to the very top shelf of all. It'll puzzle it to go through the ceiling, I expect!'

But even this plan failed: the 'thing' went through the ceiling as quietly as possible, as if it were quite used to it.[9]

'Are you a child or a teetotum?' the Sheep said, as she took up another pair of needles. 'You'll make me giddy

10. *Feathering* and *crab-catching* are, of course, terms of art among oarsmen, adapted as metaphors from the ordinary vocabulary. Since Alice knows only their literal meanings, she is inevitably misled, and can make nothing of the advice they are used to convey. (Sutherland, p. 159; Gardner, p. 254)

soon, if you go on turning round like that.' She was now working with fourteen pairs at once, and Alice couldn't help looking at her in great astonishment.

'How *can* she knit with so many?' the puzzled child thought to herself. 'She gets more and more like a porcupine every minute!'

'Can you row?' the Sheep asked, handing her a pair of knitting-needles as she spoke.

'Yes, a little — but not on land — and not with needles ——' Alice was beginning to say, when suddenly the needles turned into oars in her hands, and she found they were in a little boat, gliding along between banks: so there was nothing for it but to do her best.

'Feather!' cried the Sheep, as she took up another pair of needles.

This didn't sound like a remark that needed any answer, so Alice said nothing, but pulled away. There was something very queer about the water, she thought, as every now and then the oars got fast in it, and would hardly come out again.

'Feather! Feather!' the Sheep cried again, taking more needles. 'You'll be catching a crab directly.'

'A dear little crab!' thought Alice. 'I should like that.'[10]

'Didn't you hear me say "Feather"?' the Sheep cried angrily, taking up quite a bunch of needles.

'Indeed I did,' said Alice: 'you've said it very often — and very loud. Please, where *are* the crabs?'

'In the water, of course!' said the Sheep, sticking some of the needles into her hair, as her hands were full. 'Feather, I say!'

'*Why* do you say "Feather" so often?' Alice asked at last, rather vexed. 'I'm not a bird!'

'You are,' said the Sheep: 'you're a little goose.'

This offended Alice a little, so there was no more conversation for a minute or two, while the boat glided gently on, sometimes among beds of weeds (which made the oars stick fast in the water, worse than ever), and sometimes under trees, but always with the same tall river banks frowning over their heads.

'Oh, please! There are some scented rushes!' Alice cried

in a sudden transport of delight. 'There really are — and *such* beauties!'

'You needn't say "please" to *me* about 'em,' the Sheep said, without looking up from her knitting: 'I didn't put 'em there, and I'm not going to take 'em away.'

'No, but I meant — please, may we wait and pick some?' Alice pleaded. 'If you don't mind stopping the boat for a minute.'

'How am *I* to stop it?' said the Sheep. 'If you leave off rowing, it'll stop of itself.'

So the boat was left to drift down the stream as it would, till it glided gently in among the waving rushes. And then the little sleeves were carefully rolled up, and the little arms were plunged in elbow-deep, to get hold of the rushes a good long way down before breaking them off — and for a while Alice forgot all about the Sheep and the knitting, as she bent over the side of the boat, with just the ends of her tangled hair dipping into the water — while with bright eager eyes she caught at one bunch after another of the darling scented rushes.

'I only hope the boat won't tipple over!' she said to herself. 'Oh, *what* a lovely one! Only I couldn't quite reach it.' And it certainly *did* seem a little provoking ('almost as if it happened on purpose,' she thought) that, though she managed to pick plenty of beautiful rushes as the boat glided by, there was always a more lovely one that she couldn't reach.

'The prettiest are always further!' she said at last, with a sigh at the obstinacy of the rushes in growing so far off, as, with flushed cheeks and dripping hair and hands, she scrambled back into her place, and began to arrange her new-found treasures.

11. Alice is lured into teleological explanation to account for her frustrations, and soon lapses into the pathetic fallacy (of attributing purposes and feelings to inanimate nature). The rushes' obstinacy is merely a reflection of her own failure to get what she wants.

12. The dream-rushes are peculiar in having, as it were, a feebler reality than other looking-glass items, and betraying their dream status within the dream itself. The whole episode suggests, in fact, a dream within a dream, though that is no reason why, within their context, the rushes should behave less reliably than anything else. Aesthetic symbolism is doubtless responsible for the inconsistency here. (Gardner, p. 257)

What mattered it to her just then that the rushes had begun to fade, and to lose all their scent and beauty, from the very moment that she picked them? Even real scented rushes, you know, last only a very little while — and these, being dream-rushes, melted away almost like snow, as they lay in heaps at her feet — but Alice hardly noticed this, there were so many other curious things to think about.[12]

They hadn't gone much farther before the blade of one of the oars got fast in the water and *wouldn't* come out again (so Alice explained it afterwards), and the consequence was that the handle of it caught her under the chin, and, in spite of a series of little shrieks of 'Oh, oh, oh!' from poor Alice, it swept her straight off the seat, and down among the heap of rushes.

However, she wasn't a bit hurt, and was soon up again: the Sheep went on with her knitting all the while, just as if nothing had happened. 'That was a nice crab you caught!' she remarked, as Alice got back into her place, very much relieved to find herself still in the boat.

'Was it? I didn't see it,' said Alice, peeping cautiously over the side of the boat into the dark water. 'I wish it hadn't let go — I should so like a little crab to take home with me!' But the Sheep only laughed scornfully, and went on with her knitting.

'Are there many crabs here?' said Alice.

'Crabs, and all sorts of things,' said the Sheep: 'plenty of choice, only make up your mind. Now, what *do* you want to buy?'

'To buy!' Alice echoed in a tone that was half astonished and half frightened — for the oars, and the boat, and the river, had vanished all in a moment, and she was back again in the little dark shop.

'I should like to buy an egg, please,' she said timidly. 'How do you sell them?'

'Fivepence farthing for one — twopence for two,' the Sheep replied.

'Then two are cheaper than one?' Alice said in a surprised tone, taking out her purse.

'Only you *must* eat them both, if you buy two,' said the Sheep.

'Then I'll have *one*, please,' said Alice, as she put the money down on the counter. For she thought to herself, 'They mightn't be at all nice, you know.'[13]

The Sheep took the money, and put it away in a box: then she said, 'I never put things into people's hands — that would never do — you must get it for yourself.' And so saying, she went off to the other end of the shop, and set the egg upright on a shelf.

'I wonder *why* it wouldn't do?' thought Alice, as she groped her way among the tables and chairs, for the shop was very dark towards the end. 'The egg seems to get further away the more I walk towards it. Let me see, is this a chair? Why, it's got branches, I declare! How very odd to find trees growing here! And actually here's a little brook! Well, this is the very queerest shop I ever saw!'

*   *   *   *   *
*   *   *   *
*   *   *   *   *

So she went on, wondering more and more at every step, as everything turned into a tree the moment she came up to it, and she quite expected the egg to do the same.

13. If the Sheep were selling white elephants, aircraft prototypes, sibylline books, works of art, or exclusive fashion creations, there might be a certain justification in charging more for one than for two. As it is, she makes low-priced eggs into less of a bargain than expensive ones only by imposing an unwelcome, though unenforceable, condition of sale. Alice is wasting her money. Her proper course is to buy two and threaten the vendor with one of them, until it is bought back at the higher price.

1. To assert of someone—even an apparently inanimate someone—that he is exactly like an egg is to say more than that he looks like one, and yet it is not to say that he *is* one. Nor is it to call him one, though it offers some justification for doing so. For if two things are *exactly* alike, they normally go by the same (general) name. Alice may not have intended to draw this conclusion, but on past form her chances of confusing sameness of resemblance with sameness of identity are certainly not negligible. Humpty Dumpty's suspicions have some excuse.

CHAPTER VI

HUMPTY DUMPTY

HOWEVER, the egg only got larger and larger, and more and more human: when she had come within a few yards of it, she saw that it had eyes and a nose and mouth; and when she had come close to it, she saw clearly that it was HUMPTY DUMPTY himself. 'It can't be anybody else!' she said to herself. 'I'm as certain of it as if his name were written all over his face!'

It might have been written a hundred times, easily, on that enormous face. Humpty Dumpty was sitting with his legs crossed, like a Turk, on the top of a high wall — such a narrow one that Alice quite wondered how he could keep his balance — and, as his eyes were steadily fixed in the opposite direction, and he didn't take the least notice of her, she thought he must be a stuffed figure.

'And how exactly like an egg he is!' she said aloud, standing with her hands ready to catch him, for she was every moment expecting him to fall.

'It's *very* provoking,' Humpty Dumpty said after a long silence, looking away from Alice as he spoke, 'to be called an egg — *very*!'

'I said you *looked* like an egg, sir,' Alice gently explained.[1] 'And some eggs are very pretty, you know,' she added, hoping to turn her remark into a sort of compliment.

'Some people,' said Humpty Dumpty, looking away from her as usual, 'have no more sense than a baby!'

Humpty Dumpty

Alice didn't know what to say to this: it wasn't at all like conversation, she thought, as he never said anything to *her*; in fact, his last remark was evidently addressed to a tree — so she stood and softly repeated to herself: —

> '*Humpty Dumpty sat on a wall:*
> *Humpty Dumpty had a great fall.*
> *All the King's horses and all the King's men*
> *Couldn't put Humpty Dumpty in his place again.*'

'That last line is much too long for the poetry,' she added, almost out loud, forgetting that Humpty Dumpty would hear her.

'Don't stand chattering to yourself like that,' Humpty Dumpty said, looking at her for the first time, 'but tell me your name and your business.'

'My *name* is Alice, but ——'

'It's a stupid name enough!' Humpty Dumpty interrupted impatiently. 'What does it mean?'

'*Must* a name mean something?' Alice asked doubtfully.

'Of course it must,' Humpty Dumpty said with a short laugh: '*my* name means the shape I am — and a good handsome shape it is, too. With a name like yours, you might be any shape, almost.'[2]

'Why do you sit out here all alone?' said Alice, not wishing to begin an argument.

'Why, because there's nobody with me!' cried Humpty Dumpty. 'Did you think I didn't know the answer to *that*?[3] Ask another.'

'Don't you think you'd be safer down on the ground?' Alice went on, not with any idea of making another riddle, but simply in her good-natured anxiety for the queer creature. 'That wall is so *very* narrow!'

2. As Alexander (p. 558) was the first to notice, Humpty Dumpty's theory is that, contrary to the common belief, proper names mean, or ought to mean, something about their owners (whereas general words have any meaning he chooses to give them). His complaint about Alice, or Tweedledum, could be put by saying not that they do not respond to their names, but that they do not *correspond* to them. Like Hatta and Haigha, Humpty Dumpty himself corresponds pretty well, which is one reason why Alice had no trouble in recognizing and naming him for what he is: a humanoid ovoid, the only one of his class, and known to history by 'connotative individual name' (Mill). The old patronymics based on trades and territorial connections, like Mr. Bun the Baker in the game of 'Happy Families,' did no doubt once have this useful property. But outside Plato's Republic it is futile to insist that everyone should live up to his name, or otherwise ensure that it is descriptive of himself. (Gardner, p. 263; Holmes, pp. 136-37; Sutherland, pp. 136*ff*.)

3. The question is taken to be asking for the cause or reason of Humpty Dumpty's solitude, rather than his purpose in seeking it. Since the answer given is a logical truism, Alice is left no wiser than before. (Sutherland, p. 169; Purtill [35], p. 21)

'What tremendously easy riddles you ask!' Humpty Dumpty growled out. 'Of course I don't think so! Why, if ever I *did* fall off — which there's no chance of — but *if* I did ——' Here he pursed up his lips, and looked so solemn and grand that Alice could hardly help laughing. '*If* I did fall,' he went on, '*the King has promised me* — ah, you may turn pale, if you like! You didn't think I was going to say that, did you? *The King has promised me — with his own mouth* — to — to ——'

'To send all his horses and all his men,' Alice interrupted, rather unwisely.

'Now I declare that's too bad!' Humpty Dumpty cried, breaking into a sudden passion. 'You've been listening at doors — and behind trees — and down chimneys — or you couldn't have known it!'

'I haven't, indeed!' Alice said very gently. 'It's in a book.'

'Ah, well! They may write such things in a *book*,' Humpty Dumpty said in a calmer tone. 'That's what you call a History of England, that is. Now, take a good look at me! I'm one that has spoken to a King, *I* am: mayhap you'll never see such another: and to show you I'm not proud, you may shake hands with me!' And he grinned almost from ear to ear, as he leant forwards (and as nearly as possible fell off the wall in doing so) and offered Alice his hand. She watched him a little anxiously as she took it. 'If he smiled much more, the ends of his mouth might meet behind,' she thought: 'and then I don't know what would happen to his head! I'm afraid it would come off!'

'Yes, all his horses and all his men,' Humpty Dumpty went on. 'They'd pick me up again in a minute, *they* would! However, this conversation is going on a little too

4. (Kemeny [24], p. 105, [chapter heading])

5. An early example of the notion of a 'language game,' later made fashionable by Wittgenstein. Humpty Dumpty's game, unlike the Mock Turtle's (p. 93), is not to accuse Alice of saying something she has just denied having said, but to convict her of failing to say something which his leading question implies that she *has* just said. (Sutherland, p. 196)

fast: let's go back to the last remark but one.'[4]

'I'm afraid I can't quite remember it,' Alice said very politely.

'In that case we may start fresh,' said Humpty Dumpty, 'and it's my turn to choose a subject ——' ('He talks about it just as if it was a game!' thought Alice.) 'So here's a question for you. How old did you say you were?'[5]

Alice made a short calculation, and said 'Seven years and six months.'

'Wrong!' Humpty Dumpty exclaimed triumphantly. 'You never said a word like it.'

6. Alice does not see how prevention of the inevitable can be a suitable subject for advice; but as Humpty Dumpty unkindly points out, growth and aging are by no means impossible to prevent, though in a sense that Alice is scarcely likely to appreciate. (Gardner, p. 266)

7. An awkward example of the difficulties of classification in what is certainly a borderline case. The interpenetration of opposites involved in a synthesis of belt and cravat has been taken (by Jourdain, p. 11) to show that Humpty Dumpty is a Hegelian, an identification further attested by his fondness for riddles and mathematical incompetence (p. 192). This evidence is by no means conclusive, however. His later thesis (echoing Mill) that definitions are nominal (p. 195) and his refusal to admit anything not yet verified (p. 199) tend to make him out an empiricist, while his confident philology and shaky mathematics are even stronger clues to his true identity, as an early, if eccentric, ally of the linguistic analysts. (Sutherland, pp. 107ff.)

'I thought you meant "How old *are* you?"' Alice explained.

'If I'd meant that, I'd have said it,' said Humpty Dumpty.

Alice didn't want to begin another argument, so she said nothing.

'Seven years and six months!' Humpty Dumpty repeated thoughtfully. 'An uncomfortable sort of age. Now if you'd asked *my* advice, I'd have said "Leave off at seven" —but it's too late now.'

'I never ask advice about growing,' Alice said indignantly.[6]

'Too proud?' the other enquired.

Alice felt even more indignant at this suggestion. 'I mean,' she said, 'that one can't help growing older.'

'*One* can't, perhaps,' said Humpty Dumpty, 'but *two* can. With proper assistance, you might have left off at seven.'

'What a beautiful belt you've got on!' Alice suddenly remarked. (They had had quite enough of the subject of age, she thought: and if they were really to take turns in choosing subjects, it was her turn now.) 'At least,' she corrected herself on second thoughts, 'a beautiful cravat, I should have said — no, a belt, I mean — oh, I *beg* your pardon!' she added in dismay, for Humpty Dumpty looked thoroughly offended, and she began to wish she hadn't chosen that subject. 'If only I knew,' she thought to herself, 'which was neck and which was waist!'[7]

Evidently Humpty Dumpty was very angry, though he said nothing for a minute or two. When he *did* speak again, it was in a deep growl.

'It is a — *most* — *provoking* — thing,' he said at last, 'when a person doesn't know a cravat from a belt!'

'I know it's very ignorant of me,' Alice replied, in so humble a tone that Humpty Dumpty relented.

'It's a cravat, child, and a beautiful one, as you say. It's a present from the White King and Queen. There now!'

'Is it really?' said Alice, quite pleased to find she *had* chosen a good subject, after all.

'They gave it me,' Humpty Dumpty continued thoughtfully, as he crossed one knee over the other and clasped his hands round it, '— for an un-birthday present.'

'I beg your pardon?' Alice said with a puzzled air.

'I'm not offended,' said Humpty Dumpty.[8]

'I mean, what *is* an un-birthday present?'

'A present given when it isn't your birthday, of course.'

Alice considered a little. 'I like birthday presents best,' she said at last.

'You don't know what you're talking about!' cried Humpty Dumpty. 'How many days are there in a year?'

'Three hundred and sixty-five,' said Alice.

'And how many birthdays have you?'

'One.'

'And if you take one from three hundred and sixty-five, what remains?'

'Three hundred and sixty-four, of course.'

Humpty Dumpty looked doubtful. 'I'd rather see that done on paper,' he said.[9]

Alice couldn't help smiling as she took out her memorandum-book, and worked the sum for him:

$$
\begin{array}{r}
3\,6\,5 \\
1 \\
\hline
3\,6\,4
\end{array}
$$

8. The idiomatic use of this formula appears to be unknown beyond the looking-glass. Humpty Dumpty's construction of it, though literal-minded, is not so crassly uncomprehending as that of the White King (p. 201). (Sutherland, p. 197)

9. One logical truth which seems to escape Humpty Dumpty—or is he, like Descartes, sceptical not so much of the truth of such propositions as of the fallible human claim to have stated, proved, or computed any of them correctly? (Kemeny [24], p. 14; Purtill [35], p. 21)

10. This famous passage has immortalized Humpty Dumpty among philosophers of language as the leading exponent of what might be called 'subjective nominalism,' a theory in which two familiar views about language are somewhat extravagantly amalgamated. Ever since the issue between *phusis* and *nomos* (nature and law, or custom) was first fully joined in Plato's *Cratylus*, dissension has continued between those who believe that the meanings of words are rooted in the nature of things, and those who see them as a product of human choice and convention. Humpty Dumpty is on this point clearly a conventionalist, and to that extent a nominalist, since he believes it is words, and not things, that possess meaning. But he also claims that words mean just what *he* chooses them to mean. He is the master, they the servants; the conventions that govern his employment of them are arbitrarily laid down by himself, and he sees no reason for informing anyone beforehand what his stipulations are to be. His language is not private in the sense of referring only to private objects or in disdaining the use of the ordinary vocabulary, but it is so in making word-meaning dependent on

private acts of choice. Wittgenstein ([48] § 665, p. 18; [49], pp. 34ff., 41, 145; see also Pitcher [in Fann], pp. 327-28) persistently assails this view of meaning, whose extremer forms would manifestly be fatal, in practice, to any form of verbal communication. Conventions imply agreement and a willingness to conform with others, though not the opposing folly of attributing word-meanings to a ceremonial compact between language-users. For most purposes, obviously, such meanings are social products, created unwittingly by many generations of choice and conformity among earlier users of language. Once they are established, the individual has to accept them *as if* they were part of the natural order, and departs from them only at his peril. Nevertheless (or so Carroll thought) he still has a right of departure, either in creating new words, or in attaching new meanings to old ones; and so long as he exercises this right sparingly and announces his intention in advance, logicians, at least, can have no quarrel with him (*cf.* Carroll's *Symbolic Logic,* p. 165, quoted by Gardner, pp. 268-69).

Humpty Dumpty, it may be noticed, reverts to a more normal view in defining the words from *Jabberwocky,* which he does not claim to be endowing with private meanings of his own. His present dictatorial attitude results from superimposing a picture of the speaker's private and spontaneous act of selecting words to express his meaning on the fact that it is the existing and publicly accepted meanings of words that make them suitable or not for selection. *We* mean (and say) whatever we want by the use of words, but *they* mean what they have always meant, not whatever we want them to mean in a particular given case. (Alexander, p. 558; Holmes, p. 137; Pitcher, [in Fann], pp. 327-28, 331; Spacks, p. 94; Sutherland,

Humpty Dumpty took the book, and looked at it very carefully. 'That *seems* to be done right ——' he began.

'You're holding it upside down!' Alice interrupted.

'To be sure I was!' Humpty Dumpty said gaily, as she turned it round for him. 'I thought it looked a little queer. As I was saying, that *seems* to be done right — though I haven't time to look it over thoroughly just now — and that shows that there are three hundred and sixty-four days when you might get un-birthday presents ——'

'Certainly,' said Alice.

'And only *one* for birthday presents, you know. There's glory for you!'

'I don't know what you mean by "glory",' Alice said.

Humpty Dumpty smiled contemptuously. 'Of course you don't — till I tell you. I meant "there's a nice knock-down argument for you!"'

'But "glory" doesn't mean "a nice knock-down argument",' Alice objected.

'When *I* use a word,' Humpty Dumpty said in rather a scornful tone, 'it means just what I choose it to mean — neither more nor less.'

'The question is,' said Alice, 'whether you *can* make words mean different things.'

'The question is,' said Humpty Dumpty, 'which is to be master — that's all.'[10]

Alice was too much puzzled to say anything, so after a minute Humpty Dumpty began again. 'They've a temper, some of them — particularly verbs, they're the proudest — adjectives you can do anything with, but not verbs — however, *I* can manage the whole lot! Impenetrability! That's what *I* say!'

'Would you tell me, please,' said Alice, 'what that means?'

'Now you talk like a reasonable child,' said Humpty Dumpty, looking very much pleased. 'I meant by "impenetrability" that we've had enough of that subject, and it would be just as well if you'd mention what you mean to do next, as I suppose you don't intend to stop here all the rest of your life.'

'That's a great deal to make one word mean,' Alice said in a thoughtful tone.

'When I make a word do a lot of work like that,' said Humpty Dumpty, 'I always pay it extra.'[11]

'Oh!' said Alice. She was too much puzzled to make any other remark.

'Ah, you should see 'em come round me of a Saturday night,' Humpty Dumpty went on, wagging his head gravely from side to side: 'for to get their wages, you know.'

(Alice didn't venture to ask what he paid them with; and so you see I can't tell *you*.)

'You seem very clever at explaining words, sir,' said Alice. 'Would you kindly tell me the meaning of the poem "Jabberwocky"?'

'Let's hear it,' said Humpty Dumpty. 'I can explain all the poems that ever were invented — and a good many that haven't been invented just yet.'

This sounded very hopeful, so Alice repeated the first verse:

> *''Twas brillig, and the slithy toves*
> *Did gyre and gimble in the wabe:*
> *All mimsy were the borogoves,*
> *And the mome raths outgrabe.'*

pp. 97, 154-56; Austin [2], p. 62; Blanshard [6], p. 256; Broad [8], p. 26; Carney and Scheer [11], p. 85; Flew [17], p. 18; Morris [33], p. 21; Ritchie [37], pp. 259-60; Robinson [38], pp. 59, 72, 75, 76, 80; Woozley [50], p. 89)

11. *Impenetrability*—normally the equivalent of Locke's term *solidity* for the alleged simple idea most characteristic of matter—is certainly put here to hard and unaccustomed work, though no more than is done by a number of technical terms employed in the sciences. The main objection to it is not, indeed, that it is overtasked, but that its duties are too specialized for it to serve any useful purpose as part of the linguistic work force. Who needs a word so little in demand as that? (Sutherland, pp. 156-57; Holmes, p. 137; Kemeny [24], p. 3)

12. The concept of a 'portmanteau word' is Humpty Dumpty's most enduring contribution to the science of philology. His only actual examples of it are *slithy* and *mimsy*, though others (e.g., *frumious, burble, galumph,* and *chortle*) occur in the Jabberwocky poem. Of the other words discussed, *brillig, gyre,* and *gimble* are back-formations, while *mome* and *wabe* are mere phonetic abridgments; the remainder seem arbitrary. A portmanteau word is, broadly speaking, the opposite of a pun. It packs two meanings *into* a single word (or rather, nonword) whereas a pun gets two meanings *out of* one. (Sutherland, pp. 148-52; Gardner, p. 271; Partridge, pp. 162-88).

'That's enough to begin with,' Humpty Dumpty interrupted: 'there are plenty of hard words there. "*Brillig*" means four o'clock in the afternoon — the time when you begin *broiling* things for dinner.'

'That'll do very well,' said Alice: 'and "*slithy*"?'

'Well, "*slithy*" means "lithe and slimy". "Lithe" is the same as "active". You see, it's like a portmanteau — there are two meanings packed up into one word.'[12]

'I see it now,' Alice remarked thoughtfully: 'and what are "*toves*"?'

'Well, "*toves*" are something like badgers — they're something like lizards — and they're something like corkscrews.'

'They must be very curious creatures.'

'They are that,' said Humpty Dumpty: 'also they make their nests under sun-dials — also they live on cheese.'

'And what's to "*gyre*" and to "*gimble*"?'

'To "*gyre*" is to go round and round like a gyroscope. To "*gimble*" is to make holes like a gimlet.'

'And "*the wabe*" is the grass plot round a sun-dial, I suppose?' said Alice, surprised at her own ingenuity.

'Of course it is. It's called "*wabe*", you know, because it goes a long way before it, and a long way behind it ——'

'And a long way beyond it on each side,' Alice added.

'Exactly so. Well then, "*mimsy*" is "flimsy and miserable" (there's another portmanteau for you). And a "*borogove*" is a thin shabby-looking bird with its feathers sticking out all round — something like a live mop.'

'And then "*mome raths*"?' said Alice. 'If I'm not giving you too much trouble.'

'Well, a "*rath*" is a sort of green pig: but "*mome*" I'm

and when you've once heard it you'll be *quite* content. Who's been repeating all that hard stuff to you?'

'I read it in a book,' said Alice. 'But I had some poetry repeated to me, much easier than that, by — Tweedledee, I think.'

'As to poetry, you know,' said Humpty Dumpty, stretching out one of his great hands, '*I* can repeat poetry as well as other folk if it comes to that ——'

'Oh, it needn't come to that!' Alice hastily said, hoping to keep him from beginning.

'The piece I'm going to repeat,' he went on without noticing her remark, 'was written entirely for your amusement.'

Alice felt that in that case she really *ought* to listen to it, so she sat down, and said 'Thank you' rather sadly.

> '*In winter, when the fields are white,*
> *I sing this song for your delight ——*

only I don't sing it,' he explained.

'I see you don't,' said Alice.

'If you can *see* whether I'm singing or not, you've sharper eyes than most,' Humpty Dumpty remarked severely. Alice was silent.

> '*In spring, when woods are getting green,*
> *I'll try and tell you what I mean.*'

'Thank you very much,' said Alice.

> '*In summer, when the days are long,*
> *Perhaps you'll understand my song:*

not certain about. I think it's short for "from home" — meaning that they'd lost their way, you know.'

'And what does "*outgrabe*" mean?'

'Well, "*outgribing*" is something between bellowing and whistling, with a kind of sneeze in the middle: however, you'll hear it done, maybe — down in the wood yonder —

13. The prelude of Humpty Dumpty's song contains echoes of Alice's earlier conversation with the black kitten (p. 130). In the narrative proper, as in other accounts of diplomatic negotiations, the reasons for the squabble, the content of the ultimatum, and the precise nature of the final *démarche* are never clearly made out. In addition to the dearth of pronominal referents, already familiar from the evidence at the Knave of Hearts' trial, a further source of obscurity is created by the use of aposiopesis (breaking-off short) at crucial moments throughout.

Humpty Dumpty

In autumn, when the leaves are brown,
Take pen and ink and write it down ' [13]

'I will, if I can remember it so long,' said Alice.
'You needn't go on making remarks like that,' Humpty Dumpty said: 'they're not sensible, and they put me out.'

'I sent a message to the fish:
I told them "This is what I wish."

The little fishes of the sea,
They sent an answer back to me.

The little fishes' answer was
"We cannot do it, Sir, because ——"'

'I'm afraid I don't quite understand,' said Alice.
'It gets easier further on,' Humpty Dumpty replied.

'I sent to them again to say
"It will be better to obey."

The fishes answered with a grin,
"Why, what a temper you are in!"

I told them once, I told them twice:
They would not listen to advice.

I took a kettle large and new,
Fit for the deed I had to do.

My heart went hop, my heart went thump;
I filled the kettle at the pump.

Then some one came to me and said
"The little fishes are in bed."

I said to him, I said it plain,
"Then you must wake them up again."

I said it very loud and clear;
I went and shouted in his ear.'

'But he was very stiff and proud;
He said "You needn't shout so loud!"

And he was very proud and stiff;
He said "I'd go and wake them, if ——"

I took a corkscrew from the shelf:
I went to wake them up myself.

And when I found the door was locked,
I pulled and pushed and kicked and knocked.

And when I found the door was shut,
I tried to turn the handle, but ——'

There was a long pause.

'Is that all?' Alice timidly asked.

'That's all,' said Humpty Dumpty. 'Good-bye.'

This was rather sudden, Alice thought: but, after such a *very* strong hint that she ought to be going, she felt that it would hardly be civil to stay. So she held out her hand. 'Good-bye, till we meet again!' she said as cheerfully as she could.

'I shouldn't know you again if we *did* meet,' Humpty Dumpty replied in a discontented tone, giving her one of his fingers to shake; 'you're so exactly like other people.'

'The *face* is what one goes by, generally,' Alice remarked in a thoughtful tone.

'That's just what I complain of,' said Humpty Dumpty. 'Your face is the same as everybody has — the two eyes, so ——' (marking their places in the air with his thumb) 'nose in the middle, mouth under. It's always the same. Now if you had the two eyes on the same side of the nose,

Humpty Dumpty raised his voice almost to a scream as he repeated this verse, and Alice thought with a shudder, 'I wouldn't have been the messenger for *anything*!'

14. Victims of myopia apart, there are many to whom orientals, business executives, film stars and so forth all look exactly alike. Humpty Dumpty, however, is a uniquely defective case. Preoccupied as he is with generic similarities of facial arrangement, he cannot or will not attend to specific differences, and hence, so far as people are concerned, he has no *principium individuationis* whatever. (Sutherland, pp. 76*ff*.; Carney and Scheer [11], p. 5)

15. Having learned the trick of it, Alice indulges in a little aposiopesis on her own account, as well as taking comfort in the use of a polysyllable for therapeutic relief. If she knew how to swear, this would have been the very place for it; within the limits of a ladylike education, she does in fact do her best. (Sutherland, p. 221)

for instance — or the mouth at the top — that would be *some* help.'[14]

'It wouldn't look nice,' Alice objected. But Humpty Dumpty only shut his eyes and said 'Wait till you've tried.'

Alice waited a minute to see if he would speak again, but as he never opened his eyes or took any further notice of her, she said 'Good-bye!' once more, and, on getting no answer to this, she quietly walked away: but she couldn't help saying to herself as she went, 'Of all the unsatisfactory ——' (she repeated this aloud, as it was a great comfort to have such a long word to say) 'of all the unsatisfactory people I *ever* met ——'[15] She never finished the sentence, for at this moment a heavy crash shook the forest from end to end.

CHAPTER VII

THE LION AND THE UNICORN

THE next moment soldiers came running through the wood, at first in twos and threes, then ten or twenty together, and at last in such crowds that they seemed to fill the whole forest. Alice got behind a tree, for fear of being run over, and watched them go by.

She thought that in all her life she had never seen soldiers so uncertain on their feet: they were always tripping over something or other, and whenever one went down, several more always fell over him, so that the ground was soon covered with little heaps of men.

Then came the horses. Having four feet, these managed rather better than the foot-soldiers: but even *they* stumbled now and then; and it seemed to be a regular rule that, whenever a horse stumbled, the rider fell off instantly. The confusion got worse every moment, and Alice was very glad to get into an open place, where she found the White King seated on the ground, busily writing in his memorandum-book.

'I've sent them all!' the King cried in a tone of delight, on seeing Alice. 'Did you happen to meet any soldiers, my dear, as you came through the wood?'

'Yes, I did,' said Alice: 'several thousand, I should think.'

'Four thousand two hundred and seven, that's the exact number,' the King said, referring to his book. 'I couldn't send all the horses, you know, because two of them are wanted in the game. And I haven't sent the two Messengers, either. They're both gone to the town. Just look along the road, and tell me if you can see either of them.'

'I see nobody on the road,' said Alice.

'I only wish *I* had such eyes,' the King remarked in a

1. This passage, and its reprise a page or two later, are a perennial standby for philosophers who wish to horrify their readers with the dangers of hypostatizing the null class, and so fabricating nonentities. Because *nobody* functions grammatically very like *somebody*, there is a temptation to believe it the name of a peculiar, diaphanous sort of somebody, who is then unnecessarily added to a list of the world's inhabitants. In such ways does the language of abstraction darken counsel, corrupt communications, and beget bad philosophy, a theme much insisted on by Bacon, Hobbes, Locke, Berkeley, Hume, Kant, and their many modern successors. Most of the White King's critics among the latter simply dismiss him as a reifying idiot, and thus deny him such credit as he deserves for a perfectly explicit distinction between visible nobodies and visible real people. Russell ([40], p. 148) makes the more interesting point that Alice's 'I see nobody' is a genuine report of observation. It is not reducible to 'I do not see anybody,' which she could equally well say with her eyes shut, and which therefore fails to settle whether anyone is there or not. Alice is reporting that she has looked, but not seen anyone, and this really does provide evidence that there is not anyone in sight. (Alexander, p. 563; Holmes, p. 135; Pitcher [in Fann], p. 333; Sutherland, p. 199; Laird [25], p. 97; Terrell and Baker [46], p. 78)

2. If Haigha (see note 1, p. 66) is indeed G. E. Moore, the much-disputed problem of his behavior is solved at once. All Cambridge philosophers gesticulate and contort themselves in argument, whether they are happy or not; hence the name 'analytic movement.' Moore was unrivaled as

fretful tone. 'To be able to see Nobody! And at that distance too! Why, it's as much as *I* can do to see real people, by this light!'[1]

All this was lost on Alice, who was still looking intently along the road, shading her eyes with one hand. 'I see somebody now!' she exclaimed at last. 'But he's coming very slowly — and what curious attitudes he goes into!' (For the Messenger kept skipping up and down, and wriggling like an eel, as he came along, with his great hands spread out like fans on each side.)

'Not at all,' said the King. 'He's an Anglo-Saxon Messenger — and those are Anglo-Saxon attitudes. He only does them when he's happy. His name is Haigha.'[2] (He pronounced it so as to rhyme with 'mayor'.)

'I love my love with an H,' Alice couldn't help beginning, 'because he is Happy. I hate him with an H, because he is Hideous. I fed him with — with — with Ham-sandwiches and Hay.[3] His name is Haigha, and he lives ——'

'He lives on the Hill,' the King remarked simply, without the least idea that he was joining in the game, while Alice was still hesitating for the name of a town beginning with H. 'The other Messenger's called Hatta. I must have *two*, you know — to come and go. One to come, and one to go.'[4]

'I beg your pardon?' said Alice.

'It isn't respectable to beg,' said the King.

'I only meant that I didn't understand,' said Alice. 'Why one to come and one to go?'

'Don't I tell you?' the King repeated impatiently. 'I must have *two* — to fetch and carry. One to fetch, and one to carry.'

At this moment the Messenger arrived: he was far too much out of breath to say a word, and could only wave his hands about, and make the most fearful faces at the poor King.

'This young lady loves you with an H,' the King said, introducing Alice in the hope of turning off the Messenger's attention from himself — but it was no use — the Anglo-Saxon attitudes only got more extraordinary every moment, while the great eyes rolled wildly from side to side.

'You alarm me!' said the King. 'I feel faint — Give me a ham-sandwich!'

On which the Messenger, to Alice's great amusement, opened a bag that hung round his neck, and handed a sandwich to the King, who devoured it greedily.

a gesticulator. Nobody's attitudes *could* have been more Anglo-Saxon than his. But it has to be admitted that they were not.

3. Alice's words are again prophetic; indeed, as Spacks remarks (p. 98), they virtually create the event that follows. The same is true of her proleptic account of the battle between the Lion and the Unicorn. She does not initiate this encounter, but she either determines, or has foreknowledge of, its outcome.

4. An unlikely, if not impossible, division of labor between activities logically complementary to each other. For the misunderstanding of Alice's query on the matter, see note 8, p. 192. She extricates herself, as before, by paraphrase and restatement of the question. (Sutherland, p. 197)

5. In common with such equivalents as *peerless, unequalled, incomparable, nonpareil,* the phrase *nothing like* has long since been escalated into a term of commendation (meaning 'nothing so good as'), though it can still function merely to express a judgment of nonsimilarity, or uniqueness at a given level. The King interprets it in this more literal and conservative sense, to Alice's discomfiture. A riposte, as it happens, lies ready to hand, if only it had occurred to her: if nothing is like hay, it would clearly do just as well instead. (Alexander, p. 557; Sutherland, p. 196)

6. While the King still adheres obsessively to the idea of nobody as a walking nonentity, the Messenger, like Alice, takes a more conventional view. He detects a rebuke,

therefore, in what the King conceives as a mild compliment, or harmless statement of fact. His attempted self-exculpation is again misconstrued, however, as a would-be claim of fact, which the King, to his own satisfaction, is able to refute. The conceptual finagling here has a distant but disturbing resemblance to St. Anselm's ontological argument for God's existence, whereby a being 'greater than which none other can be conceived' is argued into reality on the ground that a nonexisting being, however great, would not meet the case, since an existing being, otherwise its equal, would be greater still. If valid, this could also provide a knock-down ontological argument for nobody himself, since 'nobody is greater than God' is by definition necessarily true. Vain disputations of this sort are, however, precisely what the present proceedings are intended to satirize, and prevent. For a profane version of the argument, see the remarks of Herr Niemand in Dodgson's *Euclid and his Modern Rivals* (pp. 181*ff*). The 'nobody' joke itself is as old as Homer's *Outis* (*Odyssey*, Bk. IX). (Alexander, p. 563; Holmes, p. 135; Pitcher [in Fann], p. 334, citing Wittgenstein [49], p. 69; Spacks, p. 94; Sutherland, pp. 199*ff*.; Ayer [3], p. 213; Barnes [5], p. 50; Carney and Scheer [11], p. 138; Flew [16], p. 7; Lazerowitz [26], p. 79; Stebbing [45], p. 139; Wells [47], pp. 129*ff*.)

'Another sandwich!' said the King.

'There's nothing but hay left now,' the Messenger said, peeping into the bag.

'Hay, then,' the King faintly murmured.

Alice was glad to see that it revived him a good deal. 'There's nothing like eating hay when you're faint,' he remarked to her, as he munched away.

'I should think throwing cold water over you would be better,' Alice suggested: '— or some sal-volatile.'

'I didn't say there was nothing *better*,' the King replied. 'I said there was nothing *like* it.' Which Alice did not venture to deny.[5]

'Who did you pass on the road?' the King went on, holding out his hand to the Messenger for some more hay.

'Nobody,' said the Messenger.

'Quite right,' said the King: 'this young lady saw him too. So of course Nobody walks slower than you.'

'I do my best,' the Messenger said in a sullen tone. 'I'm sure nobody walks much faster than I do!'

'He can't do that,' said the King, 'or else he'd have been here first.[6] However, now you've got your breath, you may tell us what's happened in the town.'

'I'll whisper it,' said the Messenger, putting his hands to his mouth in the shape of a trumpet and stooping so as to get close to the King's ear. Alice was sorry for this, as she wanted to hear the news too. However, instead of whispering, he simply shouted at the top of his voice 'They're at it again!'

'Do you call *that* a whisper!' cried the poor King, jumping up and shaking himself. 'If you do such a thing again I'll have you buttered! It went through and through my head like an earthquake!'

'It would have to be a very tiny earthquake!' thought Alice. 'Who are at it again?' she ventured to ask.

'Why, the Lion and the Unicorn, of course,' said the King.

'Fighting for the crown?'

'Yes, to be sure,' said the King: 'and the best of the joke is, that it's *my* crown all the while! Let's run and see them.' And they trotted off, Alice repeating to herself, as she ran, the words of the old song:—

'The Lion and the Unicorn were fighting for the crown;
The Lion beat the Unicorn all round the town.
Some gave them white bread and some gave them brown;
Some gave them plum-cake and drummed them out of town.'

'And does — the one — that wins — get the crown?' she asked, as well as she could, for the long run was putting her quite out of breath.

'Dear me, no!' said the King. 'What an idea!'

'Would you — be good enough ——' Alice panted out, after running a little further, 'to stop a minute — just to get — one's breath?'

'I'm *good* enough,' the King said, 'only I'm not strong enough. You see, a minute goes by so fearfully quick. You might as well try to stop a Bandersnatch!'⁷

Alice had no more breath for talking, so they trotted on in silence, till they came in sight of a great crowd, in the middle of which the Lion and Unicorn were fighting. They were in such a cloud of dust that at first Alice could not make out which was which: but she soon managed to distinguish the Unicorn by his horn.

They placed themselves close to where Hatta, the other

7. The King is as reliably literal-minded as ever. Misconstruing his task as that of arresting a runaway *object* of some sort, rather than his own progress, he sees only a practical difficulty, to which he is physically, though not morally, unequal. Like the Hatter (p. 70) he is also a subscriber to the now-despised 'river' theory of time. It does not strike him that if a minute goes by so rapidly, it must needs require *another* time in which to do so; and that the same question, How fast does it go? can now be asked about *this* time, thus calling for a third time, and so on ad infinitum. (Monro [28], p. 69)

'Speak, can't you!' Haigha cried impatiently. But Hatta only munched away, and drank some more tea.

'Speak, won't you!' cried the King. 'How are they getting on with the fight?'

Hatta made a desperate effort, and swallowed a large piece of bread-and-butter. 'They're getting on very well,' he said in a choking voice: 'each of them has been down about eighty-seven times.'

'Then I suppose they'll soon bring the white bread and the brown?' Alice ventured to remark.

'It's waiting for 'em now,' said Hatta: 'this is a bit of it as I'm eating.'

There was a pause in the fight just then, and the Lion and the Unicorn sat down, panting, while the King called out 'Ten minutes allowed for refreshments!' Haigha and Hatta set to work at once, carrying round trays of white and brown bread. Alice took a piece to taste, but it was *very* dry.

'I don't think they'll fight any more to-day,' the King said to Hatta: 'go and order the drums to begin.' And Hatta went bounding away like a grasshopper.

For a minute or two Alice stood silently watching him. Suddenly she brightened up. 'Look, look!' she cried, pointing eagerly. 'There's the White Queen running across the country! She came flying out of the wood over yonder — How fast those Queens *can* run!'

'There's some enemy after her, no doubt,' the King said, without even looking round. 'That wood's full of them.'

'But aren't you going to run and help her?' Alice asked, very much surprised at his taking it so quietly.

'No use, no use!' said the King. 'She runs so fearfully

Messenger, was standing watching the fight, with a cup of tea in one hand and a piece of bread and butter in the other.

'He's only just out of prison, and he hadn't finished his tea when he was sent in,' Haigha whispered to Alice: 'and they only give them oyster-shells in there — so, you see, he's very hungry and thirsty. How are you, dear child?' he went on, putting his arm affectionately round Hatta's neck.

Hatta looked round and nodded, and went on with his bread-and-butter.

'Were you happy in prison, dear child?' said Haigha.

Hatta looked round once more, and this time a tear or two trickled down his cheek: but not a word would he say.

quick. You might as well try to catch a Bandersnatch! But I'll make a memorandum about her, if you like — She's a dear good creature,' he repeated softly to himself, as he opened his memorandum-book. 'Do you spell "creature" with a double "e"?'

At this moment the Unicorn sauntered by them, with his hands in his pockets. 'I had the best of it this time!' he said to the King, just glancing at him as he passed.

'A little — a little,' the King replied, rather nervously. 'You shouldn't have run him through with your horn, you know.'

'It didn't hurt him,' the Unicorn said carelessly, and he was going on, when his eye happened to fall upon Alice: he turned round instantly, and stood for some time looking at her with an air of the deepest disgust.

'What — is — this?' he said at last.

'This is a child!' Haigha replied eagerly, coming in front of Alice to introduce her, and spreading out both his hands towards her in an Anglo-Saxon attitude. 'We only found it to-day. It's as large as life, and twice as natural!'

'I always thought they were fabulous monsters!' said the Unicorn. 'Is it alive?'

'It can talk,' said Haigha solemnly.

The Unicorn looked dreamily at Alice, and said 'Talk, child.'

Alice could not help her lips curling up into a smile as she began: 'Do you know, I always thought Unicorns were fabulous monsters, too! I never saw one alive before!'

'Well, now that we *have* seen each other,' said the Unicorn, 'if you'll believe in me, I'll believe in you. Is that a bargain?'[8]

'Yes, if you like,' said Alice.

8. A bad bargain, from Alice's point of view. Having survived her identity crisis, and recovered from Tweedledum's aspersions on her claim to reality, she ought by now to have acquired a solidly Cartesian conviction of her own existence. The Jamesian 'will to believe' of a notorious nonentity can therefore have no reassurance to offer her; yet for this she is prepared to barter away her own right to scepticism.

This Unicorn, by the way, was a great favorite with G. E. Moore, who practically kept it as a philosophical pet. Wherever the topic of the real versus the imaginary occurs in his works, it is regularly trotted forth; nor will just any old unicorn do (as it does for most philosophers); it has to be, and always is, the one from *Alice*. (Moore [29], pp. 211-18; [30], p. 120; [31], pp. 243-45; [32], pp. 24-27)

'Come, fetch out the plum-cake, old man!' the Unicorn went on, turning from her to the King. 'None of your brown bread for me!'

'Certainly — certainly!' the King muttered, and beckoned to Haigha. 'Open the bag!' he whispered. 'Quick! Not that one — that's full of hay!'

Haigha took a large cake out of the bag, and gave it to Alice to hold, while he got out a dish and carving-knife. How they all came out of it Alice couldn't guess. It was just like a conjuring trick, she thought.

The Lion had joined them while this was going on: he looked very tired and sleepy, and his eyes were half shut. 'What's this!' he said, blinking lazily at Alice, and speaking in a deep hollow tone that sounded like the tolling of a great bell.

'Ah, what *is* it, now?' the Unicorn cried eagerly. 'You'll never guess! *I* couldn't.'

The Lion looked at Alice wearily. 'Are you animal — or vegetable — or mineral?' he said, yawning at every other word.

'It's a fabulous monster!' the Unicorn cried out, before Alice could reply.

'Then hand round the plum-cake, Monster,' the Lion said, lying down and putting his chin on his paws. 'And sit down, both of you,' (to the King and the Unicorn): 'fair play with the cake, you know!'

The King was evidently very uncomfortable at having to sit down between the two great creatures: but there was no other place for him.

'What a fight we might have for the crown, *now*!' the Unicorn said, looking slyly up at the crown, which the poor King was nearly shaking off his head, he trembled so much.

'I should win easy,' said the Lion.

'I'm not so sure of that,' said the Unicorn.

'Why, I beat you all round the town, you chicken!' the Lion replied angrily, half getting up as he spoke.

Here the King interrupted, to prevent the quarrel going on: he was very nervous, and his voice quite quivered. 'All round the town?' he said. 'That's a good long way. Did you go by the old bridge, or the market-place? You get the best view by the old bridge.'

'I'm sure I don't know,' the Lion growled out as he lay down again. 'There was too much dust to see anything. What a time the Monster is, cutting up that cake!'

Alice had seated herself on the bank of a little brook, with the great dish on her knees, and was sawing away diligently with the knife. 'It's very provoking!' she said, in reply to the Lion (she was getting quite used to being called "the Monster"). 'I've cut off several slices already, but they will always join on again!'

'You don't know how to manage Looking-glass cakes,' the Unicorn remarked. 'Hand it round first, and cut it afterwards.'

This sounded nonsense, but Alice very obediently got up, and carried the dish round, and the cake divided itself into three pieces as she did so. '*Now* cut it up,' said the Lion, as she returned to her place with the empty dish.[9]

'I say, this isn't fair!' cried the Unicorn, as Alice sat with the knife in her hand, very much puzzled how to begin. 'The Monster has given the Lion twice as much as me!'

'She's kept none for herself, anyhow,' said the Lion. 'Do you like plum-cake, Monster?'

But, before Alice could answer him, the drums began.

Where the noise came from, she couldn't make out: the air seemed full of it, and it rang through and through her

9. The most resolute attempt in the narrative at a reversal of normal time order; but as an account of action it taxes credulity to the limit. If the cake divides itself, how can Alice be blamed for misapportioning it? And how is she to cut what has already been dispersed and distributed? In fact she never does so, and this ought, if it is her action, to have prevented the previous division. Whether an effect can precede its cause has been seriously debated. But if the cause never occurs, it is hard to see how anything, either before or after it, can be regarded as its effect. (Holmes, p. 146)

head till she felt quite deafened. She started to her feet, and in her terror she sprang across the brook,

*   *   *   *   *
*   *   *   *
*   *   *   *

and had just time to see the Lion and Unicorn rise to their feet, with angry looks at being interrupted in their feast, before she dropped to her knees, and put her hands over her ears, vainly trying to shut out the dreadful uproar.

'If *that* doesn't "drum them out of town",' she thought to herself, 'nothing ever will!'

CHAPTER VIII

'IT'S MY OWN INVENTION'

AFTER a while the noise seemed gradually to die away, till all was dead silence, and Alice lifted up her head in some alarm. There was no one to be seen, and her first thought was that she must have been dreaming about the Lion and the Unicorn and those queer Anglo-Saxon Messengers. However, there was the great dish still lying at her feet, on which she had tried to cut the plum-cake, 'So I wasn't dreaming, after all,' she said to herself, 'unless — unless we're all part of the same dream. Only I do hope it's *my* dream, and not the Red King's! I don't like belonging to another person's dream,' she went on in a rather complaining tone: 'I've a great mind to go and wake him, and see what happens!'

At this moment her thoughts were interrupted by a loud shouting of 'Ahoy! Ahoy! Check!' and a Knight, dressed in crimson armour, came galloping down upon her, brandishing a great club. Just as he reached her, the horse stopped suddenly: 'You're my prisoner!' the Knight cried, as he tumbled off his horse.

Startled as she was, Alice was more frightened for him than for herself at the moment, and watched him with some anxiety as he mounted again. As soon as he was comfortably in the saddle, he began once more 'You're my ——' but here another voice broke in 'Ahoy! Ahoy! Check!' and Alice looked round in some surprise for the new enemy.

The Philosopher's Alice

209

'It's My Own Invention'

This time it was a White Knight. He drew up at Alice's side, and tumbled off his horse just as the Red Knight had done: then he got on again, and the two Knights sat and looked at each other without speaking. Alice looked from one to the other in some bewilderment.

'She's *my* prisoner, you know!' the Red Knight said at last.

'Yes, but then *I* came and rescued her!' the White Knight replied.

'Well, we must fight for her, then,' said the Red Knight, as he took up his helmet (which hung from the saddle, and was something the shape of a horse's head), and put it on.

'You will observe the Rules of Battle, of course?' the White Knight remarked, putting on his helmet too.

'I always do,' said the Red Knight, and they began banging away at each other with such fury that Alice got behind a tree to be out of the way of the blows.

'I wonder, now, what the Rules of Battle are,' she said to herself, as she watched the fight, timidly peeping out from her hiding-place:[1] 'one Rule seems to be that, if one Knight hits the other, he knocks him off his horse, and if he misses, he tumbles off himself — and another Rule seems to be that they hold their clubs in their arms, as if they were Punch and Judy. What a noise they make when they tumble. Just like fire-irons falling into the fender! And how quiet the horses are! They let them get on and off them just as if they were tables!'

Another Rule of Battle, that Alice had not noticed, seemed to be that they always fell on their heads, and the battle ended with their both falling off in this way, side by side: when they got up again, they shook hands, and then the Red Knight mounted and galloped off.

1. To an ignorant observer, the Rules of Battle—as distinct from its regularities—are liable to be just as mysterious as those of croquet (p. 82) or chess (p. 130). Prohibitions, in particular, are likely to remain undetectable, since so long as the Knights fight fairly there will be nothing to indicate what they are not allowed to do. Alice has the further problem of discriminating, on Kantian lines, between legal and moral actions, that is, those in which the contestants merely act within the rules and those in which they consciously observe and obey them. A converse distinction is similarly needed to mark the difference between an error and a foul, and although the general object may be clear enough to her, only the end of the contest can tell her what officially counts as victory or defeat. (Pitcher [in Fann], p. 327, citing Wittgenstein [48], § 54, and [49], p. 13)

manage by himself: however, she managed to shake him out of it at last.

'Now one can breathe more easily,' said the Knight, putting back his shaggy hair with both hands, and turning his gentle face and large mild eyes to Alice. She thought she had never seen such a strange-looking soldier in all her life.

He was dressed in tin armour, which seemed to fit him very badly, and he had a queer little deal box fastened across his shoulders upside-down, and with the lid hanging open. Alice looked at it with great curiosity.

'I see you're admiring my little box,' the Knight said in a friendly tone. 'It's my own invention — to keep clothes and sandwiches in. You see I carry it upside-down, so that the rain can't get in.'

'But the things can get *out*,' Alice gently remarked. 'Do you know the lid's open?'

'I didn't know it,' the Knight said, a shade of vexation passing over his face. 'Then all the things must have fallen out! And the box is no use without them.' He unfastened it as he spoke, and was just going to throw it into the bushes, when a sudden thought seemed to strike him, and he hung it carefully on a tree. 'Can you guess why I did that?' he said to Alice.

Alice shook her head.

'In hopes some bees may make a nest in it — then I should get the honey.'

'But you've got a bee-hive — or something like one — fastened to the saddle,' said Alice.

'Yes, it's a very good bee-hive,' the Knight said in a discontented tone, 'one of the best kind. But not a single bee has come near it yet. And the other thing is a mouse-

'It was a glorious victory, wasn't it?' said the White Knight, as he came up panting.

'I don't know,' Alice said doubtfully. 'I don't want to be anybody's prisoner. I want to be a Queen.'

'So you will, when you've crossed the next brook,' said the White Knight. 'I'll see you safe to the end of the wood — and then I must go back, you know. That's the end of my move.'

'Thank you very much,' said Alice. 'May I help you off with your helmet?' It was evidently more than he could

trap. I suppose the mice keep the bees out — or the bees keep the mice out, I don't know which.'

'I was wondering what the mouse-trap was for,' said Alice. 'It isn't very likely there would be any mice on the horse's back.'

'Not very likely, perhaps,' said the Knight; 'but, if they *do* come, I don't choose to have them running all about.'[2]

'You see,' he went on after a pause, 'it's as well to be provided for *everything*. That's the reason the horse has anklets round his feet.'

'But what are they for?' Alice asked in a tone of great curiosity.

'To guard against the bites of sharks,' the Knight replied. 'It's an invention of my own. And now help me on. I'll go with you to the end of the wood — What's that dish for?'

'It's meant for plum-cake,' said Alice.

'We'd better take it with us,' the Knight said. 'It'll come in handy if we find any plum-cake. Help me to get it into this bag.'

This took a long time to manage, though Alice held the bag open very carefully, because the Knight was so *very* awkward in putting in the dish: the first two or three times that he tried he fell in himself instead. 'It's rather a tight fit, you see,' he said, as they got it in at last; 'there are so many candlesticks in the bag.' And he hung it to the saddle, which was already loaded with bunches of carrots, and fire-irons, and many other things.

'I hope you've got your hair well fastened on?' he continued, as they set off.

'Only in the usual way,' Alice said, smiling.

2. As Jourdain puts it (p. 56), 'the need to devote great care to the elimination of difficulties which rarely occur' is a common duty of philosophers, and especially of logicians. The White Knight's practices are compared to those of Boole, a fellow pioneer in mathematical logic, though both are suspected of wanting to base logic on psychology. Broad sees a resemblance to McTaggart, a similarly meticulous and precautionary metaphysician. (Broad [9], p. 129; [10], p. 8)

3. An inept comparison, founded on an equivocation in which pungency is mistaken as a standard of violence. A similar folly is perpetrated below (p. 215); and yet many such comparisons (e.g., 'weak as water') are tolerated in language, presumably because the shift from a physical to a mental application is accepted as a metaphor, rather than a genuinely equivocal use of the term. (Sutherland, p. 167)

4. An illustration of the ineffectiveness of purely conceptual remedies in the solution of practical problems. The White Knight's disinterested inventiveness has led such commentators as Empson and Taylor to treat him as an archetype of the Victorian scientist. There is more warrant, however, for Jourdain's description of him (p. 13) as a practical idealist (of the T. H. Green type). Most of his difficulties, after all, arise from an inability to accept or adjust to the laws of Newtonian mechanics. Gravity (as Taylor observes) is his main enemy, as Time is that of

the Hatter, and his energies are largely spent in vain attempts to defeat it.

5. There is a lurking paradox here, ignored by author, illustrator, and commentators alike. If the Knight falls off behind whenever the horse moves on, it is quite impossible for him ever to fall off in front when it stops, let alone sideways at other times, since by then he will no longer be aboard. The rules as stated are mutually inconsistent, and admit of but one outcome, the other options being vacuous. The *only* time the Knight spends in the saddle is when the horse is stationary. Hence he never actually rides it at all. For a similar, though more complex, Carrollian puzzle concerning comings and goings in a barber's shop, which has provoked the attention of Russell, W. E. Johnson, and a number of later logicians, see "A Logical Paradox" (*Mind* July 1894, reprinted in *Diversions and Digressions of Lewis Carroll*, Dover ed. [1961], pp. 312-16).

'It's My Own Invention'

'That's hardly enough,' he said anxiously. 'You see, the wind is so *very* strong here. It's as strong as soup.'[3]

'Have you invented a plan for keeping one's hair from being blown off?' Alice enquired.

'Not yet,' said the Knight. 'But I've got a plan for keeping it from *falling* off.'

'I should like to hear it very much.'

'First you take an upright stick,' said the Knight. 'Then you make your hair creep up it, like a fruit-tree. Now the reason hair falls off is because it hangs *down* — things never fall *upwards*, you know.[4] It's my own invention. You may try it if you like.'

It didn't sound a comfortable plan, Alice thought, and for a few minutes she walked on in silence, puzzling over the idea, and every now and then stopping to help the poor Knight, who certainly was *not* a good rider.

Whenever the horse stopped (which it did very often), he fell off in front; and whenever it went on again (which it generally did rather suddenly), he fell off behind. Otherwise he kept on pretty well, except that he had a habit of now and then falling off sideways;[5] and as he generally did this on the side on which Alice was walking, she soon found that it was the best plan not to walk *quite* close to the horse.

'I'm afraid you've not had much practice in riding,' she ventured to say, as she was helping him up from his fifth tumble.

The Knight looked very much surprised, and a little offended at the remark. 'What makes you say that?' he asked, as he scrambled back into the saddle, keeping hold of Alice's hair with one hand, to save himself from falling over on the other side.

'Because people don't fall off quite so often, when they've had much practice.'

'I've had plenty of practice,' the Knight said very bravely: 'plenty of practice!'

Alice could think of nothing better to say than 'Indeed?' but she said it as heartily as she could. They went on a little way in silence after this, the Knight with his eyes shut, muttering to himself, and Alice watching anxiously for the next tumble.

'The great art of riding,' the Knight suddenly began in a loud voice, waving his right arm as he spoke, 'is to keep ——' Here the sentence ended as suddenly as it had begun, as the Knight fell heavily on the top of his head

exactly in the path where Alice was walking. She was quite frightened this time, and said in an anxious tone, as she picked him up, 'I hope no bones are broken?'

'None to speak of,' the Knight said, as if he didn't mind breaking two or three of them. 'The great art of riding, as I was saying, is — to keep your balance. Like this, you know ——'

He let go the bridle, and stretched out both his arms to show Alice what he meant, and this time he fell flat on his back, right under the horse's feet.

'Plenty of practice!' he went on repeating, all the time that Alice was getting him on his feet again. 'Plenty of practice!'

'It's too ridiculous!' cried Alice, getting quite out of patience. 'You ought to have a wooden horse on wheels, that you ought!'

'Does that kind go smoothly?' the Knight asked in a tone of great interest, clasping his arms round the horse's neck as he spoke, just in time to save himself from tumbling off again.

'Much more smoothly than a live horse,' Alice said, with a little scream of laughter, in spite of all she could do to prevent it.

'I'll get one,' the Knight said thoughtfully to himself. 'One or two — several.'

There was a short silence after this; then the Knight went on again. 'I'm a great hand at inventing things. Now, I dare say you noticed, the last time you picked me up, that I was looking thoughtful?'

'You *were* a little grave,' said Alice.

'Well, just then I was inventing a new way of getting over a gate — would you like to hear it?'

6. A worse comparison than before, since it fuses not merely two meanings, but two distinct (though related) words. Alexander (pp. 556-57) credits the White Knight with sharing Plato's opinion that if different things have the same name, there must be good reason for it, in that they must have something in common. (Sutherland, p. 167)

'Very much indeed,' Alice said politely.

'I'll tell you how I came to think of it,' said the Knight. 'You see, I said to myself, "The only difficulty is with the feet: the *head* is high enough already". Now, first I put my head on the top of the gate — then the head's high enough — then I stand on my head — then the feet are high enough, you see — then I'm over, you see.'

'Yes, I suppose you'd be over when that was done,' Alice said thoughtfully: 'but don't you think it would be rather hard?'

'I haven't tried it yet,' the Knight said gravely: 'so I can't tell for certain — but I'm afraid it *would* be a little hard.'

He looked so vexed at the idea, that Alice changed the subject hastily. 'What a curious helmet you've got!' she said cheerfully. 'Is that your invention too?'

The Knight looked down proudly at his helmet, which hung from the saddle. 'Yes,' he said, 'but I've invented a better one than that — like a sugar-loaf. When I used to wear it, if I fell off the horse, it always touched the ground directly. So I had a *very* little way to fall, you see — But there *was* the danger of falling *into* it, to be sure. That happened to me once — and the worst of it was, before I could get out again, the other White Knight came and put it on. He thought it was his own helmet.'

The Knight looked so solemn about it that Alice did not dare to laugh. 'I'm afraid you must have hurt him,' she said in a trembling voice, 'being on the top of his head.'

'I had to kick him, of course,' the Knight said, very seriously. 'And then he took the helmet off again — but it took hours and hours to get me out. I was as fast as — as lightning, you know.'[6]

'But that's a different kind of fastness,' Alice objected.

The Knight shook his head. 'It was all kinds of fastness with me, I can assure you!' he said. He raised his hands in some excitement as he said this, and instantly rolled out of the saddle, and fell headlong into a deep ditch.

Alice ran to the side of the ditch to look for him. She was rather startled by the fall, as for some time he had kept on very well, and she was afraid that he really *was* hurt this time. However, though she could see nothing but the soles of his feet, she was much relieved to hear that he was talking on in his usual tone. 'All kinds of fastness,' he repeated: 'but it was careless of him to put another man's helmet on — with the man in it, too.'

'How *can* you go on talking so quietly, head downwards?' Alice asked, as she dragged him out by the feet, and laid him in a heap on the bank.

The Knight looked surprised at the question. 'What does it matter where my body happens to be?' he said. 'My mind goes on working all the same. In fact, the more head downwards I am, the more I keep inventing new things.'[7]

'Now the cleverest thing that I ever did,' he went on after a pause, 'was inventing a new pudding during the meat-course.'

'In time to have it cooked for the next course?' said Alice. 'Well, that *was* quick work, certainly.'

'Well, not the *next* course,' the Knight said in a slow thoughtful tone; 'no, certainly not the next *course*.'

'Then it would have to be the next day. I suppose you wouldn't have two pudding-courses in one dinner.'

'Well, not the *next* day,' the Knight repeated as before: 'not the next *day*. In fact,' he went on, holding his head down, and his voice getting lower and lower, 'I don't believe that pudding ever *was* cooked! In fact, I don't believe that pudding ever *will* be cooked! And yet it was a very clever pudding to invent.'

'What did you mean it to be made of?' Alice asked, hoping to cheer him up, for he seemed quite low-spirited about it.[8]

'It began with blotting-paper,' the Knight answered with a groan.

'That wouldn't be very nice, I'm afraid ——'

'Not very nice *alone*,' he interrupted, quite eagerly: 'but you've no idea what a difference it makes, mixing it with other things — such as gunpowder and sealing-wax. And here I must leave you.'

Alice could only look puzzled: she was thinking of the pudding.

'You are sad,' the Knight said in an anxious tone: 'let me sing you a song to comfort you.'

7. The White Knight's assertions appear, at first sight, to imply a thoroughgoing acceptance of old-fashioned Cartesian dualism, in which mind and body are regarded as separate and distinct substances, entirely independent of one another. In maintaining, however, that his mind actually works better when he is head downwards, the Knight in effect concedes, as did Descartes himself, that the empirical evidence is all in favor of interaction between them. Present-day opinion would still disdain this view as outmoded, since it clings, however incoherently, to the notion that mind is a substance. But no theory on this subject is entirely free from difficulties. Even the fashionable modern belief that mind-events and brain-events are in some sense identical has the problem of explaining how it is to avoid saying, in the present case, that the Knight's mind is upside down. (Holmes, p. 143)

8. The divorce between theory and practice is always dispiriting to idealists. As Marx said of Hegel —whom *he* claimed to have found standing on his head—the problem is not simply to interpret the world, but to change it (*Theses on Feuerbach,* No. XI).

   The Knight's hypothetical pudding illustrates the soundly idealist 'law of the transformation of quantity into quality,' subsequently restated by G. E. Moore as the 'principle of organic wholes': elements in combination exhibit new, 'toti-resultant' properties, which are not reducible to a mere aggregation of those they possessed individually before amalgamation.

'Is it very long?' Alice asked, for she had heard a good deal of poetry that day.

'It's long,' said the Knight, 'but it's very, *very* beautiful. Everybody that hears me sing it — either it brings the *tears* into their eyes, or else ——'

'Or else what?' said Alice, for the Knight had made a sudden pause.

'Or else it doesn't, you know.[9] The name of the song is called "*Haddocks' Eyes*".'

'Oh, that's the name of the song, is it?' Alice said, trying to feel interested.

'No, you don't understand,' the Knight said, looking a little vexed. 'That's what the name is *called*. The name really *is* "*The Aged Aged Man*".'

'Then I ought to have said "That's what the *song* is called"?' Alice corrected herself.

'No, you oughtn't: that's another thing. The *song* is called "*Ways and Means*": but that's only what it's *called*, you know!'

'Well, what *is* the song, then?' said Alice, who was by this time completely bewildered.

'I was coming to that,' the Knight said. 'The song really is "*A-sitting On a Gate*": and the tune's my own invention.'[10]

So saying, he stopped his horse and let the reins fall on its neck: then, slowly beating time with one hand, and with a faint smile lighting up his gentle, foolish face, he began.

Of all the strange things that Alice saw in her journey Through The Looking-Glass, this was the one that she always remembered most clearly. Years afterwards she could bring the whole scene back again, as if it had been

9. An essentially vacuous claim, since it merely sets forth the logical truism, *p* or not-*p*, embodied in the 'law of excluded middle.' Where two alternatives are mutually exclusive and collectively exhaustive of a given universe of discourse, their disjunctive assertion conveys no information whatever. Being true of everything, always, in all possible worlds, it is interesting only to logicians. (Alexander, pp. 557-58; Gardner, p. 306; Pitcher [in Fann], p. 320, citing Wittgenstein, *Tractatus*, 4.461; Purtill [35], p. 21)

10. Since anything can be given a name, including a name itself, and since the name of a thing is not necessarily the same as what it is called, the White Knight has a perfect right to the distinctions here enumerated, though it is not obvious what reasons he has for making them. The distinctions themselves, between what the song's name is called, the song's name itself, what the song is called, and the designated song-*an-sich*, are not only legitimate, but actually useful to logicians who need to refer separately to different 'levels' of language in order to avoid paradoxes. Their importance, as Jourdain remarks (p. 22), was first made clear to logicians by Russell and Frege, though neither of them, unaccountably, admits to having been anticipated by the White Knight. Some have argued that the Knight is at fault in identifying the song as 'A-sitting On A Gate,' since the latter is still a title of some sort, and not a song; his duty at this point was therefore to prevaricate no further, but simply to deliver the selection as advertised. For a logically exhaustive analysis of the passage, see Nagel pp. 1878*ff*. (Gardner, p. 306; Holmes, pp. 138-39; Pitcher [in Fann], pp. 324-25; Spacks, p. 96; Sutherland, pp. 119*ff*.; Keene [23], pp. vii-viii)

only yesterday — the mild blue eyes and kindly smile of
the Knight — the setting sun gleaming through his hair,
and shining on his armour in a blaze of light that quite
dazzled her — the horse quietly moving about, with the
reins hanging loose on his neck, cropping the grass at her
feet — and the black shadows of the forest behind — all
this she took in like a picture, as, with one hand shading
her eyes, she leant against a tree, watching the strange
pair, and listening, in a half-dream, to the melancholy
music of the song.

'But the tune *isn't* his own invention,' she said to herself: 'it's *"I give thee all, I can no more"*.' She stood and
listened very attentively, but no tears came into her eyes.

> *'I'll tell thee everything I can;*
> *There's little to relate.*
> *I saw an aged aged man,*
> *A-sitting on a gate.*
> *"Who are you, aged man?" I said.*
> *"And how is it you live?"*
> *And his answer trickled through my head*
> *Like water through a sieve.*
>
> *He said "I look for butterflies*
> *That sleep among the wheat:*
> *I make them into mutton pies,*
> *And sell them in the street.*
> *I sell them unto men," he said,*
> *"Who sail on stormy seas;*
> *And that's the way I get my bread —*
> *A trifle, if you please."*
>
> *But I was thinking of a plan*
> *To dye one's whiskers green,*

'It's My Own Invention'

And always use so large a fan
  That they could not be seen.[11]
So, having no reply to give
  To what the old man said,
I cried "Come, tell me how you live!"
  And thumped him on the head.

His accents mild took up the tale:
  He said "I go my ways,
And when I find a mountain-rill,
  I set it in a blaze;
And thence they make a stuff they call
  Rowlands' Macassar Oil —
Yet twopence-halfpenny is all
  They give me for my toil."

But I was thinking of a way
  To feed oneself on batter,
And so go on from day to day
  Getting a little fatter.
I shook him well from side to side,
  Until his face was blue:
"Come, tell me how you live," I cried,
  "And what it is you do!"

He said "I hunt for haddocks' eyes
  Among the heather bright,
And work them into waistcoat-buttons
  In the silent night.
And these I do not sell for gold
  Or coin of silvery shine,
But for a copper halfpenny,
  And that will purchase nine.

11. Idle as it may seem to adopt an extravagant line of conduct only to conceal it by another hardly less far-fetched, the practice has been known to pay dividends in the history of logic and science. When ordinary principles lead to improbable consequences, extraordinary ones may sometimes lead back to acceptable results. Jourdain (p. 13) instances the treatment of reflexive paradoxes in logic; Russell ([39], p. 26), the recourse to the Fitzgerald contraction in prerelativity physics. Eddington ([13], p. 39) uses the White Knight's fan as a general emblem for the secretiveness of Nature.

"*I sometimes dig for buttered rolls,*
Or set limed twigs for crabs;
I sometimes search the grassy knolls
For wheels of Hansom-cabs.
And that's the way" (*he gave a wink*)
"*By which I get my wealth —*
And very gladly will I drink
Your Honour's noble health."

I heard him then, for I had just
Completed my design
To keep the Menai bridge from rust
By boiling it in wine.
I thanked him much for telling me
The way he got his wealth,
But chiefly for his wish that he
Might drink my noble health.

'*It's My Own Invention*'

And now, if e'er by chance I put
My fingers into glue,
Or madly squeeze a right-hand foot
Into a left-hand shoe,
Or if I drop upon my toe
A very heavy weight,
I weep, for it reminds me so
Of that old man I used to know —
Whose look was mild, whose speech was slow,
Whose hair was whiter than the snow,
Whose face was very like a crow,
With eyes, like cinders, all aglow,
Who seemed distracted with his woe,
Who rocked his body to and fro,
And muttered mumblingly and low,
As if his mouth were full of dough,
Who snorted like a buffalo —
That summer evening long ago,
A-sitting on a gate.'

As the Knight sang the last words of the ballad, he gathered up the reins, and turned his horse's head along the road by which they had come. 'You've only a few yards to go,' he said, 'down the hill and over that little brook, and then you'll be a Queen — But you'll stay and see me off first?' he added as Alice turned away with an eager look. 'I shan't be long. You'll wait and wave your handkerchief when I get to that turn in the road? I think it'll encourage me, you see.'

'Of course I'll wait,' said Alice: 'and thank you very much for coming so far — and for the song — I liked it very much.'

'I hope so,' the Knight said doubtfully: 'but you didn't cry so much as I expected.'

So they shook hands, and then the Knight rode slowly away into the forest. 'It won't take long to see him *off*, I expect,' Alice said to herself, as she stood watching him.[12] 'There he goes! Right on his head as usual! However, he gets on again pretty easily — that comes of having so many things hung round the horse ——' So she went on talking to herself, as she watched the horse walking leisurely along the road, and the Knight tumbling off, first on one side and then on the other. After the fourth or fifth tumble he reached the turn, and then she waved her handkerchief to him, and waited till he was out of sight.

'I hope it encouraged him,' she said, as she turned to run down the hill: 'and now for the last brook, and to be a Queen! How grand it sounds!' A very few steps brought her to the edge of the brook. 'The Eighth Square at last!' she cried, as she bounded over and threw herself down to

rest on a lawn as soft as moss, with little flower-beds dotted all about it here and there. 'Oh, how glad I am to get here! And what *is* this on my head?' she exclaimed in a tone of dismay, as she put her hands up to something very heavy, that fitted tight round her head.

'But how *can* it have got there without my knowing it?' she said to herself, as she lifted it off, and set it on her lap to make out what it could possibly be.

It was a golden crown.

*   *   *   *   *

*   *   *   *   *

*   *   *   *   *

12. One of the rare instances in which Alice not only detects an ambiguity, but actually turns it into a joke. (Sutherland, p. 172)

CHAPTER IX

QUEEN ALICE

'WELL, this *is* grand!' said Alice. 'I never expected I should be a Queen so soon — and I'll tell you what it is, your Majesty,' she went on in a severe tone (she was always rather fond of scolding herself), 'it'll never do to loll about on the grass like that! Queens have to be dignified, you know!'

So she got up and walked about — rather stiffly just at first, as she was afraid that the crown might come off: but she comforted herself with the thought that there was nobody to see her, 'and if I really am a Queen,' she said as she sat down again, 'I shall be able to manage it quite well in time.'

Everything was happening so oddly that she didn't feel a bit surprised at finding the Red Queen and the White Queen sitting close to her, one on each side: she would have liked very much to ask them how they came there, but she feared it would not be quite civil. However, there would be no harm, she thought, in asking if the game was over. 'Please, would you tell me ——' she began, looking timidly at the Red Queen.

'Speak when you're spoken to!' the Red Queen sharply interrupted her.

'But if everybody obeyed that rule,' said Alice, who was always ready for a little argument, 'and if you only spoke when you were spoken to, and the other person always waited for *you* to begin, you see, nobody would ever say anything, so that ——'[1]

'Ridiculous!' cried the Queen. 'Why, don't you see, child ——' here she broke off with a frown, and, after thinking for a minute, suddenly changed the subject of the conversation. 'What do you mean by "If you really are a Queen"? What right have you to call yourself so? You can't be a Queen, you know, till you've passed the proper examination. And the sooner we begin it, the better.'

'I only said "if"!' poor Alice pleaded in a piteous tone.

The two Queens looked at each other, and the Red Queen remarked, with a little shudder, 'She *says* she only said "if" ——'

'But she said a great deal more than that!' the White Queen moaned, wringing her hands. 'Oh, ever so much more than that!'[2]

'So you did, you know,' the Red Queen said to Alice. 'Always speak the truth — think before you speak — and write it down afterwards.'

'I'm sure I didn't mean ——' Alice was beginning, but the Red Queen interrupted.

'That's just what I complain of! You *should* have meant! What do you suppose is the use of a child without any meaning? Even a joke should have some meaning —and a child's more important than a joke, I hope.[3] You couldn't deny that, even if you tried with both hands.'

'I don't deny things with my *hands*,' Alice objected.

'Nobody said you did,' said the Red Queen. 'I said you couldn't if you tried.'[4]

'She's in that state of mind,' said the White Queen, 'that she wants to deny *something* — only she doesn't know what to deny!'

1. Alice has obviously been reading Kant's ethics—in a nursery edition, no doubt—for her 'little argument' is squarely based on his first formulation of the cate-gori-cal imp-era-tive: 'Act only on that maxim which you can at the same time will to be a universal law.' The Red Queen's maxim cannot be universalized without contradiction since its general adoption would prevent her from even enunciating it. Hence it is self-defeating, and so morally unsound. Capsized by this thrust, the Queen (like the March Hare and Gryphon) has no recourse but to change the subject.

2. Alice means only to recall that her original statement was hypothetical, not categorical. But her ellipsis is taken to be an incorrect verbatim report of everything she said. (Sutherland, pp. 195-96)

3. A triple equivocation on *meaning*. Alice's intention, the significance of a child, and the point of a joke are all meanings of a kind, but not of the same kind. Hence because a joke should have some meaning, it does not follow that Alice (who is more meaningful) should *a fortiori* have meant something, any more than it follows that she must have meant nothing in saying that there was something she did not mean. (Kemeny [24], p. 36)

4. The Red Queen is asserting what logicians now know as a counterfactual conditional. Alice misses the point of it by mistakenly disputing the factual truth of the antecedent, and is justly rebuked for irrelevance. 'If Lewis Carroll were alive today, he would be the oldest don in Oxford' is contested *not* by insisting that he died in 1898, but by

producing an academic ancient born in 1831. Alice also fails to take note that the Queen's condition is not just factually untrue but conceptually impossible, since denying is not in principle a manual occupation. This by no means entails, however, that her total assertion is false. If 'trying with both hands' is simply not a way of denying things, clearly no attempts at denial by *that* method have any chance of success; this is far from saying, of course, that the Red Queen's original statement is in other ways beyond dispute. As noted by Jourdain (p. 29), the White Queen's observations indicate a general disapproval of critics, whether they are justified or not. (Alexander, p. 557)

---

5. Alice is repeatedly victimized by the fallacy of *secundum quid*. Failure to hit off the answer to a trick question is treated as evidence of general incapacity throughout the field under review.

'A nasty, vicious temper,' the Red Queen remarked; and then there was an uncomfortable silence for a minute or two.

The Red Queen broke the silence by saying to the White Queen, 'I invite you to Alice's dinner-party this afternoon.'

The White Queen smiled feebly, and said 'And I invite *you*.'

'I didn't know I was to have a party at all,' said Alice; 'but if there is to be one, I think *I* ought to invite the guests.'

'We gave you the opportunity of doing it,' the Red Queen remarked: 'but I dare say you've not had many lessons in manners yet?'

'Manners are not taught in lessons,' said Alice. 'Lessons teach you to do sums, and things of that sort.'

'Can you do Addition?' the White Queen asked. 'What's one and one and one and one and one and one and one and one and one and one?'

'I don't know,' said Alice. 'I lost count.'

'She can't do Addition,' the Red Queen interrupted. 'Can you do Subtraction? Take nine from eight.'

'Nine from eight I can't, you know,' Alice replied very readily: 'but ——'

'She can't do Substraction,' said the White Queen.[5] 'Can you do Division? Divide a loaf by a knife — what's the answer to that?'

'I suppose ——' Alice was beginning, but the Red Queen answered for her. 'Bread-and-butter, of course. Try another Subtraction sum. Take a bone from a dog. What remains?'

Alice considered. 'The bone wouldn't remain, of course,

if I took it — and the dog wouldn't remain; it would come to bite me — and I'm sure *I* shouldn't remain!'

'Then you think nothing would remain?' said the Red Queen.

'I think that's the answer.'

'Wrong, as usual,' said the Red Queen; 'the dog's temper would remain.'

'But I don't see how ——'

'Why, look here!' the Red Queen cried. 'The dog would lose its temper, wouldn't it?'

'Perhaps it would,' Alice replied cautiously.

'Then if the dog went away, its temper would remain!' the Queen exclaimed.[6]

Alice said, as gravely as she could, 'They might go different ways.' But she couldn't help thinking to herself, 'What dreadful nonsense we *are* talking!'

'She can't do sums a *bit*!' the Queens said together, with great emphasis.

6. The dog's temper, like the Cat's grin, is an attribute allowed to masquerade as a thing—a piece of lost property, as it were, that can thus be thought to subsist independently when its owner is no longer about. Alice meekly accepts the presuppositions of the argument, but even she can see that it will not do.

7. Before contemning the White Queen too hastily for her want of literacy, it is worth recalling that these are not necessarily the easiest words to read, and that two out of the three of them in English (*a* and *I*) are words of much depth and difficulty from a philosophical point of view.

8. Homophonic ambiguity once more; and Alice, as usual, is unable to restrain the confusion that follows.

9. *Ignoratio elenchi* again, denying (as in note 4, p. 224) what the question does not have to assume. Alice has her facts all wrong in any case. *Fiddle-de-dee* (reduplicated form of E. *fiddle*, O.E. *fithele*, M.L. *fidula*, backformation of L. *fides*, lyre-strings; or, as some maintain, from L. *vitula*, an instrument, *vitulari*, to celebrate) is a perfectly good old English word, used by (no prizes for guessing) Dr. Johnson, not to mention De Quincey, Trollope, the Young Lady of Lucca, and the Pobble who has no Toes. The French for it (if anyone cares) is *turlututu*, or *tatata*; German, *Larifari*, *Quatsch*—information that would obviously be news to both parties. It is sad that a sensible question (for once) cannot get (for once) a sensible answer. (Sutherland, p. 196)

Through the Looking-glass

'Can *you* do sums?' Alice said, turning suddenly on the White Queen, for she didn't like being found fault with so much.

The Queen gasped and shut her eyes. 'I can do Addition,' she said, 'if you give me time — but I can't do Substraction under *any* circumstances!'

'Of course you know your A B C?' said the Red Queen.

'To be sure I do,' said Alice.

'So do I,' the White Queen whispered. 'We'll often say it over together, dear. And I'll tell you a secret — I can read words of one letter! Isn't *that* grand?[7] However, don't be discouraged. You'll come to it in time.'

Here the Red Queen began again. 'Can you answer useful questions?' she said. 'How is bread made?'

'I know *that*!' Alice cried eagerly. 'You take some flour —— '

'Where do you pick the flower?' the White Queen asked. 'In a garden, or in the hedges?'

'Well, it isn't *picked* at all,' Alice explained: 'it's ground —— '[8]

'How many acres of ground?' said the White Queen. 'You mustn't leave out so many things.'

'Fan her head!' the Red Queen anxiously interrupted. 'She'll be feverish after so much thinking.' So they set to work and fanned her with bunches of leaves, till she had to beg them to leave off, it blew her hair about so.

'She's all right again now,' said the Red Queen. 'Do you know Languages? What's the French for fiddle-de-dee?'

'Fiddle-de-dee's not English,' Alice replied gravely.[9]

'Who said it was?' said the Red Queen.

Alice thought she saw a way out of the difficulty this time. 'If you'll tell me what language "fiddle-de-dee"

Philosopher's
Alice

227

is, I'll tell you the French for it!' she exclaimed triumphantly.

But the Red Queen drew herself up rather stiffly, and said 'Queens never make bargains.'

'I wish Queens never asked questions,' Alice thought to herself.

'Don't let us quarrel,' the White Queen said in an anxious tone. 'What is the cause of lightning?'

'The cause of lightning,' Alice said very decidedly, for she felt quite sure about this, 'is the thunder — no, no!' she hastily corrected herself. 'I meant the other way.'[10]

'It's too late to correct it,' said the Red Queen: 'when you've once said a thing, that fixes it, and you must take the consequences.'

'Which reminds me —' the White Queen said, looking down and nervously clasping and unclasping her hands, 'we had *such* a thunderstorm last Tuesday — I mean one of the last set of Tuesdays, you know.'

'In *our* country,' Alice remarked, 'there's only one day at a time.'

The Red Queen said, 'That's a poor thin way of doing things. Now *here*, we mostly have days and nights two or three at a time, and sometimes in the winter we take as many as five nights together — for warmth, you know.'[11]

'Are five nights warmer than one night, then?' Alice ventured to ask.

'Five times as warm, of course.'

'But they should be five times as *cold*, by the same rule ——'

'Just so!' cried the Red Queen. 'Five times as warm, *and* five times as cold — just as I'm five times as rich as you are, *and* five times as clever!'

10. Facts wrong again. And even on her amended theory, Alice is committed to a naively Humean view of causation as consisting merely in regularity of succession. The Red Queen's insistence on the determining influence of a statement once it is made represents a sweeping anticipation of J. L. Austin's discovery that certain word-utterances are 'performative' in character. Saying 'I will' to a clergyman in a church creates *ipso facto* the bond of matrimony. That fixes it, and you must take the consequences. Fortunately, the world at large does not always conform so willingly to the descriptions we choose to give it. The consequences would be quite untakeable if it did. (Sutherland, p. 224)

11. Virtually anything can be put into sets by the mathematician, including Tuesdays, or, for that matter, other sets. (Russell's set of all sets that are not members of themselves is a notorious exception. Is it, or is it not, a member of itself?) The license to form sets out of items necessarily successive does not, however, entitle the latter to be reckoned as simultaneous. Even if days and nights *could* be thus bundled together, like blankets, it would in any case be committing a fallacy of composition to suppose that their properties are invariably cumulative in the same way. Five blankets may be five times as warm as one; they are not therefore five times as woolly, or washable, or white. Alice sees that the multiplicative enhancement of a property may well be a doubtful blessing, but she fails to notice that many properties are anyway not of this type. (Kemeny [24], p. 141)

12. So much for memories that work both ways. Considering her own past anxieties in the matter of name-losing, Alice's utilitarian reaction to the White Queen's predicament seems a trifle insensitive. Attempting to remember one's name may be no way to tackle a crisis, but was it ever conceived as such by the Queen? (Sutherland, p. 133*n*; Spacks, p. 97)

13. Alice's abysmal examination performance has surely given her no right to be addressed as 'Your Majesty.' Like a 'Failed B.A. (Calcutta),' she ought to be known as a 'Failed Queen.' Either the examination was a fraud, or the Red Queen has forgotten its outcome, or—more likely—the way to pass examinations beyond the looking-glass is to come hopelessly to grief on them.

Alice sighed and gave it up. 'It's exactly like a riddle with no answer!' she thought.

'Humpty Dumpty saw it too,' the White Queen went on in a low voice, more as if she were talking to herself. 'He came to the door with a corkscrew in his hand ——'

'What for?' said the Red Queen.

'He said he *would* come in,' the White Queen went on, 'because he was looking for a hippopotamus. Now, as it happened, there wasn't such a thing in the house, that morning.'

'Is there generally?' Alice asked in an astonished tone.

'Well, only on Thursdays,' said the Queen.

'I know what he came for,' said Alice: 'he wanted to punish the fish, because ——'

Here the White Queen began again. 'It was *such* a thunderstorm, you can't think!' ('She *never* could, you know,' said the Red Queen.) 'And part of the roof came off, and ever so much thunder got in — and it went rolling round the room in great lumps — and knocking over the tables and things — till I was so frightened, I couldn't remember my own name!'[12]

Alice thought to herself, 'I never should *try* to remember my name in the middle of an accident! Where would be the use of it?' But she did not say this aloud, for fear of hurting the poor Queen's feelings.

'Your Majesty must excuse her,' the Red Queen said to Alice, taking one of the White Queen's hands in her own, and gently stroking it: 'she means well, but she can't help saying foolish things, as a general rule.'[13]

The White Queen looked timidly at Alice, who felt she

ought to say something kind, but really couldn't think of anything.

'She never was really well brought up,' the Red Queen went on: 'but it's amazing how good-tempered she is! Pat her on the head, and see how pleased she'll be!' But this was more than Alice had courage to do.

'A little kindness — and putting her hair in papers — would do wonders with her ——'

The White Queen gave a deep sigh, and laid her head on Alice's shoulder. 'I *am* so sleepy!' she moaned.

'She's tired, poor thing!' said the Red Queen. 'Smooth her hair — lend her your nightcap — and sing her a soothing lullaby.'

'I haven't got a nightcap with me,' said Alice, as she tried to obey the first direction: 'and I don't know any soothing lullabies.'

'I must do it myself, then,' said the Red Queen, and she began:

> '*Hush-a-by lady, in Alice's lap!*
> *Till the feast's ready, we've time for a nap:*
> *When the feast's over, we'll go to the ball —*
> *Red Queen, and White Queen, and Alice, and all!*

'And now you know the words,' she added, as she put her head down on Alice's other shoulder, 'just sing it through to *me*. I'm getting sleepy too.' In another moment both Queens were fast asleep, and snoring loud.

'What *am* I to do?' exclaimed Alice, looking about in great perplexity, as first one round head, and then the other, rolled down from her shoulder, and lay like a heavy lump in her lap. 'I don't think it *ever* happened before, that any one had to take care of two Queens asleep at

once! No, not in all the History of England — it couldn't, you know, because there never was more than one Queen at a time.[14] Do wake up, you heavy things!' she went on in an impatient tone; but there was no answer but a gentle snoring.

The snoring got more distinct every minute, and sounded more like a tune: at last she could even make out words, and she listened so eagerly that, when the two great heads suddenly vanished from her lap, she hardly missed them.

She was standing before an arched doorway, over which were the words QUEEN ALICE in large letters, and on each side of it there was a bell-handle; one marked 'Visitors' Bell', and the other 'Servants' Bell'.

'I'll wait till the song's over,' thought Alice, 'and then I'll ring the — the — *which* bell must I ring?' she went on, very much puzzled by the names. 'I'm not a visitor,

14. The set designated by the phrase 'present Queen of England' is of necessity always a set with one or no elements. But if Queen-mothers and visiting royalties are admitted, to form the set of 'Queens presently *in* England,' the probability of having two or more such elements in one's care at once, though negligible, is not zero.

Queen Alice

and I'm not a servant. There *ought* to be one marked "Queen", you know ——'[15]

Just then the door opened a little way, and a creature with a long beak put its head out for a moment and said 'No admittance till the week after next!' and shut the door again with a bang.

Alice knocked and rang in vain for a long time, but at last a very old Frog, who was sitting under a tree, got up and hobbled slowly towards her: he was dressed in bright yellow, and had enormous boots on.

15. A further problem about sets. If the set of potential entrants to Alice's palace is exclusively but not exhaustively partitioned into 'visitors' and 'servants,' Alice herself, who is a potential entrant but not an element of either subset, has no means of securing admittance. (Sutherland p. 106*ff*.)

'What is it, now?' the Frog said in a deep hoarse whisper.

Alice turned round, ready to find fault with anybody. 'Where's the servant whose business it is to answer the door?' she began.

'Which door?' said the Frog.[16]

Alice almost stamped with irritation at the slow drawl in which he spoke. '*This* door, of course!'

The Frog looked at the door with his large dull eyes for a minute: then he went nearer and rubbed it with his thumb, as if he were trying whether the paint would come off; then he looked at Alice.

'To answer the door?' he said. 'What's it been asking of?'[17] He was so hoarse that Alice could scarcely hear him.

'I don't know what you mean,' she said.

'I speaks English, doesn't I?' the Frog went on. 'Or are you deaf? What did it ask you?'

'Nothing!' Alice said impatiently. 'I've been knocking at it!'

'Shouldn't do that — shouldn't do that —' the Frog muttered. 'Wexes it, you know.' Then he went up and gave the door a kick with one of his great feet. 'You let *it* alone,' he panted out, as he hobbled back to his tree, 'and it'll let *you* alone, you know.'

At this moment the door was flung open, and a shrill voice was heard singing:

'*To the Looking-Glass world it was Alice that said
    "I've a sceptre in hand, I've a crown on my head;
Let the Looking-Glass creatures, whatever they be,
    Come and dine with the Red Queen, the White Queen, and
    me!"*'

16. Alice accepts the well-known doctrine of Russell, according to which *the door* is a definite description, denoting, and implying the existence of, one and only one door. As it stands, however, it is not an identifying description. The Frog, a more up-to-date logician, has been reading Strawson on referring; or else Strawson has been reading the Frog. Both of them recognize, at all events, that *the door* requires to be supplemented by information drawn from the context of utterance, or by more exact specification, or (as here) by use of a demonstrative pronoun, if it is to function as a uniquely referring expression.

17. Having identified the door and assured himself of its real existence, the Frog makes an ill-considered leap into ordinary language philosophy. The contextual implications of the word *answer* commit him, as a native speaker of standard English, to a variety of distinctly nonstandard conclusions about the habits, feelings, rights and so forth of doors. When you've once said a thing, that fixes it. A general erosion of the categorial differences between things and persons ensues almost immediately, creating a series of embarrassing social problems (with talking puddings and so on) to which Alice can find no adequate answer. (Alexander, p. 557; Spacks, p. 94)

18. A naively egocentric view of the habits and functions of royalty. If Alice supposes that such personages ever have the remotest idea of who most of the guests at state banquets are, she certainly has much to learn about her station and its duties.

And hundreds of voices joined in the chorus:

> '*Then fill up the glasses as quick as you can,*
> *And sprinkle the table with buttons and bran:*
> *Put cats in the coffee, and mice in the tea —*
> *And welcome Queen Alice with thirty-times-three!*'

Then followed a confused noise of cheering, and Alice thought to herself, 'Thirty times three makes ninety. I wonder if any one's counting?' In a minute there was silence again, and the same shrill voice sang another verse:

> '"*O Looking-Glass creatures," quoth Alice, "draw near!*
> '*Tis an honour to see me, a favour to hear:*
> '*Tis a privilege high to have dinner and tea*
> *Along with the Red Queen, the White Queen, and me!*"'

Then came the chorus again:

> '*Then fill up the glasses with treacle and ink,*
> *Or anything else that is pleasant to drink;*
> *Mix sand with the cider, and wool with the wine —*
> *And welcome Queen Alice with ninety-times-nine!*'

'Ninety times nine!' Alice repeated in despair. 'Oh, that'll never be done! I'd better go in at once —' and in she went, and there was a dead silence the moment she appeared.

Alice glanced nervously along the table, as she walked up the large hall, and noticed that there were about fifty guests, of all kinds: some were animals, some birds, and there were even a few flowers among them. 'I'm glad they've come without waiting to be asked,' she thought: 'I should never have known who were the right people to invite!'[18]

There were three chairs at the head of the table; the Red and White Queens had taken two of them, but the middle one was empty. Alice sat down, rather uncomfortable at the silence, and longing for someone to speak.

At last the Red Queen began. 'You've missed the soup and fish,' she said. 'Put on the joint!' And the waiters set a leg of mutton before Alice, who looked at it rather anxiously, as she had never had to carve one before.

'You look a little shy; let me introduce you to that leg of mutton,' said the Red Queen. 'Alice — Mutton; Mutton — Alice.' The leg of mutton got up in the dish and made a little bow to Alice; and she returned the bow, not knowing whether to be frightened or amused.

'May I give you a slice?' she said, taking up the knife and fork, and looking from one Queen to the other.

'Certainly not,' the Red Queen said, very decidedly: 'it isn't etiquette to cut any one you've been introduced to.[19] Remove the joint!' And the waiters carried it off, and brought a large plum-pudding in its place.

'I won't be introduced to the pudding, please,' Alice said rather hastily, 'or we shall get no dinner at all. May I give you some?'

19. A well-planted equivocation, based on the lexical ambiguity of *cut*. But Alice, if she wished, could even the score by pointing out that, etiquette or no, it is logically impossible to cut anyone to whom you have *not* been introduced. You cannot repudiate the acquaintance of persons you do not already know. (Spacks, p. 94)

20. Arguably the most deplorable pun in the entire book, though its context—that of a typical, if slightly incongruous, Victorian rhymed conundrum—is in this case perfectly apt. The answer, by the way, is an oyster.

But the Red Queen looked sulky, and growled 'Pudding — Alice; Alice — Pudding. Remove the pudding!' and the waiters took it away before Alice could return its bow.

However, she didn't see why the Red Queen should be the only one to give orders, so, as an experiment, she called out 'Waiter! Bring back the pudding!' and there it was again in a moment like a conjuring trick. It was so large that she couldn't help feeling a *little* shy with it, as she had been with the mutton; however, she conquered her shyness by a great effort, and handed a slice to the Red Queen.

'What impertinence!' said the Pudding. 'I wonder how you'd like it, if I were to cut a slice out of *you*, you creature!'

Alice could only look at it and gasp.

'Make a remark,' said the Red Queen: 'it's ridiculous to leave all the conversation to the pudding!'

'Do you know, I've had such a quantity of poetry repeated to me to-day,' Alice began, a little frightened at finding that, the moment she opened her lips, there was dead silence, and all eyes were fixed upon her; 'and it's a very curious thing, I think — every poem was about fishes in some way. Do you know why they're so fond of fishes, all about here?'

She spoke to the Red Queen, whose answer was a little wide of the mark. 'As to fishes,' she said, very slowly and solemnly, putting her mouth close to Alice's ear, 'her White Majesty knows a lovely riddle — all in poetry — all about fishes. Shall she repeat it?'

'Her Red Majesty's very kind to mention it,' the White Queen murmured into Alice's other ear, in a voice like the cooing of a pigeon. 'It would be *such* a treat! May I?'

'Please do,' Alice said very politely.

The White Queen laughed with delight, and stroked Alice's cheek. Then she began:

> '"*First the fish must be caught.*"
> *That is easy: a baby, I think, could have caught it.*
> "*Next, the fish must be bought.*"
> *That is easy: a penny, I think, would have bought it.*
>
> "*Now cook me the fish!*"
> *That is easy, and will not take more than a minute.*
> "*Let it lie in a dish!*"
> *That is easy, because it already is in it.*
>
> "*Bring it here! Let me sup!*"
> *It is easy to set such a dish on the table.*
> "*Take the dish-cover up!*"
> *Ah,* that is so hard that I fear I'm unable!
>
> *For it holds it like glue* ——
> *Holds the lid to the dish, while it lies in the middle:*
> *Which is easiest to do,*
> *Un-dish-cover the fish, or dishcover the riddle?*' [20]

'Take a minute to think about it, and then guess,' said the Red Queen. 'Meanwhile, we'll drink your health — Queen Alice's health!' she screamed at the top of her voice, and all the guests began drinking it directly, and very queerly they managed it: some of them put their glasses upon their heads like extinguishers, and drank all that trickled down their faces — others upset the decanters, and drank the wine as it ran off the edges of the table — and three of them (who looked like kangaroos) scrambled into the dish of roast mutton, and began to lap up the gravy, 'just like pigs in a trough!' thought Alice.

'You ought to return thanks in a neat speech,' the Red Queen said, frowning at Alice as she spoke.

'We must support you, you know,' the White Queen whispered, as Alice got up to do it, very obediently, but a little frightened.

'Thank you very much,' she whispered in reply, 'but I can do quite well without.'

'That wouldn't be at all the thing,' the Red Queen said very decidedly: so Alice tried to submit to it with a good grace.

('And they *did* push so!' she said afterwards, when she was telling her sister the history of the feast. 'You would have thought they wanted to squeeze me flat!')

In fact it was rather difficult for her to keep in her place while she made her speech: the two Queens pushed her so, one on each side, that they nearly lifted her up into the air: 'I rise to return thanks —' Alice began: and she really *did* rise as she spoke, several inches; but she got hold of the edge of the table, and managed to pull herself down again.[21]

'Take care of yourself!' screamed the White Queen, seizing Alice's hair with both her hands. 'Something's going to happen!'[22]

And then (as Alice afterwards described it) all sorts of things happened in a moment. The candles all grew up to the ceiling, looking something like a bed of rushes with fireworks at the top. As to the bottles, they each took a pair of plates, which they hastily fitted on as wings, and so, with forks for legs, went fluttering about: 'and very like birds they look,' Alice thought to herself, as well as she could in the dreadful confusion that was beginning.

The Philosopher's Alice

236

21. More word-play, on the figurative and literal meanings of 'support' and 'rise.' Alice expects moral and gets physical support; expects merely to stand, but finds herself levitated.

22. A necessary truth about experience, and hence a plausible example of a Kantian synthetic a priori proposition. For at whatever time it is uttered, at least one further event is bound to lie ahead of it, namely (at worst) the end of the world, or some suitably similar cataclysm. Though not a mere logical truism, it is thus universally and necessarily true. 'All sorts of things' happen after its utterance on the present occasion; but the end is not far off.

At this moment she heard a hoarse laugh at her side, and turned to see what was the matter with the White Queen; but, instead of the Queen, there was the leg of mutton sitting in the chair. 'Here I am!' cried a voice from the soup-tureen, and Alice turned again, just in time to see the Queen's broad good-natured face grinning at her for a moment over the edge of the tureen, before she disappeared into the soup.

There was not a moment to be lost. Already several of the guests were lying down in the dishes, and the soup-ladle was walking up the table to Alice, and signing to her to get out of its way.

'I can't stand this any longer!' she cried, as she seized the table-cloth with both hands: one good pull, and plates, dishes, guests, and candles came crashing down together in a heap on the floor.

'And as for *you*,' she went on, turning fiercely upon the Red Queen, whom she considered as the cause of all the mischief — but the Queen was no longer at her side — she had suddenly dwindled down to the size of a little doll, and was now on the table, merrily running round and round after her own shawl, which was trailing behind her.

At any other time, Alice would have felt surprised at this, but she was far too much excited to be surprised at anything *now*. 'As for *you*,' she repeated, catching hold of the little creature in the very act of jumping over a bottle which had just lighted upon the table, 'I'll shake you into a kitten, that I will!'

CHAPTER X

SHAKING

S<small>HE</small> took her off the table as she spoke, and shook her backwards and forwards with all her might.

The Red Queen made no resistance whatever; only her face grew very small, and her eyes got large and green; and still, as Alice went on shaking her, she kept on growing shorter — and fatter — and softer — and rounder — and ——

CHAPTER XI

WAKING

—— and it really *was* a kitten, after all.

CHAPTER XII

WHICH DREAMED IT?

'YOUR Red Majesty shouldn't purr so loud,' Alice said, rubbing her eyes, and addressing the kitten respectfully, yet with some severity. 'You woke me out of — oh! such a nice dream! And you've been along with me, Kitty — all through the Looking-Glass world. Did you know it, dear?'

It is a very inconvenient habit of kittens (Alice had once made the remark) that, whatever you say to them, they *always* purr. 'If they would only purr for "yes", and mew for "no", or any rule of that sort,' she had said, 'so that one could keep up a conversation! But how *can* you talk with a person if they always say the same thing?'[1]

On this occasion the kitten only purred: and it was impossible to guess whether it meant "yes" or "no".

So Alice hunted among the chessmen on the table till she had found the Red Queen: then she went down on her knees on the hearthrug, and put the kitten and the Queen to look at each other. 'Now, Kitty!' she cried, clapping her hands triumphantly. 'You've got to confess that that was what you turned into!'

('But it wouldn't look at it,' she said, when she was explaining the thing afterwards to her sister: 'it turned away its head, and pretended not to see it: but it looked a *little* ashamed of itself, so I think it *must* have been the Red Queen.')

'Sit up a little more stiffly, dear!' Alice cried with a merry laugh. 'And curtsey while you're thinking what to

1. A language with only one symbol can convey no meaning, and is, in fact, no language at all. From the point of view of communication theory, the kitten is a Boolean two-state switching device, with the on/off switch permanently locked in the 'on' position. (Sutherland, pp. 68, 89)

2. Excellent advice for young ladies, and no doubt also for kittens (if curtsey they can). Philosophers (who cannot) are accustomed in such situations to fiddle with their pipes, fill, light or clean them, conduct a frantic search for tobacco, matches, etc., all with a similar purpose in view: not so much to save as to buy or make time, while thinking what to purr next.

3. As at the end of *Wonderland*, there is a brief attempt to suggest a naturalistic interpretation of the dream. Humpty Dumpty and the two Queens are at least tentatively to be regarded as subliminal representations of Dinah and her kittens, who share the same order of (fictionally) real existence as the waking Alice herself. Who, then, is the Red King, on whose imagination the whole story, waking-period and all, may still conceivably depend? If he is not just a projection of Alice's unconscious, and she, after all, is only a projection of his, he cannot be identified with anyone subsisting on her (merely fictional) level, and must inhabit a plane of existence more authentic and inclusive still. On this hypothesis, the only plausible candidate for the role can be none other than Carroll himself. (Spacks, p. 99)

— what to purr. It saves time, remember!'[2] And she caught it up in her arms, and gave it one little kiss 'just in honour of its having been a Red Queen, you know!'

'Snowdrop, my pet!' she went on, looking over her shoulder at the White Kitten, which was still patiently undergoing its toilet, 'when *will* Dinah have finished with your White Majesty, I wonder? That must be the reason you were so untidy in my dream. — Dinah! Do you know that you're scrubbing a White Queen? Really, it's most disrespectful of you, and I'm quite surprised at you!'

'And what did *Dinah* turn to, I wonder?' she prattled on, as she settled comfortably down, with one elbow on the

rug, and her chin in her hand, to watch the kittens. 'Tell me, Dinah, did you turn to Humpty Dumpty? I *think* you did — however, you'd better not mention it to your friends just yet, for I'm not sure.[3]

'By the way, Kitty, if only you'd been really with me in my dream, there was one thing you *would* have enjoyed — I had such a quantity of poetry said to me, all about fishes! To-morrow morning you shall have a real treat. All the time you're eating your breakfast, I'll repeat "The Walrus and the Carpenter" to you; and then you can make believe it's oysters, my dear!

'Now, Kitty, let's consider who it was that dreamed it all. This is a serious question, my dear, and you should *not* go on licking your paw like that — as if Dinah hadn't washed you this morning! You see, Kitty, it *must* have been either me or the Red King. He was part of my dream, of course — but then I was part of his dream, too! *Was* it the Red King, Kitty? You were his wife, my dear, so you ought to know — Oh, Kitty, *do* help to settle it! I'm sure your paw can wait!' But the provoking kitten only began on the other paw, and pretended it hadn't heard the question.

Which do *you* think it was?

Which Dreamed It?

A BOAT, beneath a sunny sky,
Lingering onward dreamily
In an evening of July —

Children three that nestle near,
Eager eye and willing ear,
Pleased a simple tale to hear —

Long has paled that sunny sky:
Echoes fade and memories die:
Autumn frosts have slain July.

Still she haunts me, phantomwise,
Alice moving under skies
Never seen by waking eyes.

Children yet, the tale to hear,
Eager eye and willing ear,
Lovingly shall nestle near.

In a Wonderland they lie,
Dreaming as the days go by,
Dreaming as the summers die:

Ever drifting down the stream —
Lingering in the golden gleam —
Life, what is it but a dream?

THE END

Appendix A:

SELECT BIBLIOGRAPHY
OF COMMENTATORS

ALEXANDER, PETER, "Logic and the Humour of Lewis Carroll," *Proceedings of the Leeds Philosophical and Literary Society*, VI (1951), 551-66.

BARTLEY, W. W., III, "Lewis Carroll's Lost Book on Logic," *Scientific American*, 227, 1 (July 1972), 38-46.

————, "Lewis Carroll as Logician," *Times Literary Supplement*, 3719 (June 1973), 665-66.

BRAITHWAITE, R. B., "Lewis Carroll as Logician," *Mathematical Gazette*, XVI (July 1932), 174-78 (reprinted in Gray).

EMPSON, WILLIAM, "Alice in Wonderland: The Child as Swain," in *Some Versions of Pastoral* (London: Chatto & Windus, 1935; Norfolk, Conn.: New Directions Paperbooks, 1960; reprinted in Gray, Phillips, and Rackin).

EPERSON, D. B., "Lewis Carroll, Mathematician," *Mathematical Gazette*, XVII (May 1933), 92-100.

FENSCH, THOMAS, *Alice in Acidland* (New York: A. S. Barnes, 1970).

GARDNER, MARTIN, *The Annotated Alice* (New York: Clarkson N. Potter, 1960; rev. ed., Harmondsworth, Eng.: Penguin Books, 1970).

GRAY, DONALD J., *Lewis Carroll: Alice in Wonderland* (New York: W. W. Norton, 1971).

GREEN, ROGER L., ed., *Alice's Adventures in Wonderland* and *Through the Looking-Glass* (London: Oxford University Press [Oxford English Novels], 1971).

————, *Lewis Carroll* (London: The Bodley Head, 1960).

GREENACRE, PHYLLIS, *Swift and Carroll: A Psychoanalytic Study of Two Lives* (New York: International Universities Press, 1955; extracts in Gray and Rackin).

HEATH, PETER, "Carroll, Lewis," *Encyclopedia of Philosophy*, Vol. 2, ed. Paul Edwards (New York: Macmillan 1967), 36-37.

HENKLE, ROGER B., "The Mad Hatter's World," *Virginia Quarterly Review*, 49, 1 (Winter 1973), 99-117.

HINZ, JOHN, "Alice Meets the Don," *South Atlantic Quarterly*, LII (1953), 253-66 (reprinted in Phillips and Rackin).

HOLMES, ROGER W., "The Philosopher's *Alice in Wonderland*," *Antioch Review*, XIX (1959), 133-49 (reprinted in Phillips and Rackin).

HUDSON, DEREK, *Lewis Carroll* (London: Constable, 1954).

JOURDAIN, P. E. B., *The Philosophy of Mr. B*rtr*nd R*ss*ll* (London: Allen & Unwin, 1918).

KINCAID, JAMES R., "Alice's Invasion of Wonderland," *Proceedings of the Modern Language Association*, LXXXVIII (January 1973), 92-99.

KIRK, DANIEL F., *Charles Dodgson, Semeiotician* (Gainesville, Fla.: University of Florida Press, 1963; University of Florida Monographs, Humanities No. 11, 1962).

LENNON, FLORENCE B., *The Life of Lewis Carroll* (New York: Dover, 1973; rev. ed. of *Victoria Through the Looking-Glass* [New York: Simon & Schuster, 1945]).

NAGEL, ERNEST, "Symbolic Notation, Haddocks' Eyes and the Dogwalking Ordinance," in *The World of Mathematics*, Vol. III, ed. J. R. Newman (New York: Simon & Schuster, 1956), 1878-1900.

PARTRIDGE, ERIC, "The Nonsense Words of Edward Lear and Lewis Carroll," in *Here, There and Everywhere* (London: H. Hamilton 1950), 162-88.

PHILLIPS, ROBERT, *Aspects of Alice: Lewis Carroll's Dreamchild as seen through the Critics' Looking-Glasses, 1865-1971* (New York: Vanguard Press, 1971).

PITCHER, GEORGE, "Wittgenstein, Nonsense and Lewis Carroll," *Massachusetts Review*, VI, 3 (1965), 591-611; reprinted in *Ludwig Wittgenstein, the Man and his Philosophy*, ed. K. T. Fann (New York: Dell, 1967), 315-35 (also in Gray).

RACKIN, DONALD, *Alice's Adventures in Wonderland: A Critical Handbook* (Belmont, Calif.: Wadsworth, 1969).

———, "Alice's Journey to the End of the Night," *PMLA* LXXXI (October 1966), 313-26 (reprinted in Phillips and Rackin).

RUSSELL, BERTRAND, "Lewis Carroll: *Alice in Wonderland*," discussion with Katherine Anne Porter and Mark Van Doren in *The New Invitation to Learning*, ed. M. Van Doren (New York: Random House, 1942), 206-20.

SEWELL, ELIZABETH, *The Field of Nonsense* (London: Chatto & Windus, 1952; extracts in Gray and Rackin).

SHIBLES, WARREN A., "A Philosophical Commentary on *Alice's Adventures in Wonderland*," in *Wittgenstein, Language and Philosophy* (Dubuque, Iowa: Wm.C. Brown, 1969), 14-45.

SPACKS, PATRICIA M., "Logic and Language in *Through the Looking-Glass*," *ETC: A Review of General Semantics*, XVIII, 1 (April 1961), 91-100 (reprinted in Phillips).

SUTHERLAND, ROBERT D., *Language and Lewis Carroll* (The Hague: Mouton, 1970; Janua Linguarum: Series Major, 26).

TAYLOR, ALEXANDER L. *The White Knight: A Study of C. L. Dodgson (Lewis Carroll)* (London: Oliver & Boyd, 1952; extracts in Gray).

WEAVER, WARREN., "Lewis Carroll: Mathematician," *Scientific American*, CXCIV (April 1956), 116-28 (reprinted in his *Science and Imagination* [New York: Basic Books, 1967], 268-78).

————, *Alice in Many Tongues: The Translations of Alice in Wonderland* (Madison, Wis.: University of Wisconsin Press, 1964).

WILLIAMS, GLANVILLE L., "A Lawyer's *Alice*," *Cambridge Law Journal*, IX, 2 (1946), 171-84.

WILLIAMS, S. H. AND MADAN, F., *The Lewis Carroll Handbook*, revised and augmented by R. L. Green (London: Dawsons of Pall Mall, 1970).

WOOLLEN, C. J., "Lewis Carroll: Philosopher," *The Hibbert Journal*, XLVI, 1 (October 1947), 63-68.

Appendix A

246

This list is only a beginning, and could easily be extended. Additions are invited from devotees of useless research.

1. AUSTIN, J. L., "The Meaning of a Word," in *Philosophical Papers* (Oxford, Eng.: Clarendon Press, 1961).
2. ——, *Sense and Sensibilia* (Oxford, Eng.: Clarendon Press, 1962).
3. AYER, A. J., *Metaphysics and Commonsense* (London: Macmillan, 1969).
4. BAKER, ROBERT, "Alice, Bergmann and the Mad Hatter," *Review of Metaphysics*, XXIV, 4, 96 (1971), 707-36.
5. BARNES, W. H. F., *The Philosophical Predicament* (London: A. & C. Black, 1950).
6. BLANSHARD, BRAND, *Reason and Analysis* (London: Allen & Unwin, 1962).
7. BRADBURY, F. R., ed, *Words and Numbers* (Edinburgh: Edinburgh University Press, 1969).
8. BROAD, C. D., *Scientific Thought* (London: Routledge & Kegan Paul, 1923).
9. ——, *Examination of McTaggart's Philosophy*, Vol. I (Cambridge, Eng.: Cambridge University Press, 1933).
10. ——, *Religion, Philosophy and Psychical Research* (London: Routledge & Kegan Paul, 1953).
11. CARNEY, JAMES D. AND SCHEER, RICHARD K., *Fundamentals of Logic*. (New York: Macmillan, 1964).
12. EDDINGTON, A. S., *Space, Time and Gravitation*. (Cambridge, Eng.: Cambridge University Press, 1920).
13. ——, *The Nature of the Physical World*. London: Dent [Everyman ed.], 1935).
14. ——, *New Pathways in Science* (Cambridge, Eng.: Cambridge University Press, 1935).
15. FINDLAY, J. N., *The Discipline of the Cave* (London: Allen & Unwin, 1966).
16. FLEW, A. G. N., ed., *Logic and Language*, First Series (Introduction) (Oxford, Eng.: Blackwell, 1951).
17. ——, "Philosophy and Language," in *Essays in Conceptual Analysis* (London: Macmillan, 1956).
18. ——, "Can an Effect Precede its Cause?" in *Aristotelian Society, Supplementary Vol.* XXVIII (1954).

Appendix B:

SELECT LIST OF PHILOSOPHICAL AUTHORS WHO QUOTE OR ALLUDE TO ALICE

Appendix B

———

19. GEACH, P. T., "Russell's Theory of Descriptions," in *Philosophy and Analysis,* ed. M. MacDonald (Oxford, Eng.: Blackwell, 1954).
20. HARRISON, J., "The Third Dimension," in *Proceedings of the Aristotelian Society,* 1960-61.
21. HIGH, DALLAS M. *Language, Persons and Belief* (New York: Oxford University Press, 1967).
22. HOFFMAN, ROBERT, *Language, Minds and Knowledge* (New York: Humanities Press, 1970).
23. KEENE, G. B., *Language and Reasoning* (London: Van Nostrand, 1961).
24. KEMENY, JOHN G., *A Philosopher Looks at Science* (Princeton, N. J.: Van Nostrand, 1959).
25. LAIRD, JOHN, *Theism and Cosmology* (London: Allen & Unwin, 1940).
26. LAZEROWITZ, M., "Negative Terms," in *Philosophy and Analysis,* ed. M. MacDonald (Oxford, Eng.: Blackwell, 1954).
27. MANICAS, P. T. AND KRUGER, A. N., *Essentials of Logic* (New York: Van Nostrand, Reinhold, 1968).
28. MONRO, D. H., *Argument of Laughter* (Melbourne: Melbourne University Press, 1951).
29. MOORE, G. E., *Philosophical Studies* (London: Routledge & Kegan Paul, 1922).
30. ———, *Philosophical Papers* (London: Allen & Unwin, 1959).
31. ———, *Commonplace Book* (London: Allen & Unwin, 1962).
32. ———, *Lectures on Philosophy* (London: Allen & Unwin, 1966).
33. MORRIS, C. R., *Idealistic Logic* (London: Macmillan, 1933).
34. PEARS, D. F., "Time, Truth and Inference," in *Essays in Conceptual Analysis,* ed. A. G. N. Flew (London: Macmillan, 1956).
35. PURTILL, R. L., *Logic for Philosophers* (New York: Harper & Row, 1971).
36. QUINE, W. V. O., *Philosophy of Logic* (Englewood Cliffs, N. J.: Prentice-Hall, 1970).
37. RITCHIE, A. D., *The Natural History of Mind* (London: Longmans Green, 1936).
38. ROBINSON, RICHARD, *Definition* (Oxford, Eng.: Clarendon Press, 1950).
39. RUSSELL, BERTRAND, *The ABC of Relativity* (London: Allen & Unwin 1925; 3rd ed. 1969).
40. ———, *Human Knowledge, its Scope and Limits* (London: Allen & Unwin, 1948).
41. ———, "Mind and Matter," in *Portraits from Memory* (London: Allen & Unwin, 1956).
42. RYLE, GILBERT, "Categories," in *Collected Papers,* Vol. II (London: Hutchinson, 1971).
43. ———, "Use, Usage and Meaning," in *Collected Papers,* Vol. II (London: Hutchinson, 1971).

Appendix B

44. SMART, J. J. C., *Philosophy and Scientific Realism* (London: Routledge & Kegan Paul, 1963).
45. STEBBING, L. S., *A Modern Introduction to Logic*, 7th ed. (London: Methuen, 1950).
46. TERRELL D. B. AND BAKER, R., *Exercises in Logic* (New York: Holt, Rinehart & Winston, 1967).
47. WELLS, RULON, "Meaning and Use," in *Theory of Meaning*, ed. A. and K. Lehrer (Englewood Cliffs, N. J.: Prentice-Hall, 1970).
48. WITTGENSTEIN, L., *Philosophical Investigations* (Oxford, Eng.: Blackwell, 1953).
49. ———, *The Blue and Brown Books* (Oxford, Eng.: Blackwell, 1958).
50. WOOZLEY, A. D., *Theory of Knowledge* (London: Hutchinson, 1949).